**TRADE POLICY AND CORPORATE
BUSINESS DECISIONS**

International Business Education
and Research Program

Trade Policy and Corporate Business Decisions

Edited by
TAMIR AGMON
and
CHRISTINE R. HEKMAN

A Research Book from the
International Business Education
and Research Program
University of Southern California

New York · Oxford
OXFORD UNIVERSITY PRESS
1989

Oxford University Press

Oxford New York Toronto
Delhi Bombay Calcutta Madras Karachi
Petaling Jaya Singapore Hong Kong Tokyo
Nairobi Dar es Salaam Cape Town
Melbourne Auckland

and associated companies in
Berlin Ibadan

Copyright © 1989 by Oxford University Press, Inc.

Published by Oxford University Press, Inc.,
200 Madison Avenue, New York, New York 10016

Oxford is a registered trademark of Oxford University Press.

Library of Congress Cataloging-in-Publication Data
Trade policy and corporate business decisions/edited by Tamir Agmon
and Christine R. Hekman.
p. cm.
Proceedings of the IBEAR Research Conference,
held 4/7–9/87 at USC.
Bibliography: p. Includes index.
"An IBEAR research book."
ISBN 0-19-505538-1
1. International business enterprises—Management—Congresses.
2. United States—Commercial policy—Congresses. I. Agmon, Tamir.
II. Hekman, Christine Ries, 1947– . III. IBEAR Research
Conference (1st: 1987: University of Southern California)
HD62.4.T7 1989
658′.049—dc19 88-36854 CIP

9 8 7 6 5 4 3 2 1
Printed in the United States of America
on acid-free paper

Foreword

This volume represents the work of the first IBEAR Research Conference. The IBEAR (International Business Education and Research) Program serves as the focal point for the promotion of international business teaching and research in the Graduate School of Business Administration at the University of Southern California.

IBEAR began in 1978 as an executive MBA program for midcareer managers from Asia Pacific. In the 11 years since, more than 250 executives from countries in Asia and elsewhere have graduated from the IBEAR MBA program. As IBEAR has grown, the program has broadened to include the Pacific Rim Research Program and the Pacific Rim Management Program. The first is the research arm of IBEAR, the second deals with nondegree management development activities.

Over the years it has become apparent that many of the key issues faced by the firms and enterprises of our various societies are not ones about which definitive resolutions are yet apparent. It is clear that as the world is becoming an increasingly transnational place, many issues are coming to be framed in ways that are new and nonroutine. IBEAR has responded to this development by designing activities within the Pacific Rim Research Program that will provide information and knowledge pertaining to these issues.

During the 1986–87 academic year, IBEAR chose as its focus the relationship between trade policies and corporate business decisions. With respect to the trade policies, special attention was paid to the United States. With respect to the corporate business decisions, special attention was paid to the experiences of firms in Japan and other Pacific Rim nations. In addition to making this theme central to the year's work, IBEAR committed itself to a Spring conference as the culmination of this work. The volume, then, is a multiauthored book drawing from the work of that year and the interchange made possible by the discussion of the papers at that conference.

The interplay between policies and outcomes is, of course, always a subtle one. Trade policies may be set with varying degrees of consistency. Moreover, what is achieved may or may not relate directly and positively to the original intentions. In any event, from the point of view of the individual firm or enterprise, those trade policies represent an environment of expectations, opportunities, and constraints within which their own decisions must be taken. It is remarkable how little is known about this intersection between intention and outcome with respect to trade policies and what individual firms make of them.

This lack of knowledge about the relationship between the decisions of individual firms and enterprises and the broader trade policies within which they work is quite surprising, given the time we have been at these matters as a species. Some would suggest that human communication and trade are in fact synonymous. Some would suggest that the development of elaborated language that seems to have occurred across the world some 40,000 years ago— associated as it was with the increasingly elaborate use of artifacts that became the basis of trade between those emerging human societies—was as much the consequence of the emergence of trade as it was its corollary.

Few activities appear as distinctively human as do the processes of language or the trade that language may have, in part, evolved to handle. The University of Southern California and the government of Bahrain have for years had a contract through which jointly identified projects of interest can be pursued. It is striking how the business correspondence of an earlier series of business houses located where Manama is today with branch offices in places like Ur of the Chaldees some 4000 years ago parallel the concerns we recognize today— how standards of quality are understood, how financing questions are handled, and other such matters.

The processes by which human trade has then gone forward for many millenia thus predate any of the policy-setting instruments (principally national governments) with which we are now most familiar. These policy-setting instruments are, in turn, being sharply challenged by the transnational world in which we find ourselves. The policy environment for trade is increasingly interactive with the broadest array of effects and decreasingly responsive to the framing of individual national specifications.

Thus, each firm and enterprise must make choices about its own behavior that are governed not by the specific constraints of its own national policies but by the interactive effects of these policies as they are modified and shaped by the policies of other nations. Policymakers, in turn, find themselves needing a clearer understanding of how the individual firms and enterprises constructively deal with the opportunities and constraints of their own circumstances as these are shaped in the policy arena.

It is thus imperative that we know a great deal more about how individual firms shape their own decisions in response to the trade policies they experience—and in turn how these decisions alter the desirability and feasibility of alternative trade policies that might be available to us. It is to this gap in our knowledge about how actual firm decision-making strategies interact with trade policies that this work is directed.

The University of Southern California, through our School of Business Administration, is pleased to have been able to encourage this important work. For many years the university in the United States with the largest number of international students, USC has come to recognize the international dimensions of the Southern California region and our linkage through it as a nation to the critically important Pacific Rim societies.

The research reported in this volume represents an important contribution to a set of issues best approached collegially and collaboratively in the way a research university can at its best support. The work is informed by knowledgeable persons from many universities. While taking the overall questions of foreign trade policy seriously, it constantly asks how these matters are to be understood when disciplined by data about the choices made by real firms in response to those policies.

It is one thing to note the remarkable continuity of United States trade policy over the past 50 years. It is another to note how disparate are the effects of this policy on different sectors through this period and therefore on the decisions of individual firms. It is certainly another to inquire about how more effective trade policies might in the future be shaped—and how higher-quality individual firm decisions might be forged—not by treating those questions in isolation but by trying to see them in the common frame that the scholars developing this work have begun.

The research university builds on the steady linking of research and educational goals. While IBEAR began principally with an educational mission, it is no accident that it finds itself now turning to a closer integration of that educational objective with the educational program. The linking of theory and practice that this work now supported by IBEAR makes possible, particularly in the crossnational and crosscultural context that IBEAR represents, can be of extraordinary importance. This is a task in which the strongest universities in many societies should increasingly be engaged. We are proud of the important contribution IBEAR is making to that work.

Robert P. Biller
Vice President, External Affairs
University of Southern California

Preface

Research at its best is a collaborative effort, based on an exchange of ideas. This is even more true when an attempt is made to examine an issue from different points of view. Many important issues of the world in which we live require such a multidisciplinary approach. Yet, much of the research done in universities and other research organizations is aimed toward a narrowly defined, disciplinary group.

This book brings together for the first time some of the best disciplinary work on the impact of trade policies on the various aspects of corporate business activities. In bringing together the different disciplinary studies and providing an overall theme and some linking, we provide a multidisciplinary approach to a complex problem that cannot be dealt with on any single disciplinary basis.

The present volume is a multidisciplinary effort to investigate the complex issue of the impact trade policies on corporate business decisions. International trade issues, like the recent trade deficit of the United States, that give rise to trade policies have occupied the center stage of the public debate stage for quite some time. However, for the most part they have been domain of policymakers and those who study policy issues. There is also a common feeling in the business community, in the United States and elsewhere, that something has to be done about the international trade position of the United States and other countries, and that a good way to do it is to mobilize the corporate sector in the United States and make it "more competitive." A good way to approach both the "macro" policy aspects of international trade and the "micro" corporate business decisions in the sphere of international business is by exploring the interface between trade policy and business as is done in this volume.

Given the nature of the problem, we approached the research in the following three steps. In the first stage, the issues were identified and a preliminary research plan was drawn. In the second stage, we identified a number of researchers at USC and elsewhere who were interested in the subject matter and were engaged in doing research in the different relevant disciplines. A group of such researchers met at USC for the First Annual IBEAR Research Conference, April 7–9, 1987. For $2\frac{1}{2}$ days the issue of the relationship between trade policy and corporate business decisions was discussed by the researchers, by the IBEAR IX participants (a group of executives in the IBEAR MBA Program), and by a small group of top-level executives. In the third stage, following the conference, we put together this volume in which the individual researchers act as contributing authors and which we devised and coordinated as a cohesive book rather than a conference volume.

The book is organized in three parts. In Part I, the focus is on the nature of the United States trade policy. The United States trade policy is the environment in which corporations must form their strategy and implement that strategy through the various functional fields of management. The studies presented in this part set the stage for the rest of the book. In Part II, the relationship between aggregate trade policy and the various expressions of corporate performance is explored. Corporate performance is expressed through the functional fields of management like investment decisions, marketing and operational policies, risk management, and organizational structure. Part III comprises three empirical studies: one deals with the effects of trade policy on the semiconductor industry; one considers the effects of the decline of the dollar on Japanese exports to the United States; and one treats the effects of protectionism on the performance of protected industry in the United States. Each chapter is preceded by a header written by us. The purpose of the headers is to weave the different chapters into one consistent and cohesive book.

A long-term effort like devising, coordinating, and writing such a book requires the cooperation and the goodwill of many individuals. We are fortunate in having such help. The 16 contributing authors make this multidisciplinary undertaking possible. Moreover, individually and as a group they have made it both instructive and enjoyable to us. The School of Business Administration at USC and the IBEAR program made this complex and expensive effort possible. Richard L. Drobnick, the IBEAR Director, provided us with encouragement and support. Coordinating the preliminary stage, the conference, and the writing of the book has been a difficult and sometimes frustrating task. Maggie Hunt of the IBEAR staff accomplished this job with much efficiency, good spirit, and grace. Michele Cassingham's editorial assistance is also appreciated.

Writing a book is at times are all-consuming effort. Often it requires a lot of cooperation from the family members of the authors. As our spouses and children can testify, this case was no exception. We appreciate their cooperation in giving up time and attention that they deserve.

Los Angeles   T.A.
Claremont   C.R.H.
December 1988

Contents

III. Corporate Responses to Trade Policies: Three Case Histories

Contributors

Tamir Agmon
University of Southern California
and Tel Aviv University

Jonathan D. Aronson
University of Southern California

Victor A. Canto
A.B. Laffer & Associates

Thomas G. Cummings
University of Southern California

William H. Davidson
University of Southern California

J. Kimbal Dietrich
University of Southern California

Richard L. Drobnick
University of Southern California

Selwyn Enzer
University of Southern California

Christine R. Hekman
Claremont Graduate School

Reuven Horesh
The Management College, Tel Aviv

Johny K. Johansson
University of Washington

Wesley Johnston
University of Southern California

Maria Nathan
University of Southern California

John Odell
University of Southern California

Thomas A. Pugel
New York University

Ingo Walter
New York University and INSEAD

Clas Wihlborg
University of Southern California
and Gothenburg University

Thomas D. Willett
Claremont Graduate School
and Claremont McKenna College

TRADE POLICY AND CORPORATE BUSINESS DECISIONS

1

Trade Policies and Corporate
Business Decisions: Insights and Lessons

TAMIR AGMON

CHRISTINE R. HEKMAN

Issues of international trade have occupied the center stage of the world in the post–World War II period. The fast growth of many countries was associated with an increase in their exports. The most notable examples of such export-led growth are Japan, South Korea, Taiwan, and Singapore. At the same time international trade has become an important component of the business scene in the United States. The rise in the volume and importance of international trade has brought issues of trade policy to the forefront. This is particularly true in the United States, where the recent continuing deficit in the trade balance and its consequences have made trade policy a subject of many discussions and arguments in both the political and economic arenas.

Most of the discussions and arguments about trade policies have focused on the macro policy issues. Questions such as Should the United States follow a more protectionistic policy? Are United States corporations treated fairly in the world's markets? There has been relatively little discussion of the implications of the international trade situation in general, and the United States trade policy in particular, for the corporate sector in the United States and elsewhere. Yet this is an extremely important issue. Whatever the trade policy is, the vehicle by which much of the policy will be carried out is the corporate sector (particularly in the Pacific Rim nations). For the economist and the policymaker dealing with trade policy, what matters are the exports, imports, and other aggregate items of the balance of payments. But exports and imports as well as financial and capital investments do not occur in an abstract way. They are all the result of corporate business decisions. More than that, they are the result of many decisions by marketing managers, plant managers, financial managers, and senior executives in a large number of business firms.

A meaningful analysis of trade policy cannot stop at the macro policy level and assume that the managerial decisions will take care of themselves. If we wish to gain a real understanding of how trade policy is carried out in the marketplace, how the intentions of the policymakers are turned into actual outcomes, often very different from the original intentions, then we must study the way by which corporations respond to trade policy, both current and expected, and how corporate response is translated into actual business policies in the various functional fields of management.

This is not an easy undertaking. First, the subject of the interface between aggregate policy issues and corporate business decisions is a very complicated one. It requires a solid understanding of the policy, the way by which it is formed and its execution and a solid understanding of corporate strategy and the way in which the different functional fields of management operate. There is no one person who can command so many diverse fields of economics and management. Yet such research is relevant, important, and interesting. To do it properly requires a team effort. Therefore we organized a group of researchers from different fields. The group includes scholars from political science, economics, organizational behavior, finance, marketing, operations management, and strategy, who all share an interest in the interface between international trade policy and corporate business decisions. This cooperative and collaborative effort produced new knowledge which exceeded the sum total of the different fields of study of the individual researchers. The main vehicle of the collaborative research effort was a $2\frac{1}{2}$-day conference that took place April 7–9, 1987, at USC. The conference was followed by continuing research efforts by the authors of this book.

This book examines the major insights and the attendant lessons derived from the conference, from the subsequent research, and from actual experiences of American and non-American corporations. The insights deal primarily with the interface between macro economic trade policy and the corporate response through one or more of the traditional functional fields of management. The lessons are expressed as actual prescriptions, or suggestions for management that may improve their firm's competitive position. Our main premise is that a better understanding of the basic processes with the ability to draw the necessary lessons and apply them to actual situations will allow corporations not just to manage the risk inherent in international trade but to take advantage of the opportunities as well. These profit opportunities are products of the same factors that create the risks. Thus, higher risk implies higher expected rates of return. Good management entails the ability to understand, estimate, and manage risk in order to secure a consistently higher rate of return and operate efficiently in an environment characterized by a high degree of international trade risk.

Trade policies affect market access. Tariff and nontariff barriers are erected to hinder foreign corporations' ability to penetrate domestic markets. Similar results are achieved by exchange rate policies. The various taxes and barriers, direct and indirect, which we term the configuration of trade policy, create a situation of monopolistic competition. To take advantage of the potential monopolistic rent, corporations need to be able to access the protected market. This can be accomplished by marketing, production, and financial business policies. These business responses to the configuration of trade policies are costly, but if successful they will lead to higher profits. Success is a function of a correct understanding of the configuration of trade policy, its risks and potential profit opportunities, and a correct choice of a combination of managerial responses to the current and expected trade policy configuration. This is true with regard to service industries as well as the more traditionally international manufacturing industries. The applicability of the analysis of trade policy as an access to markets issue is clearly demonstrated in Chapter 10, by Ingo Walter. The current attempts to secure market access for United States financial services in the Asian markets lend additional credibility to the arguments presented by Walter in that chapter.

The first insight that we have gained is that although the aggregate trade policy in the United States has been stable since the mid-1930s and is likely to remain so, the configuration of the trade policy and its incidence are constantly changing. The effect of these changes can be significant for any particular firm or industry. The attendant risk is a function of the probability that a certain change in one of the components of the trade policy will occur: the change may involve creating or dismantling a specific nontariff barrier, a change in the tariff level or a change in the way that a certain regulation is implemented. Given a particular change in the configuration, the question then is what the effect of that change will be on a particular firm or industry. As is demonstrated in Chapter 3, by Odell and Willett; in Chapter 4, by Aronson; and in Chapter 15, by Canto and Dietrich, the configuration of macro trade policy, its implementation in terms of specific bills, regulations, and negotiated agreements, and the effects of all these steps on particular firms and industries create a substantial business risk.

The first managerial lesson to be derived from this insight is that management has first to ascertain the likely changes and, given these changes, their importance for that particular firm in the short and the long run. Once this has been done, management must determine how the firm should respond to these changes if they occur. This is a short-term response. The long-term issue is the way in which the firm should change its operating policies to make it more adaptable to possible changes in trade policies.

The first task, that of estimating possible changes in the configuration of trade policies, has to do with economics—some say political economics. The response of the firm, both in the short and in the long run, is a managerial issue that depends to a large extent on the organizational structure of the firm. For an individual firm, risk is created by the interaction of many macroeconomic and political factors—the way in which the firm responds to the risk reflects the organizational characteristics of the firm. Specifically, firms that have the capacity to respond in a more flexible way to inherent international trade risk are less vulnerable. This point is elaborated in Part II of this book. The work of Agmon and Wihlborg on investment decisions, Hekman's analysis of financial management, Davidson's treatment of operations management, Johnston's on marketing, and Cummings and Nathan on organizational structure, are all building blocks toward our understanding of how business firms should respond to trade policies.

In all of these cases it is possible to examine the issue at hand by using two paradigms: the economic and the organizational. The economic paradigm tells us the major trends as well as the basic possibilities. To use a specific example, let us look at the issue of international sourcing. In terms of operations management, the economics paradigm will indicate the overall likely developments in the costs of labor in a certain country and in a given industry. Given this general information, the organizational paradigm will tell us how a specific firm may respond to such a situation. For example, it will tell us what the likelihood is that a certain firm will respond in a passive or an aggressive way. Are the managers of this corporation more likely to sense the change or even the prospects for changes and respond effectively, or are they more likely to stick to the old policies and try to avoid the need for change? A preliminary examination of the organizational paradigm is provided in Chapter 7, but a clear lesson of this book is that there exists a need for an extensive analysis of the interface between the economic and the organizational paradigms.

The second managerial lesson is that the interface between trade policy and corporate business decisions is an issue for senior management. Successful management of that interface requires balancing and coordinating the responses of the various functions of the firm. International sourcing, marketing policies, capital budgeting, and external and internal hedging policies comprise the firm's overall response to the risks and opportunities associated with trade policy. The coordination of such a multifunctional response and the choice to be made between passive and proactive policy require the attention of senior management. This strategic choice is demonstrated in specific case histories presented in Chapter 8, by Horesh, and in Chapters 13 and 14, by Pugel and Johansson.

As always, senior management depends on information provided by the various functional fields within the firm. Here the main lesson and common thread is the tradeoff between flexibility and cost effectiveness. This is also the common denominator of all the chapters that deal with the functional management perspective. The tradeoff between cost effectiveness and flexibility is the delineation between short-term and long-term considerations, between a passive response to changes that have already occurred and a proactive response to likely changes in the future. It takes a senior management perspective and a senior management responsibility to decide to move toward greater flexibility, toward a long-term proactive view of a changing world, and toward a better positioning of the firm in the long run, even at a cost of reduced profitability in the short run.

As is demonstrated in this book, such an approach is possible and even practical. It does require some effort, however. The effort is first of all in the recognition of the problem. The second stage is to decide on the overall response of the firm. The third stage involves the translation of the overall policy to specific and concrete steps in the different functional fields of management, including investment decisions, organizational structure, marketing and operations management, and financial management. To accomplish all this we need to develop a high level of sensitivity to the problems with the interface between trade policy and corporate strategy, their effects on the firm, and the way they should be managed. Such sensitivity at all levels of management can be arrived at only as a result of substantial effort at organizing the relevant information and communicating in an effective way. This book is a step in that direction.

The multidisciplinary nature of the issues discussed in this book poses a problem: how to tell a cohesive story, while drawing on the specific expertise of the many researchers who are involved in this study. We chose the following structure. The book is divided into three parts containing 15 chapters. Each part begins with an introduction, written by us. We also wrote a "header" to each chapter. Taken together, the introductions to the three parts and the headers to the 15 chapters provide the continuing line of the story. Each chapter contains a specific article written by one or two of the contributing authors, expressing their own views and analysis of a specific issue pertaining to the general theme of the book. In this way we believe that we were able to strike a balance between the benefits of a general multidisciplinary approach and the expertise and rigor of a specialized study.

I
STABILITY AND RISK ASSOCIATED
WITH UNITED STATES TRADE POLICY

Government economic policy is determined as a result of the interface among many factors. Economics, politics, morality, and cultural considerations contribute to the process by which policy is formulated, enacted, and executed. Trade policy is no exception. If anything, trade policy is more responsive to noneconomic considerations owing to its international nature. In the United States, trade policy has been determined jointly by the legislative and executive branches. In general, one can say that the executive branch adopts an economic approach that seeks to maximize the welfare of the country as a whole. This approach leads, in most cases, to a policy of free trade. The legislative branch, true to its own nature, adopts an approach representing a narrower constituency: a state or a district. This approach often leads to restrictive trade policy with regard to a certain industry. It is important to realize that these two branches of the United States government know full well that the other branch will push toward free trade—or more restrictive trade, as the case may be. This common American process of checks and balances has provided a balanced and stable trade policy since the mid-1930s. The term "balanced and stable trade policy" refers to the overall combination of free trade policy, as expressed by a process of reduced tariffs and generally free access to the United States market, together with incidences of restrictive trade policy with regard to certain industries. The industries that are subjected to restrictive trade policies change from time to time to reflect changes in the patterns of trade, changes in the political power of various interest groups, and changes in public opinion. The changes in the incidence of restrictive United States trade policy make it risky for the individual corporation and for single industries to maintain a general macro policy stability.

The way in which the various economic, political, moralistic, and other behavioral factors interact is illustrated by the attitude toward the recent United States trade deficit with the Pacific Rim countries. The trade surplus accumulated by countries like Japan, South Korea, Taiwan, and other small countries creates political and even cultural and moralistic pressures to "correct" the situation, far beyond what would have been required by an economic analysis of the situation. In Chapter 2, Drobnick and Enzer provide a scenario analysis of the trade situation between the United States and its main trading partners in the Pacific Rim. Their analysis rests on the assumption that the trade deficit has to be eliminated, for a combination of economic and noneconomic reasons, and they proceed to examine the possible consequences of such a reversal.

The case described in the work of Drobnick and Enzer is a specialized case of the general process discussed in Chapter 3 by Odell and Willett. They provide a thorough description and analysis of the process by which United States trade policy is generated and formulated. They also provide the rationale and the evidence for the stability of the policy on the aggregate level, which is the level of analysis relevant for the political scientist and the economist interested in macro economic policy. As we will see later in this book, once we assume a managerial point of view, what is stable at the aggregate level becomes fairly risky at the micro, corporate level.

Aggregate United States trade policy is comprised of a large number of specific bills, regulations, and executive actions. There is a process of constant additions and deletions of specific trade-related actions. In Chapter 4, Aronson presents and discusses an array of such policy components. These components of future United States trade policy are not certain. They range from very probable to unlikely. The uncertainty of these events, coupled with their uncertain effects on different corporations, if and when they take place, is what makes trade policy risky.

The risk associated with trade policy in general, and with United States trade policy in particular, is the subject of Chapter 5, the last chapter in Part I. Agmon and Wihlborg begin by defining international trade risk in a potentially measurable way. They continue with a proposal for a statistically based actual measurement and then examine the possible statistical expressions of three types of common trade policies with regard to single industries or individual corporations.

From the specific case study of repairing the United States trade deficit with its major trading partners in the Pacific Rim, through the general process of political economy and its expressions in terms of specific actions, this part of the book sets the stage for the major thrust of the book as a whole: the effect of the ever-changing incidence of the generally stable United States trade policy on business firms.

2

Consequences of Balanced Trade Between the United States and Its Pacific Rim Trading Partners[1]

RICHARD L. DROBNICK

SELWYN ENZER

The growing United States trade deficit vis-à-vis the Pacific Rim nations (in particular, Japan and Korea) is one of the major issues of political economy in the 1980s. It has attracted much attention in the popular press as well as in the business, political, and academic communities, both in the United States and overseas. Many political and business leaders have spoken of the need to reduce this trade deficit. Some, particularly in the United States Congress, have spoken of balanced trade on a bilateral basis as a desirable, and feasible, policy objective.

While there are various opinions as to whether balanced trade between the United States and the other Pacific Rim nations is in fact desirable or feasible, Drobnick and Enzer contend that such an occurrence will take place in the early 1990s, and they explore the policies that may lead to it, with their attendant implications. They specify a number of possible scenarios and examine their ramifications for United States and foreign corporations.

This chapter demonstrates how policy goals at the aggregate macro policy level are translated to trade flows (exports and imports). Later, we will see how changes in trade flows generate actual investment and divestment decisions as well as other operational decisions at the corporate level.

We do not say that any one of the scenarios described below is going to occur or even that any one of them is very likely to occur; rather, these scenarios represent one set of possible outcomes. Given these trade policy scenarios, many changes will necessarily follow. In this chapter we provide, via Drobnick and Enzer, a quantitative way to evaluate the potential changes and their effect on Pacific Rim economies and on the corporations that are active in this market.

The different patterns of trade policy—which will bring balanced trade with the Pacific Rim—will also create international trade risk. This risk emanates from our inability to fully predict the future and from the probability that United States legislative and executive branches will take some action, or will continue to threaten action, to balance trade in the Pacific Rim.

This chapter deals with aggregate policy on an analytical level. Although its findings are based on data collection, the data itself are hypothetical. All the scenarios, and the different trade flows they generate, provide an estimate of the risk associated with an assumed trade policy of reducing the trade deficit between the United States and its Pacific Rim trading partners.

The large regional picture provided by Drobnick and Enzer is used here as a demonstration of the possible implications of political and economic policy goals (to be discussed later), as well as a basis against which corporate guidelines for international business policy can be set.

The recent pattern of ever-growing United States trade deficits is neither politically nor financially sustainable. The key question in international economics today is how the United States and the world will adjust to the inevitable *reversal* of America's mammoth trade deficit. That is, how will the "overconsuming" United States and its "underconsuming" trade partners rapidly transform their economies so as to convert America's recent $150 billion per year trade deficits into the $50 billion to $100 billion annual trade surpluses required to service America's international indebtedness?

Whether or not trade adjustments of the magnitude implied by eliminating the United States deficits can be made without disrupting the economic and social fabric of nations whose economic structures have become so heavily export dependent is unknown. To some extent, it depends on the nature and speed of the adjustment process. Four important questions about this adjustment are as follows[2]:

1. Will America adjust its external balance primarily by import compression (with little increase in exports), by export expansion (with little decrease in imports), or by some combination thereof?
2. Will America's adjustment process occur quickly or slowly? That is, will America achieve a regular trade surplus in the early or latter years of the 1990s, or after 2000?
3. Will America's adjustment process occur primarily as a result of market mechanisms (further United States dollar depreciation and slower United States income growth, as well as elimination, or a substantial reduction, of the federal deficit), or as a result of nonmarket mechanisms (tariffs, quotas, export subsidies, "voluntary" export restraints, and "required" purchases of United States products)?
4. Will the Japanese and German economies be expanded to offset the worldwide contractionary influence of the shrinking of the United States federal deficit and the consequent shrinking of the United States trade deficit?

The answers to these questions depend primarily on macroeconomic policies to be adopted by America.[3] However, as America begins to eliminate its macroeconomic "savings gap," the policies of its major trading partners will be of critical importance to the nature and speed of the worldwide adjustment process.

This chapter begins by explaining why the basic hypothesis—that the United States will reverse its trade deficit in the 1990s—is inevitable. Second, a discussion of the nature, timing, and adjustment mechanisms for the trade reversal is provided. Third, these views are contrasted with the expectations of many Asian experts that a United States trade reversal cannot happen in the near future. Fourth, the global, regional, and national consequences of the United States trade reversal are described.

NECESSITY OF QUICKLY REVERSING THE UNITED STATES MERCHANDISE TRADE DEFICIT

Americans have not been "paying their own way" in the world since 1982. The standard of living enjoyed by Americans has been increasingly supported by

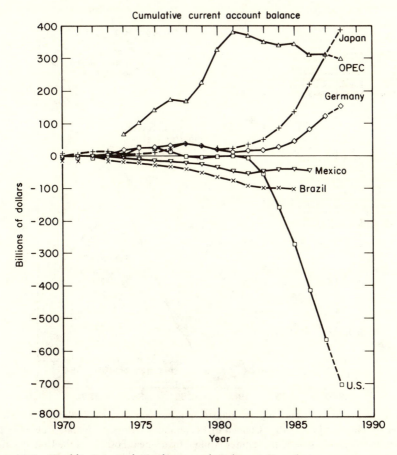

Figure 2.1 World's Principal Creditors and Debtors. Cumulative current account balance. Source: International Monetary Fund, *World Economic Outlook* (various issues); 1987 and 1988 figures are IMF estimates.

foreigners. From 1982 through 1987, Americans were able to "consume" more than they produced because their trading partners "consumed" less than they produced.[4] During this time, the United States substantially changed the nature of its economic relations with the world. The United States joined the world's debtor countries (or to be more technically correct, net capital importing countries), running current account deficits of $9 billion, $42 billion, $102 billion, $118 billion, $140 billion, and $150 billion (estimate) from 1982 to 1987 (see Fig. 2.1). This has produced the anomalous situation of the world's richest nation borrowing and attracting investment capital from poorer nations to such an extent that in just 6 years the United States transformed its net international asset position from a $140 billion surplus to a net $400 billion deficit.[5]

Furthermore, even if the United States balances its trade by 1992, America will still have to attract another $500 billion of foreign capital between 1988

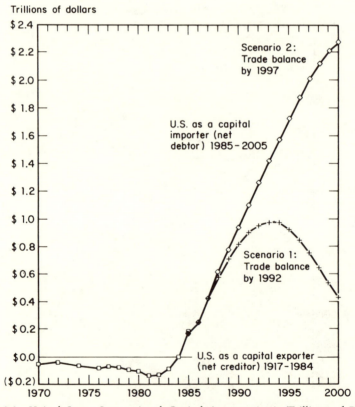

Figure 2.2   United States International Capital Account (net). Trillions of Dollars. Source: Historical data from Council of Economic Advisors, *Economic Report of the President* (various issues), Table-International Investment Position of the United States; Projections computed from tables on pp. A-9 and A-5 in Drobnick and Enzer, "Pacific Rim Trade Scenarios: 1987–1992," paper presented at the IBEAR Trade Policy Workshop at the University of Southern California, April 2–4, 1987.

and 1992 to finance its prospective trade deficit and interest and dividend obligations on an external debt of almost $1 trillion (see Fig. 2.2, scenario 1). Such an "optimistic" estimate of America's foreign capital requirements is considered quite *un*likely by most economists.[6] The consensus opinion is that 1992 is an impossibly early date for the United States to achieve trade balance; the late 1990s is considered to be much more likely (see Fig. 2.3, scenario 2). This vision of a slow trade adjustment would pur America on an external indebtedness trajectory that would exceed $2 trillion by the year 2000 (see Fig. 2.2, scenario 2).

In the fast adjustment scenario (trade balance by 1992), the United States would probably need to export more than $400 billion and import less than $350 billion worth of merchandise by 1995 in order to earn the trade surplus needed to service its trillion dollar debt (see Fig. 2.4). The 1992 interest and dividend payments required to service America's external debt in scenario 1

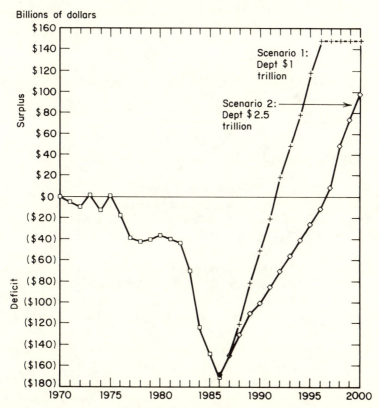

Figure 2.3 United States Merchandise Trade Balance. Billions of Dollars. Source: Historical data from Council of Economic Advisors, *Economic Report of the President* (various issues), Table-International Investment Position of the United States; Projections computed from tables on pp. A-9 and A-5 in Drobnick and Enzer, "Pacific Rim Trade Scenarios: 1987–1992," paper presented at the IBEAR Trade Policy Workshop at the University of Southern California, April 2–4, 1987.

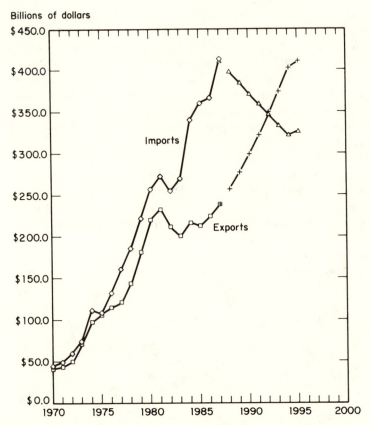

Figure 2.4   United States Import and Exports. Billions of Dollars. Source: Date from Council of Economic Advisors, *Economic Report of the President* (various issues). Data from 1987 are annualized estimates from January–October data; forecasts are from the baseline projection of the Pacific Rim Trade Scenarios project.

(trade balance by 1992) would be about $70 billion and declining in subsequent years; in scenario 2 (trade balance by 1997), these 1992 payments would be about $90 billion and rising to $170 billion by the year 2000 (see Fig. 2.5). That is, in scenario 1, America would need to achieve a $70 billion merchandise trade surplus in 1992 just to stay even—otherwise it would go deeper into debt; in scenario 2 it would need an annual trade surplus of about $170 billion after the year 2000 just to avoid going deeper in debt!

One of the penalties of a slow reversal of America's trade account is that America's external debt would peak at about $2.5 trillion shortly after the turn of the century, as opposed to peaking at about $1 trillion in the mid 1990s. This $2.5 trillion indebtedness that occurs in the slow-adjustment process that most economists and politicians anticipate is extremely unlikely. International financiers—American as well as foreign—will prevent such a slow adjustment. They will consider it too risky to continue to accumulate the ever-larger amounts of dollar-denominated assets needed for the slow-adjustment

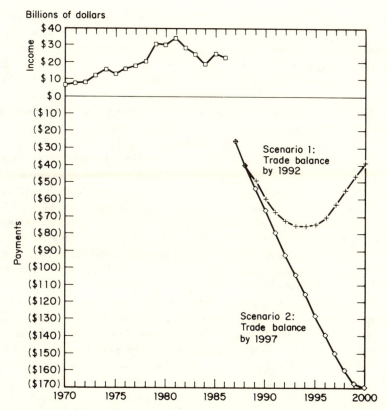

Figure 2.5   United States Investment Income and Payments (net). Billions of Dollars. Source: Historical data from Council of Economic Advisors, *Economic Report of the President* (various issues), Table-International Investment Position of the United States; Projections computed from tables on pp. A-9 and A-5 in Drobnick and Enzer, "Pacific Rim Trade Scenarios: 1987–1992," paper presented at the IBEAR Trade Policy Workshop at the University of Southern California, April 2–4, 1987. Notes: [1] An 8% average rate of return is assumed. [2] From 1974 to 1982, investment income was equal to about 1% of GNP. From 1989 to 1994, investment payments would equal 1 to 1.5% of GNP in Scenario 1.

scenario. They will sell dollars to central banks, which will in turn intensify their pressure on the United States to implement fiscal and monetary austerity programs. America's creditors will want it to follow more conservative fiscal and monetary policies in order to restore confidence in the long-term financial integrity of their most indebted client.

Perhaps this process has already begun. In 1986, $29 billion of America's $140 billion current account deficit was financed by foreign central banks; in the first half of 1987, all $78 billion was financed by official intervention.[7] Without such central bank action, the dollar would have fallen further. As seen in the stock market "Crash of '87," this process caused United States interest rates to rise, the bond market to fall, and the stock market to plummet. Until the stock market panic focused expert attention on this issue, most economists believed (and many still do) that it is *likely* that foreigners would be willing to continuously and United States dollar assets to their portfolios without demanding sharply higher yields.[8]

Meanwhile, Japan had been generating substantial current account surpluses and has become the world's preeminent capital exporter. Between 1982 and 1987, Japan recorded a cumulative current account surplus of about $300 billion. An international issue of major political and economic significance is whether or not Japan has permanently replaced the United States as the premier source of international capital, as the United States once replaced Britain.[9]

Japan's cumulative current account surplus will continue to grow even as its exports slow substantially and its imports rise rapidly (owing to the inevitable growth of its income and dividend receipts). In fact, even if the United States eliminates its trade deficit by the early 1990s, Japan's cumulative current account surplus will be in the $400 billion to $500 billion range by the early 1990s—which would be more than triple America's peak international creditor position of $140 billion in 1981.

The issue of recycling Japan's "export dollars" will dominate tomorrow's financial and political headlines, much as the recycling of "petrodollars" did in years past. But how will Japan, the United States, and the world manage this shift in financial power? Will it be accompanied by movement toward a yen-based international financial system? Or will it be accompanied by even more strident calls for trade and investment protectionism and perhaps even the collapse of the multilateral trading system? The answer is unclear, but if the United States can quickly reduce its fiscal and trade deficits, the adjustments will be made with fewer disruptions.

REVERSING THE UNITED STATES TRADE DEFICIT: TIMING AND MECHANISMS[10]

The results of a survey of 18 American and 25 Asian trade policy experts that we conducted between June and September of 1987 are summarized in Table 2.1.[11] These experts think there is only a 50 percent chance that the United States will balance its trade by 1998. The United States experts believe there is a 25 percent change of doing so by 1994, while the Asian experts did not foresee a 25 percent chance until 1996. If the United States is to balance its trade by 1992, the panel believes that this will occur as a result of export expansion (from about $240 billion in 1987 to $350 billion in 1992) and a reversal of America's import trend (from about $415 billion in 1987 to $350 billion in 1992). Given the substantial ongoing depreciation of the United States dollar, these trade estimates imply a *major* contraction of the *volume* of United States imports. As a consequence, world trade (in constant dollars) is expected to grow even more slowly than in the recent past (2.4 percent annually from 1987 to 1992 rather than 3.0 percent from 1981 to 1986). The forecasts referred to in

Table 2.1 Estimates of Economic and Trade Policy Experts[a]

	Forecasts[b]			Historical reference 1981–86 avg.
Economic indicators	Lower quartile	Median	Upper quartile	
Year of United States trade balance	1995	1998	> 2002	N.A.
Level of United States exports and imports (if balanced by 1992)	$275B	$350B	$400B	N.A.
World trade growth rate (1987–92 average in constant $)	1.2%	2.4%	4.0%	3.0%
Inflation rate for traded goods (1987–92 avg. rate)	1.7%	3.0%	4.4%	− 1.6%
United States federal deficit (FY 1992 level)	$50B	$75B	$100B	$172B
United States GNP growth (1987–92 avg. rate)	1.5%	1.75%	2.0%	2.4%
Yes/$ exchange rate (by 1992)	115	125	145	228
New Taiwan dollar/$ (by 1992)	27	29	31	39
Won/$ (by 1992)	720	770	810	790
Importance of "market" versus "nonmarket" forces in eliminating the United States trade deficit	60%	75%	90%	N.A.

[a] These are the summary results of a survey of 18 American and 25 Asian economic and trade policy experts conducted between June and September of 1987. After the stock market crash of October 1987, the lower quartile forecasts of the panel probably provide the most representative reflection of their current views. The complete results are reported in Drobnick and Enzer, "Forecast of International Trade Conditions 1987–95: Report of a Delphi Inquiry," University of Southern California, IBEAR Working Paper 12, January 1988.

[b] The median is the midpoint of the group's forecast range. The group believes that the actual value is equally likely to be at or above (below) the median. The upper and lower quartiles represent the limits of the middle 50% of the group's forecast range. In other words, the group estimates that the actual value has a 25% chance of being at or less (greater) than the quartile.

this section are the median estimates of the panel as of September 1987. After the stock market crash of October 1987, the lower-quartile forecasts of the panel probably provide a more representative reflection of their current views.)

Such a reversal of the United States trade deficit means that America would be experiencing export-led growth (as in the late 1970s), where the GNP would be expanding faster than domestic demand. The trade experts also expect the following changes in this scenario:

1. The United States federal deficit will be reduced to the $50–100 billion range by 1992.
2. United States GNP growth will slow to the 1.5 to 2 percent range from 1987–92, as compared to the 2.4 percent average rate of growth from 1981 to 1986.

3. The United States dollar will continue to depreciate. For example, by 1992, the dollar is expected to be worth only about 115 yen, 27 new Taiwan dollars, and 720 won.
4. Productivity and competitiveness of United States manufacturing firms will continue to increase. In 1986, unit labor costs (in dollar terms) declined 0.4 percent for American manufacturers and increased 42 percent and 25 percent for Japanese and German manufacturers, respectively.
5. Production by foreign companies in the United States will increase substantially e.g., Japanese automobile manufacturers are expected to produce 2,000,000 units in the United States with about 75 percent domestic content by 1990.
6. The United States will increase its use of tariffs, quotas, and export subsidies.
7. The United States will more vigorously enforce its antidumping and countervailing duty statutes, increase its use of voluntary export restraints, and increase its pressure for market openings abroad.
8. American businesses will become increasingly knowledgeable about foreign markets and culture.

On balance, the trade experts think that the changing "market" forces (items 1–5 listed above) will account for about 75 percent of America's movement toward trade balance by 1992. They think that about 25 percent of the adjustment would occur as a result of nonmarket forces (items 6–8). They also think that America's trading partners are unlikely to retaliate against these measures, even though they would vociferously complain about the unfairness of such measures.

The immediate consequence of movement toward this reversal of the United States trade account—unless accompanied by substantial economic expansion by Japan and Germany—will be to substantially slow, and perhaps derail the economic growth plans of many nations that depend on the United States as the world's economic "locomotive." In turn, this could set off a chain of events leading to a very protectionist world.

IMPOSSIBILITY OF QUICKLY REVERSING THE UNITED STATES TRADE DEFICIT: THE ASIAN VIEW

Is it plausible that the United States will significantly reduce—let alone eliminate or reverse—its trade deficit within the next few years? For the most part, Japanese, Korean, and Taiwanese trade policy experts (officials, businessmen, and academics) think it is extremely unlikely that America would be able to reduce its trade deficit even to the $80–100 billion level by the early 1990s. Their ASEAN and Chinese counterparts are not so adamant about America's inability to reverse its trade deficit. However, they are very concerned that America's trade disputes with Japan, Korea, and Taiwan will have negative spillover effects on them.

Most of the Asian experts think about the United States trade problem primarily in bilateral terms. They view their country's access to the United States market as being essential to their economic health and regard this access as a "guaranteed right or entitlement." Furthermore, they strongly believe that this entitlement should not be interfered with by United States government policy to either weaken the dollar against *their* currency or to restrict *their* products by tariffs, quotas, or other restraints. At the same time, they deeply resent any United States government pressure to open their *own* markets to the American goods and services that would be competitive with their domestic products. An often heard refrain is, "If the United States needs to improve its trade balance, it should pressure Japan, not our country."

There is little recognition of the systemic global problem that as the United States reverses its trade deficit—by market or nonmarket methods—worldwide demand for exports will be substantially reduced, and, therefore, the export-led growth strategies, which the International Monetary Fund and the World Bank have promulgated with vigor, will result in worldwide excess capacity in numerous manufacturing sectors. As mentioned previously, for the United States to balance its trade, the expert panel feels that United States growth must slow down to a 1.5 to 2 percent range from 1987 to 1992 (as compared to the 2.4 percent average growth from 1981 to 1986). As a result, world trade growth is expected to only average 2.4 percent from 1987 to 1992, as compared to 3 percent from 1981 to 1986 (see Fig. 2.6).

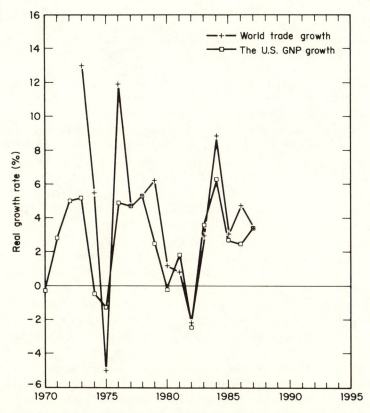

Figure 2.6 United States GNP Growth and World Trade Growth. Source: 1. Council of Economic Advisor, *Economic Report of the President*, 1987, Table B-2, p. 247. 2. International Monetary Fund, *World Economic Outlook* (various issues).

As stated above, most Asian experts believe the United States cannot eliminate—let along reverse—its trade deficit in the foreseeable future. Their beliefs are based partly on wishful thinking and partly on wrongfully ascribing much of their export success to the incompetence or laziness of American companies, rather than to America's internationally counterproductive macroeconomic policies. Their most common arguments are these:

1. America has become structurally import dependent as a result of the "hollowing out" of the economy. Econometric studies which show that over the past 4–5 years America has had a high income elasticity of imports are often used to buttress this argument. Other "evidence" is the fact that many United States firms have integrated foreign-sourced production into their operations over the past 4–5 years.
2. American consumers are addicted to the high quality and low prices of imported products.
3. America is politically incapable of substantially reducing, let alone balancing, its federal deficit.
4. American businesses do not think globally, are not organized for international business to be a priority, and are not knowledgeable about foreign markets and culture.
5. American firms produce low-quality products and do a poor job of servicing them, especially in Asia.
6. American government is incapable of implementing a strategic trade policy, because it has too many divergent goals and is too susceptible to lobbying by special interests.

The "evidence" of the Asian experts for all these arguments is the behavior of American government, businesses, and consumers during the past 4–5 years—which it is presumed will continue.

Two striking factors stand out in the comments of the Asian trade experts. First, there was widespread recognition of the unsustainability of the United States trade deficit. Yet there was little recognition of the prospects of any change in the system. In other words, despite recognition that current trade patterns could not continue, the experts and their organizations do not have contingency plans for dealing with a substantial reduction in the United States trade deficit.

Second, even though all of the experts were technically competent in economics, none of them suggested the basic macroeconomic solution— namely, for the surplus nations to reduce their exports and increase their imports. When this possibility was raised, it was generally rejected, because everyone believed it was simply not going to happen. Indeed, the one observation that everyone outside of Japan shared was that it was extremely difficult, if not impossible, to export anything except raw materials to Japan.

In our opinion, the dynamic effects of the massive exchange rate changes now in progress are not being adequately evaluated by the experts (see Fig. 2.7). Exchange rate changes are making it much more attractive for American and foreign firms to produce more of their products in the United States and are making United States products more attractive to United States consumers. Some preliminary evidence of these adjustments, in terms of recent changes in

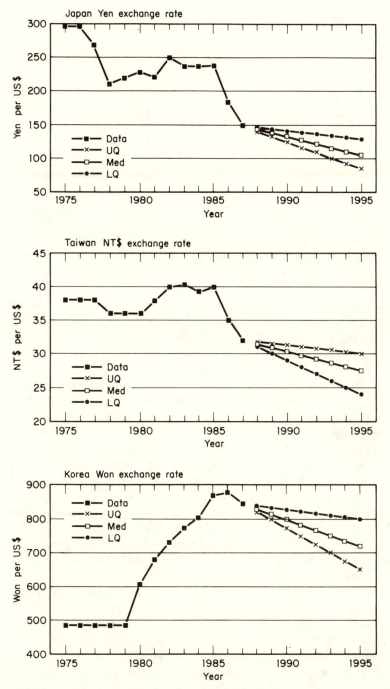

Figure 2.7 Japan Yen Exchange Rate. Taiwan nt$ Exchange Rate. Korea Won Exchange Rate. These are the median-, upper-, and lower-quartile forecasts made in September 1987 by a Delphi panel of 18 American and 25 Asian trade policy experts, reported in Drobnick and Enzer, "Forecasts of International Trade Conditions: 1987–95," U.S.C. IBEAR Working Paper No. 2, January 1988.

Table 2.2   Changing Trade Patterns (% change in volume)

Year	United States		Japan		Germany	
	Exports	Imports	Exports	Imports	Exports	Imports
1985	2.9	5.1	4.4	0.4	6.4	4.6
1986	8.0	14.8	− 1.3	7.2	1.2	5.9
1987	9.0	0.4	− 2.7	5.7	− 0.4	3.8
1988	14.6	1.2	− 0.3	5.9	2.1	4.5

SOURCE: International Monetary Fund, *World Economic Outlook*, October 1987, Table A22, p. 62.

the volume of exports and imports for the United States, Japan, and Germany, is shown in Table 2.2.

A major consequence of a declining dollar is that Americans become poorer in terms of international purchasing power. Naturally, this ongoing change in the structure of the American economy, and those of our trading partners (especially Japan's and Germany's), will not be captured by econometric models that were estimated with "yesterday's" data. The recent wave of foreign direct investment in the United States will grow rapidly in the years to come. Increasingly, foreign firms will want to serve their United States market (and some foreign markets) from a United States production base. There are two important reasons: (1) to reduce their production costs by using inexpensive American labor, land, and facilities, and (2) to ensure their access to the American market against the threat of possible protectionist actions by the United States. An obvious consequence is that America will import less and export more, although a significant amount of the changing product flow will be organized and controlled by foreign firms producing in the United States.

All serious economic thinkers realize that the United States fiscal deficit must be reduced. Even President Reagan finally acknowledged this in the aftermath of the stock market crash. Mr. Reagan pressured Republican and Democratic negotiators to produce a $30 billion and $45 billion deficit reduction plan for FY 1988 and FY 1989. Inevitably this entails raising some taxes and cutting some defense spending. The principal stimulus for this action appears to be the need to placate nervous foreign creditors about the long-term fiscal integrity of the United States.

Another factor that will contribute to the trade turnaround is that American businesses are undergoing a transformation regarding high-quality and cost-conscious production, as well as a belated awakening to the threats and opportunities of global competition. Given large investments in high-technology manufacturing capability, new management–labor relations, the weakened dollar, and more vigorous government pressure to open foreign markets, United States manufacturing firms will once again become very effective international competitors in the years to come. In fact, one can expect increasingly to hear America's trading partners complain about unfair United States competition.

CONSEQUENCES OF THE UNITED STATES TRADE DEFICIT REVERSAL

On a global basis, two major consequences of eliminating the United States trade deficit are (1) making the LDC debt problems of developing countries more intractable, and (2) encouraging a worldwide shift of production facilities to the United States. In its role as the world's biggest importer, the United States acted as the international "locomotive," pulling the world out of the economic stagnation of the early 1980s, especially the export-oriented Pacific Rim nations. This also enabled LDC debtor nations to earn the foreign exchange needed to repay their interest obligations. Thus, in the short run, America's trade deficits helped stabilize the international financial system. However, they also established unrealistic expectations and production patterns. Unless an economic expansion in Japan and Germany (which is considered to be extremely unlikely in the near term) offsets the United States trade reversal, world trade growth and economic growth will inevitably slow down. LDC debtors will be unable to generate the trade surpluses necessary to service their debts, and a systematic accommodation will need to be negotiated between the world's creditor and debtor nations.

Increasingly, Japanese, European, and other manufacturers whose currencies have appreciated against the dollar will be shifting production to the United States as well as to the ASEAN countries.[12] For the same reason, many American firms will close their "export platform" operations and return production to the United States. In addition to the exchange rate incentives, United States-based investments provide insurance against potential restrictions on access to the United States market.

On a regional basis, Asia will become ever more integrated into the financial and economic structure of Japan. In an effort to reduce production costs, medium-size and large Japanese firms are rapidly moving production facilities to ASEAN nations as well as to Korea and Taiwan.[13] Taiwanese firms and foreign firms producing in Taiwan will seek cheaper production sites in ASEAN in the next few years (as will Korean companies and foreign companies producing in Korea as the won appreciates). Japanese foreign aid and lending programs to ASEAN will also increase substantially in the years to come. Meanwhile, American firms, on balance, will not be expanding production in this area, and American aid programs are more likely to shrink than expand under the pressures of balancing the federal deficit. Japan (and to a lesser extent Taiwan and Korea) will develop "subcontractor"-type production facilities throughout ASEAN. Part of the production of these Japanese subsidiaries will be exported to Japan, and part to the rest of the world.

ASEAN leaders are concerned about this prospect of increased Japanese influence and will do what they can to limit it. Nevertheless, they are becoming resigned to the lack of alternatives. That is, nothing much is likely to come of their efforts to increase intra-ASEAN economic cooperation without capital and technology from Japan. And it is extremely unlikely that ASEAN members can cooperate enough to transform the ASEAN–United States Initiative discussions into an actual preferential trade agreement.

On a national basis, ASEAN nations will compete with each other to improve their climate for foreign investors. Japaness firms will astutely encourage and take advantage of this competition by making demands for improved investment climates. A recent example of this is the Japanese demand that Indonesia allow foreign firms to have 100 percent equity and allow foreign firms to enter Indonesia's heretofore proscribed "domestic trade" arena. All of the Asian nations will continue to seek special consideration for both better access to the United States market and relief from United States pressures to open their markets or appreciate their currencies. Resentment toward America will rise as it becomes increasingly unable to respond to these demands.

In the near term, unemployment will rise in Japan, and profits for many firms will be dismal. Consequently, the government will respond with more expansionary budgets and Asian foreign aid programs that create stronger markets for Japanese products. The often discussed economic integration of

Table 2.3 Consequences of the United States Increasing Its Indebtedness and Reversing Its Trade Deficit

---

1. United States financial, economic, and political power will erode as that of Japan's inexorably rises. This will be apparent in a decline in United States influence in international institutions such as the IMF, the World Bank, and GATT, as well as in alliance politics.

2. The United States government will find that its fiscal and monetary policy options will be increasingly constrained by its creditors, as America reaches a net capital import position of $1 trillion by the early 1990s.

3. A major reassessment of federal government tax and expenditure patterns and priorities will occur as the federal budget is forced toward balance in the early 1990s.

4. Part of the contractionary impulse of reducing the federal deficit will be offset by the positive stimulus of net exports in the $75–100 billion range by the mid-1990s and the resurgence of manufacturing production in the United States.

5. Americans will be poorer in terms of international purchasing power as the dollar falls another 10–20 percent (from its December 1987 levels) against OECD currencies and even more against the currencies of the Newly Industrializing Countries.

6. Americans will consume less than they produce in the coming era of export-led growth, reversing the pattern of 1983–87, when net imports allowed Americans to consume, on average, 2.5 percent more than they produced each year.

7. Production by foreign-owned factories in the United States will increase substantially as foreign firms locate in America to take advantage of its inexpensive labor, land, and facilities. (By itself, this will cause a substantial reduction in United States imports as well as some boost to exports.)

8. LDC debtor nations will be unable to generate the trade surpluses necessary to service their debts as the United States balances its trade account. A systemic accommodation will need to be negotiated between the world's creditor and debtor nations to reduce the export requirements of the LDCs.

9. Trade frictions will rise dramatically as America's trading partners become frustrated by their inability to continue their accustomed habits of export-led growth.

10. America will become the scapegoat for its trading partners' woes as it imports less and increasingly requires its trading partners to open their markets or lose access to the United States market.

ASEAN will occur unobserved but will be coordinated by Japanese firms as they become true multinational enterprises. ASEAN will become ever more integrated into the economic and financial structures of Japan. Japan itself will become somewhat less dependent on the United States market as it diverts some of its energy to leading a more integrated Asian economy. Thus, one can anticipate substantial economic, political, and social changes as the United States begins to "live within its means" in the years to come. Ten of the obvious implications for America are described in Table 2.3.

CONCLUSION

As the United States reverses its trade deficit—as a result of a weaker dollar, slower income growth, and less expansionary fiscal policy—world economic growth will slow substantially. In fact, unless the contractionary impulse of the United States economic slowdown is offset by expansion in Japan and Germany, a synchronized, worldwide recession is quite likely. Such a downturn would increase the spread of more protectionist trade rules throughout the world. And it is feared that a move toward more managed trade might destroy the post-World War II liberal trading order that is enshrined in the GATT. Nevertheless, if the major trading nations could quickly implement the types of policies outlined in Table 2.4, then there would be good reason to hope that a relatively open international trading environment could be maintained.

However, it would be a new international environment—one in which the economic leadership would be passing from the United States to Japan.[14] The United States would be continuously struggling to generate trade surpluses that would be sufficient to service the debts built up during its 1980s consumption

Table 2.4   Policy Prescriptions for Preserving an "Open" International Trading System

---

1. AMERICA MUST QUICKLY ELIMINATE BUDGET DEFICITS.

    The United States needs to bring its budget deficits into balance with domestic savings. This will result in a drop in interest rates which, in turn, will reduce the value of the dollar and further promote trade adjustment, as well as substantially reduce LDC debt repayment problems.

2. JAPAN AND GERMANY MUST QUICKLY EXPAND DOMESTIC-LED GROWTH.

    Japan and Germany must reorient their economies to produce more for their domestic market, and they must substantially increase manufactured imports.

3. INTERNATIONAL CREDITORS MUST QUICKLY REDUCE THE EXPORT REQUIRE-MENTS OF THE INDEBTED LDCs.

    Creditor nations must recognize the obvious with regard to the unrepayability of LDC debts, especially as worldwide growth slows. They need to make the appropriate institutional arrangements to partially "write down" the debts and convert some of the remaining debt to equity.

4. FAIR TRADE AND RECIPROCITY IN GOODS AND SERVICES.

    The world's major trading nations need to implement roughly equivalent rules for managing their international trade and capital flows. The new GATT talks on goods, services, and agriculture need to be quickly and successfully completed.

---

binge. Japan, as the word's premier creditor nation, would sit in judgment on America's efforts to maintain its credit worthiness. Japan would also be likely to be the major player in financing and supervising huge Third World development programs. If successful, such development programs might replace United States net import demand as the "locomotive" for worldwide economic growth.

America will inevitably become competitive enough to service its international debts. The issue is whether or not this increased competitiveness can be attained only by reducing wages, reducing government services, and reducing the quality of American life. Or, can sufficient international competitiveness be attained by increasing productivity while maintaining or expanding the real income of all Americans?[15] The dismal path requires little imagination or leadership; the desirable path requires a great deal of imagination and leadership. America's political and economic leaders, in cooperation with their Japanese and German counterparts, face a great challenge to rebuild the strength and stability of the international economic system.

NOTES

1. This paper is based on the preliminary results of a research project about how the economic structure in the Pacific Rim will be changing as the United States shrinks its trade and fiscal deficits. Much of the information is based on interviews and surveys conducted between May and September of 1987 with business, government, and academic leaders in nine Asian nations, stretching from Tokyo to Jakarta, and in the United States. For more information on this project, see Drobnick and Enzer, "Pacific Rim Trade Scenarios: 1987–92," a paper presented at the Trade Policy Workshop sponsored by the IBEAR Program at the University of Southern California, April 2–4, 1987, and "Pacific Rim Trade Scenarios—Delphi Questionnaire—Round 2," USC, August 1987 (mimeo).

2. The inevitable reversal of America's merchandise trade balance and these attendant issues have recently been described for international policy makers by C. Fred Bergsten, "Economic Imbalances," Foreign Affairs, Spring 1987, pp. 770–794; Martin Feldstein, "Correcting the Trade Deficit," Foreign Affairs, Spring 1987, pp. 795–806; Peter G. Peterson, "The Morning After," The Atlantic, Oct. 1987, pp. 43–69; Lester Thurow and Laura Tyson, "The Economic Black Hole," Foreign Policy, Summer 1987, pp. 3–21.

3. Policies related to the savings gap and its relation to the trade deficit are discussed by Brian Motley and Marc Charney, "The Saving Shortfall," FRBSF Weekly Letter, Jan. 1, 1988.

4. Some people have argued that a substantial part of this "excessive consumption" is the provision of free defense services to Japan, Germany, Korea, Taiwan, etc. If America modifies its defense commitments by either reducing these services or charging for them, America's current account could become much less negative.

5. If the "book value" of America's foreign assets and liabilities were adjusted to market values, America's net foreign asset position would be substantially improved. Some analysts think that America still had a positive asset position at the end of 1986. For example, see Charles Wolf Jr. and Sarah Hooker, "Who Owes Whom, and How Much?" Wall Street Journal, Jan. 6, 1988, p. 16.

6. An important exception to the consensus view is a recent statement by 33 prominent international economists that recognizes the need for the United States to eliminate its trade deficit and create a $50 billion per year surplus (to service its debts) by the early 1990s; see "Thirty Three International Economists Propose Major Policy Changes to Resolve Global Economic Crisis," Institute for International Economics, Washington, D.C.: News Release, Dec. 16, 1987, p. 2. A more detailed presentation of such a "quick" adjustment scenario is provided by Saul H. Hymans and Lawrence B. Krause, "The Outlook for the United States Economy, 1988–90," a paper prepared for the Working Group on the Economic Outlook, Pacific Economic Cooperation Conference (PECC) in Tokyo, Jan. 18, 1988. Their baseline simulation case has the United States trade deficit (on an annualized basis) falling from $137 billion in the first quarter of 1988 to $66 billion in the fourth quarter of 1990; see p. 25.

7. The Economist, Sept. 26 1987, "A Survey of the World Economy," p. 10; and Oct. 24, 1987, p. 11.

8. See Reuven Glick, "Foreign Capital Inflows," FRBSF Weekly Letter, Oct. 30, 1987. The alternative possibility of such a precipitous flight from the dollar has been described by Japan's Economic Planning Agency as the "monetary depression" scenario. See Masaru Yoshitomi, "A Growth Recession," Look Japan, August 1987, pp. 4–6.

9. For recent discussions of Japanese behavior as the premier creditor nation, see Ronald A. Morse, "Japan's Drive to Pre-eminence," Foreign Policy, Winter 1987–88, pp. 3–21; The Economist, "Where Will Wealth Propel Japan?" Oct. 17, 1987, pp. 19–22; James Flanigan, "Japan Calls the Tune in World Trade Dance," Los Angeles Times, Nov. 1, 1987, Part IV, p. 1.

10. For a review of forecasts of the United States current account deficit of five major econometric models (as of January 1987), see Ralph C. Bryant and Gerald Holtham, "The External Deficit: Why? Where Next? What Remedy?," The Brookings Review, Spring 1987, pp. 28–36. Without substantial further depreciation of the dollar, a reduction in the United States federal deficit, and expansionary policy abroad, the "average" forecast is that the current account deficit could remain about $100 billion.

11. For the complete results of this survey, see Richard Drobnick and Selwyn Enzer, "Forecasts of World Trade Conditions 1987–95; Report of a Delphi Inquiry," University of Southern California, IBEAR Working Paper 12, January 1988.

12. Concern about the "hollowing out" of Japan and the possible "boomerang effect" of Japanese firms producing abroad is described by Miyohei Shinohara, "Is Japan Doomed to Deindustrialization?" Japan Echo, Summer 1987, pp. 33–39. A recent survey of Japanese investments in America, which was produced by the Japanese Chamber of Commerce of New York, describes the big increase in Japanese investment in the United States; see "Surprise Made in America!," a special supplement in The Atlantic Monthly, February 1988.

13. Optimism about the growth prospects for ASEAN resulting from exchange rate-induced investment shifts to ASEAN are described by Bernardo M. Villegas, "The Philippines: An Emerging NIC in the Asia-Pacific Region," Manila: Center for Research and Communication (mimeo), August 1987.

14. See Paul Kennedy, "The (Relative) Decline of America," The Atlantic Monthly, August 1987, pp. 29–38, and Ronald A. Morse, "Japan's Drive to Pre-eminence," Foreign Policy, Winter 1987–88, pp. 3–21.

15. According to the Presidential Commission on Industrial Competitiveness, this is the only acceptable definition of competitiveness. That is, it should not be America's goal to compete by reducing real income; see Global Competition: The New Reality, Vol. I (Washington, D.C.: United States Government Printing Office), 1985, p. 6.

3

United States Trade Policy: Underlying Forces for Stability

JOHN ODELL

THOMAS D. WILLETT

For the past 50 years, United States trade policy has been determined by the combined forces of free trade and protectionism. Although the political and economic process by which actual policy was decided was often stormy and based on adverse relations between the legislative branch, the Administration, and a variety of interest groups, the resultant policy was very stable, and generally steered to the middle ground of a basically free trade approach, with a number of protected industries. However, the means of protection is changing from tariffs to nontariff barriers (NTBs) and the postwar trend toward reducing over all levels of protection has been reversed.

This policy, which to some may appear inconsistent, is presented by Odell and Willett as the natural outcome of the political process by which public policy is determined in the United States. It represents a compromise between the economic well-being of the country as a whole and the economic welfare of well-organized special interest groups. In this, trade policy is one more example of public policy that reflects the political structure of the country as well as basic economic realities. Therefore, for those who are interested in public policy, either because they are involved in the decision making process, or because this is their field of research, the over all thrust of United States trade policy is fairly stable and predictable.

Yet what is a stable long run policy on the whole is not necessarily without risk to specific industries or individual corporations. Indeed, the aggregate long-term stability of United States trade policy rests, to a large extent, on flexibility at the level of the components of the aggregate. In other words, changes in comparative advantage across industries over time, and cyclical as well as secular changes in the demand for various goods, may create incentives or disincentives for protection. (The footwear industry and the semiconductor industry are two specific recent cases where the former represents a case of reducing the level of protection, by the ITC, as a result of dynamic changes in comparative advantage, and the latter represents a case of an increased level of protection due to cyclical changes in demand. The semiconductor industry is discussed in part IV). Furthermore, the cooperative nature of the negotiation process, which is characteristic of the formulation of international trade policy since the end of World War II, changes the incidence of NTBs.

This chapter focuses on the continuity and stability of the underlying processes and the resultant United States trade policy. However, the reader should bear in mind that, in this case, stability at the macro policy level may be the source of international trade risk at the individual industry and corporate level. Odell and Willett argue that this situation is likely to continue in the foreseeable future: for the corporate executive, this means that international trade risk is also here to stay.

It is widely believed that United States trade policy has entered a new era of protectionism. Trade restrictions can provide benefits and reduce risks for favored sectors, but they can impose costs on the rest of the economy. At the same time, political debates and media sensationalism can also leave an exaggerated sense of the dangers down the road. Either way, the outlook of governmental trade policies should be an important aspect of the risk management policies of firms affected by international trade developments.

In this chapter we present some of the historical background and conclusions of recent political economy analysis which we believe are essential for interpreting current trade policy developments. We focus on United States trade policy but this analysis has broader relevance. Developments in the course of United States trade policies often have important impacts on the trade policies of other countries. Furthermore, in most instances the types of analysis we apply to the United States are also applicable to the trade policies in other countries.

After the 1960s the impressive postwar progress toward lowering trade barriers came to an end in the United States and many other industrial countries. While the average level of tariffs in the industrial countries has continued on a downward trend, since the 1970s this has been more than offset by the rise of nontariff barriers such as quotas and export restraints. This new protection was imposed piecemeal, product by product, in response to particular pressures. Since 1975, the United States has greatly increased its use of antidumping and antisubsidy duties to retaliate for perceived unfair foreign trading practices. And since 1985, the chief executive has increasingly turned to threats of sanctions on imports designed to force changes in other governments' policies in order to promote United States exports.

We are clearly in the midst of a swing in the orientation of United States trade policy. As Section II reminds us, major shifts between trade liberalism and protectionism are not new to United States history. Thus, one can not dismiss out of hand the commonly expressed fears that we are entering into a major new era of protectionism. We argue, however, that the outlook for United States trade policy is not as bleak as it might appear. We believe the rise in United States protectionism does not represent a decision to reverse the long-term trend toward greater opening of world markets. The United States has continued to propose and join in negotiations to reduce tariffs and to write new international rules limiting trade conflicts. At home, despite all the new import restrictions, imports have expanded substantially in the past decade. Many of the new restrictions have restrained the growth of imports rather than actually cutting them.

In 1980s something new has appeared, as Washington has turned to more aggressive export bargaining than it had used before. That is, especially beginning in 1985 the United States government has made explicit threats to retaliate by raising barriers to the goods of nations that fail to make sufficient concessions to its demands for policy changes abroad. The net effect of this trend is not obvious. If such threats are only guises under which to apply import restrictions desired regardless of other governments' practices, they are not so new. But calls for "fighting fire with fire" have come from sectors that would gain from open trade, including agriculture and high-tech manufacturing, and from political leaders who simultaneously push for trade liberalization. The shift in United States trade politics is not entirely an extension of familiar protectionism. Part of it, while departing from laissez faire, is a groping for more effective means of expanding trade. Most of the threats have not been carried out.

The institutions of United States trade policy making were changed after the protectionist horrors of the 1930s, and these institutions remain a strong factor constraining moves that would tilt policy away from a liberal direction. They are reinforced by an international political environment that, despite the frequency of current trade disputes, remains much more cooperative than in that dark period. Consequently, we argue that in the aggregate, United States trade policies are unlikely to present a highly increased source of risk for international business over the next few years. Nevertheless, at the micro level, the possibility of protectionist measures from particular industries remains significant. Thus for many firms, following trade policy trends and developing early-warning systems should be a valuable part of the risk management process.

What are the causes of the recent expansion in protectionism within an environment that is still sensitive to the gains from trade? It is becoming increasingly recognized that such issues require attention to both political and economic considerations. We are in the midst of a resurgence of interest in political economy among both economists and political scientists. As is perhaps to be expected, many of the initial contributions to the recent analysis of international political economy emphasized one particular set of considerations to the exclusion of other counterbalancing forces. In Section III we briefly present some of the major contending perspectives on international political economy, and then illustrate how we can draw upon them to begin to develop a more comprehensive framework for analysis. We conclude with a brief discussion of the outlook for United States trade policies.

HISTORICAL ROOTS OF UNITED STATES TRADE POLICY

Some of the influences that shape contemporary United States policies toward international trade, such as ideology, have roots deep in American history. In

1791, the first secretary of the treasury, Alexander Hamilton, recommended to the fledgling Congress what would today be called an industrial policy, including subsidies to manufacturers and import protection. He argued that in a mercantilist world, industries would not otherwise develop in this new mostly agricultural state, and that stronger industry would be essential for national defense. But the new government declined to follow Hamilton's advice. Its leaders had been Englishmen, and they had read and were convinced by Adam Smith. They then taught the same lessons to their descendants, who interpreted the American experience as confirmation on the virtures of laissez faire, although with significant qualifications. Even today, American leaders as a group tend to be more influenced by this ideology than leaders in almost every other country. This ideological commitment is still a valuable ally for those advocating liberal trade policies.

In the 1820s, the familiar two American political parties began to congeal, and the United States turned to national import barriers. In the 1828 race for the presidency, the factions outbid each other for support from protectionist groups, producing the famous high "tariff of abominations." After the Civil War, the (southern) Democratic and (northern) Republican parties diverged clearly into free trade and protectionist colorations, respectively. The Republicans dominated and tariffs remained high for manufacturers. When the Democrats finally regained the White House in 1913, tariffs fell. After the Republicans returned in 1921, rates rose again, reaching their all-time highs with the Smoot–Hawley Act of 1930. After 1933, tariff rates began to descend again.

This political party differentiation changed in the post–World War II period. The Republican return to power in the 1950s did not interrupt the free trade trend, and since then, the major cleavages on United States trade policy have not coincided with political party lines. Future party turnover is not likely in itself to make much difference to trade policy.

In the early twentieth-century, the domestic political system also underwent a different transformation that appears to be permanent. In many countries, urban workers and other less advantaged groups succeeded in organizing themselves for industrial and political action for the first time. Their efforts, together with the 1930s Depression, fatally undermined the nineteenth-century liberal state and replaced it with the welfare state. Since then, the idea of the unhindered free market has never been able to attract widespread allegiance, even in the United States. Organized working and middle classes have been able to compel politicians to "do something" to protect them from the pain that can be inflicted by unhindered market pressures.

During the watershed period of the 1930s and 1940s, the United States began its historic shift from a protectionist to a trade-liberalizing policy. At home, the policymaking process was changed. In the 1934 Reciprocal Trade Agreements Act, the Congress turned over to the president the authority to set specific tariff rates through negotiation. The result was to favor liberalizing forces and hinder their opponents, since the President's nationwide electoral constituency makes him much less vulnerable to pressures from a particular industry than is a member of Congress. Tariff reductions were associated with an increase in world trade in the late 1940s and 1950s. During this period the United States and its allies have designed and implemented international institutions for trade negotiations (GATT), as well as for financial negotiations (IMF).

It is important to remember, however, that from the beginning the GATT/IMF system was fitted with "escape hatches," provisions that would permit a government to restore protection if the pressure of re-opened markets became too great. The United States itself also led the way to open the escape hatches; the first large-scale waiver of obligations granted by the GATT was to the United States on behalf of its agricultural sector. Thus the current combination of official advocacy of a continued move toward increasingly liberal trade at the general level, combined with many exceptions, is not a new phenomenon.

THE POLITICAL ECONOMY OF INTERNATIONAL TRADE POLICY

In one of the first important efforts at providing a synthesis of recent international political economy analysis, Robert Gilpin (1975) focused on three major approaches: the Marxist, the modern mercantilist or realist, and the interdependence or sovereignty at bay view.[1] The two latter views held quite different beliefs about the importance of economic versus autonomous governmental political considerations in determining trade policies. The sovereignty at bay view assumed that economic efficiency considerations would dominate the political process and consequently predicted a trend toward progressive trade liberalization.[2] While this view fit well with trade policy developments in the industrial countries over the first two decades of the postwar period, the reversal of this trend in the 1970s called the cogency of this approach into question.

At first glance, this increase in trade restrictions seems consistent with the modern mercantilist or realist approach.[3] Although some of the trade restrictions adopted by the United States over the past two decades, especially the use of economic sanctions for foreign policy reasons, do reflect such modern mercantilism, most of the important trade restrictions have reflected the ability of special interest groups to generate protection for a particular sector against the desires of the Executive branch. Both Republican and Democratic presidents have supported such special-case protection, but typically only because they considered it too costly politically to do otherwise.

The Marxist approach with its emphasis on conflict between the interests of labor and capital has enjoyed some increased influence, as the AFL-CIO turned toward support for protectionism in the 1960s while most business groups remained supporters of a liberal approach. It is ironic to note that in this context the predictions of a Marxist approach can also be derived from neoclassical international trade theory. In the standard two factor model, the relatively scarce factor of production (labor in the United States loses from free trade relative to the abundant factor (capital).

It is becoming increasingly recognized, however, that most Marxist and traditional trade theory analyses focus on too aggregate a level. The business community has far from a homogeneous set of attitudes toward trade policy. While a majority of firms, especially those with multinational operations and export interests, tend to continue to favor liberal trade policies, many import-competing firms have swung strongly in a protectionist direction. Typically they join in lobbying with the workers in their industry. Thus the key to understanding the increased protectionism of the past two decades is not in aggregate conflicts between labor and capital, but rather in the combined lobbying of labor and capital in particular industries seeking protection at the expense of both labor and capital in the rest of the economy.

Over the past several decades public choice analysis has developed into a substantial subdiscipline of economics and political science. Defined broadly, this set of ideas provides a useful way of understanding the behavior of special interest groups and their interface with government at a disaggregate level. Public choice analysis helps by explaining how, because of free-rider problems, small, well-organized groups can develop greater political clout than much larger but less well organized groups.[4] Hence, contrary to the assumptions of the sovereignty at bay view, producer interests are seen to dominate consumer interests in many cases. Thus the problem from the standpoint of standard public choice analysis is not to explain why we have protection, but why we do not have more. One answer offered by public choice theorist Mancur Olson in his *Rise and Fall of Nations* (1982) is that the formation of effective interest groups is difficult, but over time the number of such groups will increase. This trend toward increased special-interest measures causes progressively reduced efficiency and the fall of nations over time. While this view appears consistent with the broad outline of United States trade policy over the postwar period, other important factors were at work as well.[5]

Free-rider problems are not so severe, however, as to prevent pro-trade sectors from organizing and bringing pressure to bear against campaigns for protections. In fact, the multiplication of protection campaigns after the mid-1970s stimulated a striking expansion of such "anti-protection" political activity in the United States. For example, retailers of automobiles, shoes, and clothing spent hundreds of thousands of dollars in the 1980s to publicize the costs of proposed barriers in each case. Farm exporters weighed in openly against new protection for steel, wine, and textiles. In most cases, the opposition is politically weaker than the proponents, and some new protection was provided in many cases. But this more vocal opposition did encourage some politicians to speak out as well, and the result may well have been more moderate change than would have occurred otherwise.[6] The recent United States campaign to penalize the Toshiba Corporation for sales to the Soviet Union mobilized hosts of American companies to lobby heavily, arguing that sanctions would hurt them.

These anti-protection pressures are not surprising considering the long-term trend toward expanding the share of the United States economy that is sensitive to trade. In the United States as well as other countries, protection cuts into the interests of organized groups—not only household consumers. This underlying interdependence on international trade and investment is likely to moderate conflictual politics.

We believe that state power objectives emphasized in the modern mercantilism approach have had an important but declining influence on United States trade policy formulation. Contrary of the traditional tendencies of the original mercantilists and of many mercantilist countries today, the United States in the postwar period followed liberal trade policies for economic as well as for foreign policy reasons (with a few major exceptions especially involving East/West trade). Foreign policy considerations are one reason why the Executive branch has been a strong advocate of liberal trade policies across both Democratic and Republican administrations. This has served as a significant counterweight to domestic protectionist pressures. Declines in the salience of traditional national security/foreign policy considerations and in the strength of the Executive branch relative to Congress have contributed to the increased incidences of protectionist policies in recent years.

The structural or hegemonic theory also helps explain the increasing incidence of protection.[7] As United States economic political and military power has declined slightly, the effectiveness of its leadership in the world economy has declined as well. Too much can be made of the decline in United States power and leadership, however. The United States retains considerable, if diminished, leadership capabilities in international economic relations, especially among the industrial countries.

This point is often missed by casual observers of the international economic scene because of the frequency of policy disagreements highlighted in the press. Although such conflict is real, to focus on it alone gives a distorted picture. These disagreements over active policy coordination take place against a backdrop of considerable passive cooperation to avoid the types of severe conflicts that so seriously damaged the world economy during the 1930s. Some protectionism of the past decade, for instance negotiated export restraints, is even considered a form of cooperation by some. While such cooperation does little if anything to cut the direct efficiency costs of protection, it does substantially reduce the likelihood of serious trade wars. Greater use of nontariff barriers in forms that transfer much of the rents generated by trade restrictions to foreign producers has been an important aspect of this process.

While the direct effectiveness of GATT has come under increasing criticism in recent years, and UNCTAD and other United Nations economic forums have become verbal battlefields over trade policy issues between the North and the South, the general fabric of international trade cooperation, while becoming increasingly frayed, has remained intact. The weathering of the shocks of the 1970s and 1980s to date without the development of widespread beggar-thy-neighbor policies has been a significant accomplishment. In general, our view is that the development of international forums for discussing economic issues and reinforcing the need for at least passive cooperation in order to avoid serious trade wars and other conflicts has been on the same order of importance in influencing trade policies as the specific international agreements that have been reached. This former influence is difficult to trace directly because it has largely taken the form of protectionist actions that were avoided, but we feel that this channel of influence has been real. In this regard, the institution of economic summits among the heads of major industrial countries has been an important innovation despite the relatively meager direct results of these meetings.

Another point often missed by casual observers is that Congress, while certainly more protectionist than the Executive branch, is in truth considerably less protectionist than typical press coverage would suggest. The tragic consequences of the Smoot–Hawley tariff showed Congress the dangers of treating trade policy in the same way as typical domestic pork barrel politics. Beginning with the Reciprocal Trade Agreements Act of 1934, Congress has deliberately limited its ability to cater to special-interest trade policy requests. Through a combination of international agreements, delegation of authority to the Executive branch and the International Trade Commission, and adoption of laws to deal with hardship cases based on general principles rather than sheer political clout, Congress has substantially diffused pressures for trade barriers.

The tendency of Congress to push for increased control in recent years has helped to obscure the fact that this is still occurring within a framework of considerable self-denial. While we believe that Robert Pastor's recent analysis (1980, 1983) or this issue paints somewhat too idealized a picture of the degree to which Congressional trade policymaking has served general rather than special interests, we find the broad outlines of his analysis to be quite important and accurate.[8] Pastor also provides considerable insight in his discussion of the "cry and sigh" paradox of Congressional trade bills. Members of Congress often have strong political incentives to introduce and/or vote for protectionist bills that they would actually not like to see enacted. This is often an effective means for signaling a danger of serious measures if the president or foreign governments refuse to take lesser steps. Recognition of this signaling process does not imply that there is no substance to this appearance of increased protectionist proclivities in Congress in recent years, but it does suggest that the dangers are not as great as they appear at first glance. Traditional ideology is still powerful.

Economic conditions have an important influence on both the amount of protectionist pressure and the extent to which government responds to this pressure. While the simplest pure rent-seeking models see no connection between economic conditions and efforts to obtain benefits from government, broader analysis suggests that poor economic conditions typically increase the incentives for groups to seek protection.[9] They also increase the likelihood that protection will be received. At least where large amounts are at stake, fairly broad support within Congress must be obtained. This is far easier to achieve if an industry has fallen on hard times. The basic philosophy of Congress has been one of favoring liberal but not free trade, with provisions for at least temporary protection or countervailing actions when American industry faces unfair practices abroad and/or seriously depressed conditions related at least in part to import competition.

In this respect, it can be argued that the increased incidence of protectionism has not reflected a major shift in this philosophy, although undoubtedly the shift of organized labor to a protectionist stance has had some influence on the traditionally liberal trade-oriented Democratic Party. More important in our judgment has been the increased international competition American industry has faced as the rest of the world has begun to catch up with us economically, and the related reduced tolerance by the United States government toward protectionist policies abroad. It is these aspects of the structuralist or hegemonic analysis of increased protectionism that we believe have the greatest cogency.

In addition to these trends and institutional considerations, short-term economic developments can also have a substantial impact on trade policies. The most significant factors in increased United States protectionism in recent years have primarily been import competition and depressed economic conditions in particular industries such as autos, steel, and textiles. The severity of depressed conditions in particular industries, however, will in turn be influenced by the state of the macroeconomy and aggregate trade developments as well as microeconomic developments specific to that industry. Thus, a number of empirical studies have found that cyclical downturns, aggregate trade deficits and strong values of the currency tend to contribute to protectionist pressures, while concern about inflation tends to generate pressure to loosen trade restrictions.[10]

There is sometimes a tendency to contrast rent-seeking and public-interest explanations of protectionism. We believe, however, that there is a good deal of complementarity between the two. Even if they do not stand up to rigorous scrutiny, the appearance of some type of public-interest argument—such as national security considerations or unfair foreign competition—substantially helps a rent seeker secure protection. On the other hand, without sizeable political clout an industry is much less likely to receive substantial protection even when it has a stronger objective case than many industries which have previously received protection. To understand and predict trade policies, the interactions between economic and political considerations must be taken into account.

THE OUTLOOK FOR TRADE POLICY

We have sketched a complex variety of influences that can shape the governmental trade environment in one direction or another. What does it add up to? The final answer varies with the analyst, of course, but on balance we remain optimistic at least that a recurrence of major trade warfare as in the 1930s can be avoided. The more likely scenario would seem to be a continuation of the United States pattern of recent years: continued general support for open trade policies and GATT negotiations, perhaps a few more exceptions for certain depressed industries, import protection provided typically in forms that minimize the danger of retaliation, and continuation of more aggressive export bargaining.

In general, pressures for exceptions are most likely in labor-intensive industries, in those with larger sunk costs in older technologies, in sectors with national defense linkages, and in those having lesser stakes in exports. Macroeconomic conditions, of course, are difficult to foresee, but major policy errors there would certainly intensify conditions that favor protectionism and international conflict. One cannot rule out entirely a substantial worsening of international debt and banking problems, or a strongly protectionist turn in the European Community that could provoke rapid adverse changes in the United States.

Having recognized all this, we have chosen to emphasize here the underlying factors that should dampen pressures for rapid growth in protectionism. These have ranged from the fact of economic interdependence and costs of protection, to the deeply rooted American cultural preference for open market competition, policy making institutions that constrain the legislature's tendency toward special interest measures, political opposition by groups who would pay the price, and the remaining fabric of international cooperation that is valued in Washington. One recent event showing that these forces are not trivial is ratification of a new trade-liberalizing agreement between Canada and the United States.

If there is one risk that particularly merits monitoring, it might be related to the new aggressive export bargaining. All negotiators would confirm that pressure is often needed in order to produce agreements that include difficult concessions, even when overall net gain would result on both sides. Advocates of a coercive strategy can also point to liberalizing changes in other countries that have taken place under pressure. At the same time, the EEC, Japan, Canada, and even developing countries do have alternatives to making such concessions, and some of them have been known to fight back. A ham-handed application of the strategy could backfire, possibly triggering retaliation against United States products or investments outside the sectors that gave rise to the dispute. Thus all trade-sensitive firms have an interest in monitoring this development.

NOTES

1. For additional surveys of various major approaches to international political economy see Frey (1984a, b), Jones (1983), Tollison and Willett (1982), and Willett (1980).
2. The Marxist approach also assumes that economics dominates politics, but has a quite different view of economic relationships.
3. Leading exponents of this approach include Calleo and Rowland (1973) and Krasner (1976).
4. See, for example, Olson (1965).
5. We should note, however, that Olson's view conflicts with those of economists who see a tendency toward greater efficiency over time; see, for example, Becker (1983) and North (1984). The generality of Olson's hypothesis has been the subject of considerable debate. See, for example, Mueller (1983).

6. See Destler and Odell (1987).
7. For presentations and criticisms of these views see Gowa (1987), Keohane (1980), Krasner (1976), Milner (1987), and Pastor (1980).
8. For recent analyses of the evolution of the institutions of United States trade policy formulation, see also Baldwin (1984), Destler (1986), and Goldstein (1986).
9. Recent examples of such broader analysis may be found in Aggarwal, Keohane, and Yoffie (1987), Cassing, McKeown and Ochs (1986), McKeown (1984), and Peltzman (1976).
10. For recent contributions and surveys of the empirical literature on the determinants of protectionist policies in the United States see Baldwin (1985), Canto (1986), Cline (1984), Coughlin (1985), Lavergne (1983), Magee and Young (1987), Pugel and Walters (1984), and Marks and McArthur (1987).

REFERENCES

Aggarwal, V.; Keohane, R.O.; and Yoffie, D.B.: "The Evolution of Cooperative Protectionism," *American Political Science Review* (June 1987), pp. 345–366.

Baldwin, Robert E.: "The Changing Nature of United States Trade Policy Since World War II," in R.E. Baldwin, and A.O. Krueger, eds, *The Structure and Evolution of Recent United States Trade Policy* (Chicago: University of Chicago Press, 1984).

Baldwin, Robert E.: "The Political Economy of Protection," in J. Bhagwati, ed., *Import Competition and Response* (Chicago: University of Chicago Press, 1982).

Baldwin, Robert E.: *The Political Economy of United States Import Policy* (Cambridge, MA: MIT Press, 1985).

Baldwin, Robert E.; and Thompson, T. Scott: "Responding to Trade-Distorting Policies of Other Countries," *American Economic Review*, 74, No. 2 (1984), pp. 271–276.

Bauer, R.A.; Pool, I.; and Dexter, L.A.: *American Business and Public Policy: The Politics of Foreign Trade*, 2d Ed. (Chicago: Aldine-Atherton, 1972).

Becker, Gary S.: "A Theory of Competition Among Pressure Groups for Political Influence," *Quarterly Journal of Economics*, 98 (1983), pp. 371–400.

Bergsten, C. Fred; and Williamson, John: "Exchange Rates and Trade Policy," in William R. Cline, ed., *Trade Policy in the 1980's* (Cambridge, MA: MIT Press for the Institute for International Economics, 1983).

Bhagwati, Jagdish N.: "Directly Unproductive Profit-Seeking (DUP) Activities," *Journal of Political Economy*, 90 pp. 988–1002.

Calleo, David P.; and Rowland, Benjamin M.: *America and the World Political Economy* (Bloomington: Indiana University Press, 1973).

Canto, Victor A.: *The Determinants and Consequences of Trade Restrictions in the United States Economy* (New York: Praeger, 1986).

Cassing, James; McKeown, Timothy J.; and Ochs, Jack: "The Political Economy of the Tariff Cycle," *American Political Science Review* (Sept. 1986), pp. 843–862.

Cline, William: "Reciprocity: A New Approach?" in William Cline, ed., *Trade Policy in the 1980s* (Cambridge, MA: MIT Press for Institute for International Economics, 1983), pp. 121–154.

Cline, William: *Exports of Manufactures from Developing Countries: Performance and Prospects for Market Access* (Washington, D.C.: Brooking Institution, 1984).

Coughlin, Cletus C.: "Domestic Content Legislation: House Voting and the Economic Theory of Regulation," *Economic Inquiry*, 23 (1985) pp. 437–448.

Destler, I.M.: *American Trade Politics: System Under Stress* (Washington, D.C.: Institute for International Economics, 1986).

Destler, I.M.; and Odell, John S.: *Anti-Protection: Changing Forces in United States Trade Politics* (Washington, D.C.: Institute for International Economics, 1987).

Dornbusch, Rudiger; and Frenkel, Jeffrey A.: "Macroeconomics and Protection," in Robert M. Stern, ed. *United States Trade Policies in a Changing World Economy* (Cambridge, MA: MIT Press, 1987), pp. 77–130.

Feigenbaum, Susan; and Willett, Thomas D.: "Domestic Versus International Influences on Protectionist Pressure in the United States," in Sven W. Arndt, Richard J. Sweeney, and Thomas D. Willett, eds, *Exchange Rates, Trade, and the United States Economy* (Washington, D.C.: American Enterprise Institute, 1985).

Feigenbaum, Susan; Ortiz, Henry; and Willett, Thomas D.: "Protectionist Pressures and Aggregate Economic Conditions: Comment on Takacs," *Economic Inquiry*, 23 (1985), pp. 175–182.

Frey, Bruno S.: *International Political Economics* (Oxford: Basil Blackwell, 1984a).

Frey, Bruno S.: "The Public Choice View of International Political Economy," *International Organization*, 38 (1984b), pp. 199–223.

Gallarotti, G.: "Toward a Business Cycle Model of Tariffs," *International Organization*, 39 (Winter 1985), pp. 155–187.

Gilpin, Robert: "Three Models of the Future," in C. Fred Bergsten, and Lawrence Krause, eds, *World Politics and International Economics* (Washington, D.C.: Brookings Institution, 1975).

Goldstein, Judith: "The Political Economy of Trade: Institutions of Protection," *American Political Science Review*, 80 (1986), pp. 161–184.

Goldstein, Judith; and Krasner, Stephen D.: "Unfair Trade Policies," *American Economic Review* (May 1984), pp. 282–287.

Gowa, Joanne: "Ships That Pass in the Night?: Neo-Classical Trade Theory in a Balance-of-Power World," paper presented at the Claremont–USC Conference on Blending Political and Economic Analysis of International Trade Policies, March 1987. Forthcoming in Odell and Willett (1989).

Jones, R.J. Barry: "Perspectives on International Political Economy," in R.J. Barry Jones, ed., *Perspectives on Political Economy* (New York: St. Martin's Press, 1983), pp. 169–208.

Kaempfer, William H.; and Willett, Thomas D.: "Why an Import Surcharge Wouldn't Help America's Trade Deficit," *The World Economy* (March 1987), pp. 27–37.

Keohane, R.: "The Theory of Hegemonic Stability and Changes in International Economic Regimes," in O. Holsti, K. Siverson, and A. George, eds, *Change in the International System* (Boulder, CO: Westview, 1980), pp. 131–162.

Krasner, Stephen D.: "State Power and the Structure of International Trade," *World Politics*, 28 (April 1976), pp. 317–347.

Lavergne, Real P.: *The Political Economy of United States Tariffs: An Empirical Analysis* (Toronto: Academic Press, 1983).

McKeown, T.: "Firms and Tariff Regime Change," *World Politics*, 36 (January 1984), pp. 215–233.

Magee, Stephen P.: "Endogenous Tariff Theory: A Survey," in D. Colander, ed., *Neoclassical Political Economy* (Cambridge, MA: Ballinger, 1984).

Magee, Stephen P.; and Young, Leslie: "Endogenous Protection in the United States, 1980–1984," in Robert M. Stern, ed., *United States Trade Policies in a Changing World Economy* (Cambridge, MA: MIT Press, 1987), pp. 145–195.

Marks, Stephen V.; and McArthur, John: "Empirical Analyses of the Determinants of Protection: A Survey and Some New Results," paper presented at the Claremont–USC Conference on Blending Political and Economic Analysis of International Trade Polices, March 1987. Forthcoming in Odell and Willett (1989).

Mayer, W.: "Endogenous Tariff Formation," *American Economic Review*, 74 (Dec. 1984), pp. 970–985.

Milner, Helen: "Trading Places. Industries for Free Trade," paper presented at the Claremont–USC Conference on Blending Political and Economic Analysis of International Trade Policies, March 1987. Forthcoming in Odell and Willett (1989).

Mueller, D.C.: ed., *The Political Economy of Growth* (New Haven, CT: Yale University Press, 1983).

North, Douglas: "Three Approaches to the Study of Institutions," in D. Collander, ed., *Neoclassical Political Economy: The Analysis of Rent-Seeking and DUP Activities* (Cambridge, MA: Ballinger Publishing Co., 1984).

Odell, John; and Willett, Thomas D.: eds, *International Trade Policies* (Ann Arber: University of Michgan Press, forthcoming).

Olson, Mancur: *The Logic of Collective Action: Public Goods and the Theory of Groups* (Cambridge: Harvard University Press, 1965).

Olson, Mancur: *The Rise and Fall of Nations* (New Haven, CT: Yale University Press, 1982).

Pastor, Robert: *Congress and the Politics of United States Foreign Economic Policy: 1929–1976* (Berkeley: University of California Press, 1980).

Pastor, R.A.: "The Cry-and-Sigh Syndrome: Congress and Trade Policy," in A. Schick, ed., *Making Economic Policy in Congress* (Washington, D.C.: American Enterprise Institute, 1983).

Peltzman, S.: "Toward a More General Theory of Regulation," *Journal of Law and Economics*, 19 (1976), pp. 211–248.

Pugel, Thomas A.; and Walter, Ingo: "United States Corporate Interests and the Political Economy of Trade Policy," *Review of Economics and Statistics*, 67 (1984), pp. 465–473.

Tollison, Robert D.; and Willett, Thomas D.: "Power, Politics, and Prosperity: Alternative Views of Economic Interdependence," in Michael J. Finger, and Thomas D. Willett, eds, "The Internationalization of the World Economy," *The Annals* (March 1982).

Willett, Thomas D.: "Some Aspects of the Public Choice Approach to International Economic Relations," Claremont CA Center for Economic Policy Studies Working Paper (January 1980).

4

Building Blocks for United States Trade Policy in the 1990s

JONATHAN D. ARONSON

United States trade policy is formulated in a dynamic process based on economic and political considerations. As was demonstrated in the last chapter, the actors remain the same, and even the process is fairly stable, yet the concrete outcomes in terms of specific policies with regard to specific sectors are uncertain. In other words, any potential Bill of Congress, Executive order, or regulatory change may or may not materialize or may do so in many different forms. For a single firm or industry, the enactment of a specific bill or the precise wording of an International Trade Commission (ITC) decision may be crucial.

The risk at the level of the single firm or industry emanates from two related aspects of the concrete steps of United States trade policy: whether a certain step will occur, and, if it does, what effect it will have on the firm or industry. For example, Aronson places high probability on the continuation of the process of tariff reduction, up to a no-tariff situation. Yet, this is not certain. A serious deterioration in the trade situation (i.e. a substantial increase in the United States trade deficit), combined with an economic recession in the United States, may reverse the process of tariff reduction. Even if tariff reduction continues, it is not clear what the net effect will be on any given firm or industry.

Another example is nontariff barriers (NTBs) and the Japanese automobile industry. At first, the precise form of NTB to be enacted or agreed upon with regard to Japanese automobile exports to the United States was far from certain. But even when the voluntary restraints were agreed upon, the long-term effects on the Japanese car industry, the United States auto manufacturers, and the Korean auto industry remained highly uncertain.

In this chapter, Aronson provides us with probabilistic estimates of the major building blocks of United States trade policy. This information also serves as an input for risk evaluation and the design of responses at the corporate level.

BASIC ASSUMPTIONS

The Trade System

Since the creation of the General Agreement on Tariffs and Trade (GATT) in the late 1940s, the trade regime has weathered many battles between free traders and protectionists. Seven rounds of multilateral trade negotiation have significantly lowered tariffs on goods and established and clarified important rules, principles, and procedures governing trade. The Tokyo Round of negotiations (1973–79) even yielded a series of new codes that begin to grapple with problems of nontariff barriers (NTBs).[1] But protectionism is fungible. When tariffs at borders were reduced or eliminated, previously irrelevant or invisible NTBs were revealed. In addition, many countries made concessions during negotiations and then immediately undermined them by erecting new regulatory obstacles that impeded trade.[2] In addition, over time, many important sectors, including agriculture, textiles, automobiles, and steel, were largely removed from the influence of the GATT. Still other sectors including energy and services never came under GATT auspices. And, even as GATT negotiations reduced tariff barriers, new obstacles were erected in those areas beyond its reach. In short, when countries reduce certain trade barriers, they do not automatically embrace free trade.

But if countries have not really changed their spots, the lair they inhabit has been transformed. During the 1950s, the trade realm had reasonably clear boundaries. Trade, monetary, investment, and aid issues were nearly independent of one another and were handled by different sets of national and international bureaucrats. At the same time, companies lived in a comfortable, predictable United States-dominated world of fixed exchange rates and low energy prices in which the fear of hostile takeovers was minimal. The business was well defined, and corporate executives knew what they wanted to accomplish.

Many things have changed for government and business leaders. The world has become more independent, and United States dominance has declined while the relative importance of countries such as Japan and West Germany has increased. Moreover, the world is facing a period of slower economic growth and higher unemployment. Trade negotiators have finished with the easiest, most transparent trade problems. What remains will be harder to conceptualize and to resolve. In addition, excess global capacity is a growing problem in sector after sector. Meanwhile, many countries are using industrial policies to try to create competitive advantage for their industries.

Business executives and government officials must also cope with considerably greater uncertainty about their environment. In the past 50 years, for example, increased foreign exchange flexibility has forced corporate executives to worry more about currency fluctuations and less about their core businesses. By the same token, higher and more volatile energy prices altered the calculus of business decisions.

Even more importantly, boundaries are blurring everywhere, and the time that officials have to react to change is shrinking. It is harder to know what to do, and it is critical that new ways of managing the world economy be developed. Put simply, the interdependence between trade, monetary, and investment issues is increasing. In addition, sectoral distinctions are breaking down. Thus, financial supermarkets are replacing separate banking, insurance, brokerage, and securities industries while the merging of telecommunications, computer, and broadcasting technologies is creating a new world information economy. At the same time, the increasingly large service component of goods and the blurring of sectoral lines make it harder for government officials to develop a clear plan for negotiating international economic accords. It is harder as well for corporations to determine what they should be doing to protect themselves in a far more uncertain economic environment.[3] Furthermore, the product cycle seems to be shortening, and unless goods and services are introduced globally on an almost simultaneous basis, companies may lose their competitive edge.[4]

One way to interpret the rising interest in international corporate arrangements on the part of leading companies from different countries is as a way of trying to manage the uncertain global economic environment. If governments cannot or will not reimpose more predictability on the global economic environment, corporations will try to reorganize themselves to accomplish this task, at least so far as it impacts them directly. (Whether or not international corporate arrangements are a long-term, stable solution for corporations is still open to question.[5])

Trade Policy Prospects

As the world economy evolves, trade policy also shifts, even if it never really keeps up to date. Tension arises because the world economy, over time, has less relevance for the system that existing trade rules were devised to manage. Today, calls for greater protectionism and efforts to promote freer trade still coexist, particularly in the United States. The United States and Israel have signed a path-breaking bilateral agreement. Significantly, this accord covers services as well as goods. Later, the United States and Canada signed a similar free trade agreement.[6] And, in September 1986, after years of preparation, the 92 members of GATT agreed to begin new, far-reaching round of multilateral trade negotiations. The Uruguay Round is meant to strengthen the rules governing the trading system and stimulate growth by further liberalizing trade. Tariffs and NTBs will receive attention. And, for the first time, GATT negotiations will focus on trade in services, intellectual property issues, and trade-related investment issues.

At the same time, saddled with a $170 billion trade deficit in 1986, the Democrat-controlled United States Congress is considering tough, protectionist legislation. To deflect Congressional criticism and initiatives, the Reagan Administration is also talking and acting tougher. Not surprisingly, many other countries are also promoting industrial policies and are considering other measures to boost their own trade position. Meanwhile, many key United States trading partners are expected to retaliate if the United States enacts protectionist measures. Even economic dogma that reveres free trade and decries protectionism is beginning to consider circumstances under which protection might actually be economically efficient.[7]

Two things are certain: neither free trade nor autarky will prevail. The result will fall somewhere in between. There are simply too many powerful domestic industry groups, each actively lobbying for its own narrow interests, to permit genuine free trade.[8] As a result, United States legislators frequently advocate strongly nationalistic policies built on reciprocity, or "tit for tat."[9] They will often vote for protectionist measures, particularly when the votes have symbolic instead of real significance.[10] But, deep down, legislators do not favor protectionist policies. The Congress has been reminded too often of the disaster that followed the Hawley–Smoot Tariff of 1930 to be genuinely tempted by heavily protectionist legislation.[11] Their preference is to adopt legislation that allows the President enough discretion that he can prevent protective activities from going into effect. However, the Congress at the same time wants to make sure that the President explains to Congress and the American people why he is not taking action. The Congress thus can shift the responsibility for actions that may later turn out to be misguided away from itself.[12]

As a result, I expect that any trade bill that becomes law during the 1980s will have more bark than bite. On the surface, it will call for stern action against United States trading partners who are "cheating" (or winning). But the President, by paying a political price, will be left with sufficient discretion to defuse all but the most innocuous protectionist actions. The worst of the protectionist fervor will also be diluted by the presence of ongoing bilateral and multilateral negotiations. While involved in negotiations, legislators and executives can more readily deflect demands for protection by concerned interest groups. Leaders can promise that every group's interests will certainly be taken into account in the final decisions and that all groups should be patient.[13]

TRADE POLICY ALTERNATIVES

This background is all very nice, but what could happen? My best estimate is that there will be a great deal of activity but not a lot of change along a spectrum from total free trade to total protection. Natural balancing mechanisms will tend to lead toward solutions somewhere in the middle.

The extreme of free trade is unthinkable, despite the best efforts of Uruguay Round negotiators, because domestic interest groups in all countries are becoming better organized in order to protect their interests. On the other hand, rising calls for protectionism, at least in the United States, may prompt those favoring free trade to begin to organize to prevent a dramatic increase in protectionism.[14] By the same token, rising protection extreme enough to prompt a crisis and collapse of the GATT trading system is also unlikely. The world economy is more complicated, and government officials may be no wiser today than 50 years ago, but their access to information about the past is better.

Two other factors are encouraging. First, government spending as a percentage of GNP is far higher today than in the past. Although this may lead to complaints of big government, it also guards against severe recessions and depressions. Second, economics (and particularly microeconomics) has made important advances at understanding how the economy works. Errors are unavoidable, but disasters are less likely.

Steps Toward Greater Liberalization

Moves that promote liberalization and protectionist activities will both take place. However, predicting a balance of gains and losses along the spectrum from free trade to autarky is insufficient. To avoid fence sitting, more specific predictions are needed.

Further Tariff Reduction
(Probability: Very Likely; Confidence: Very High)

Average tariffs are already low and will be reduced further. Seven rounds of multilateral trade negotiations have made it good politics to lower tariffs. There is not much more to reduce here; therefore, tariff reductions are less important today. The key trade obstacles are mostly NTBs. Thus I expect the process to continue. Two points are worth considering, however. First, across-the-board tariff reductions by industrial countries may hurt the competitive position of some developing countries that benefit from preferential treatment. As tariffs approach zero, there is less room for preferential treatment for developing countries. Second, accepting higher tariffs in exchange for fewer NTBs might be beneficial, because it would make trade relations more predictable.[15] Tariffs, which are transparent, usually distort the trading system less than other measures.

Strengthen Tokyo Round NTB Codes
(Probability: High; Confidence: High)

The *Government Procurement Code* was one of the major successes of the Tokyo Round negotiations. It could easily be extended to cover more purchases from more government agencies, including some PTTs.[16] More progress is possible to make sure that technical specifications are not used as barriers and that specifications are stated in terms of performance rather than design. The current code could be extended to cover services much more broadly.

The *Customs Valuation Code* tries to assure that customer value "be based on simple and equitable criteria consistent with commercial practices and that valuation should be of general application without distinction between sources of supply." This code could be strengthened.

The *Standards Code* took important steps toward minimizing the use of technical and other standards to create unnecessary obstacles to international trade. This code was a major success of the Tokyo Round but could be strengthened and extended to cover services.

The code covering *Import Licensing Procedures* began the process of simplifying and making administrative procedures more transparent and more equitable. Much more can be accomplished. In particular, work is needed to improve consultation procedures when disputes arise.

The *Code for Subsidies and Countervailing Duties* was perhaps the weakest, most ambiguous of the Tokyo Round codes. The code is not clear about exactly what constitutes a subsidy or about what types of subsidies are acceptable under what conditions. Yet subsidies are among the most common ways in which countries try to tilt the odds in their exporters' favor. I expect that negotiators will work hard and make limited progress toward strengthening the code, removing loopholes, and extending the code to services.

Complete Unfinished Tokyo Round Codes
(Probability: High; Confidence: Medium)

Differences over selectivity prevented agreement on a *Safeguards Code* during the Tokyo Round. Yet there is growing recognition that unless countries improve the rules governing when countries may legally avoid their obligations because of unforeseen economic problems—and when they must return to the fold—the trading system could grow more and more fragmented. But the nagging differences remain, so the odds of getting an agreement on safeguards during the Uruguay Round would seem to be about even. If an agreement is reached, it is likely to be quite weak, at least at first.

Industrial countries have stepped up their efforts to reach an agreement to deter *counterfeiting*. Indeed, industrial countries have extended their concerns beyond the counterfeiting of goods to related copyright, trademark, and intellectual property issues that were previously handled exclusively by the World Intellectual Property Organization. The United States has increased the pressure, particularly on Hong Kong, Singapore, Taiwan, Korea, and other NICs, to reach an agreement on counterfeiting, and a code is likely to emerge from the new round.

Liberalize Trade in Agriculture
(Probability: Medium; Confidence: Medium)

Agriculture has been a sticking point in trade negotiations for three decades. Europe and the United States both subsidize their farmers. Japan is constantly harassed to import more citrus, tobacco, and beef. The Uruguay Round seeks to improve market access and reduce import barriers, to increase discipline on the use of subsidies, and to minimize adverse effects of sanitary regulations. Domestic politics have not improved, particularly given the problems many farmers have suffered. However, two factors suggest that some progress is possible. First, the costs of the EEC's Common Agricultural Policy and of the United States' agricultural subsidies are exorbitant and are coming under increased fire. Second, a number of agricultural exporters (the Cairns Group), which includes such diverse countries as Australia, Argentina, Canada, Thailand, and Hungary, have banded together to lobby for freer trade in agriculture. The combination of inside and outside pressure for change might leave some room for compromise.

Increase Market Access for Developing Country Products
(Probability: Low to Medium; Confidence: High)

Developing countries have not gained much in the way of real concessions in recent trade rounds. This is partly because the generosity of industrial countries has waned as growth has lagged and unemployment has risen and partly because developing countries have played their hands poorly. In general, the developing countries have demanded too much relative to what they were willing to put on the table.[17] Three main product areas important to developing countries will be discussed during the upcoming round.

The Multifiber Arrangement covering *textiles and apparel* was renegotiated in mid-1986. It remains extremely protectionist, because the United States refuses to yield.[18] The EEC is somewhat more liberal, but still unlikely to open their markets significantly. Developing countries would like to reintegrate textiles and apparel into the GATT system. Industrial countries, concerned about the tremendous success of the NICs and terrified of China's potential in these markets, resist. Liberalization in this area will depend, ultimately, on cutting a bargain that favors industrial country service and high-technology manufacturing sectors and developing-country textile and apparel exporters.

Further liberalization of tariffs and NTBs affecting *tropical and natural resource-based products* is possible, but the real problem for developing countries is low world prices for most commodities. This leads to deteriorating terms of trade for countries that rely on commodity exports.[19]

Clarify Intellectual Property Rights
(Probability: Medium; Confidence: Medium)

The increased attention being given to clarifying and elaborating new rules and disciplines for intellectual property issues related to copyright, trademarks, trade secrets, and patents parallels the attempt to develop a multilateral code for counterfeiting. Previously these issues were not dealt within the GATT, but increasing concern with software protection, video pirating, and other intellectual property issues provoked the attention of trade officials. The Uruguay Round negotiations may produce a rough general framework agreement on intellectual property issues, but the significant details will probably have to wait for future negotiations.

Liberalize Trade-Related Investment Measures
(Probability: Low; Confidence: Medium)

Many firms place trade-related investment measures near the top of their priority list for a new trade round. Government negotiators, however, are more skeptical about what can be done this time. The United States delegates strongly advocated including this item on the Uruguay Round agenda but were somewhat surprised when the tired ministers agreed at the last moment to their demand. This round of discussions did no more than to help frame the issue. Effectively grappling with investment issues will require a broader approach to the management of the world economy that can only come later.

Liberalize Trade in Services
(Probability: Medium to High; Confidence Medium)
Services account for about one quarter of world trade but are not covered under the existing GATT trading system.[20] The United States (and later the EEC) staked considerable prestige on services in any new negotiations. Services were a key subject of the bilateral trade negotiations between the United States and Israel and Canada. A number of developing countries, led by Brazil and India, have consistently opposed this initiative.[21] At the Punta del Este ministerial meeting in September 1986, the trade ministers (as distinguished from the contracting parties) "decided, as part of the Multilateral Trade Negotiations, to launch negotiations on trade in services." These negotiations will "aim to establish a multilateral framework of principles and rules for trade in services, including elaboration of possible disciplines for individual sectors, with the view of the expansion of such trade under conditions of transparency and progressive liberalization and as a means of promoting economic growth of all trading partners and the development of developing countries."[22]

Whether and to what extent negotiators will reach agreement to lower barriers that hamper the international exchange of services is in doubt. However, it is increasingly clear that a multilateral agreement of principles and rules governing trade in services could probably be adopted.[23] Even though there is much disagreement on the prospects for making significant progress at a sectoral level, it seems ever more likely that telecommunications, data processing, tourism, and to some extent financial and insurance services, will be dealt with to some degree. It is less clear that progress will be made on transportation services. Moreover, despite some call by developing countries that service negotiations should consider issues related to immigration and the free flow of labor, this is unlikely. Nonetheless, if industrial countries want progress on trade in services in the GATT framework, some concession will have to be made to developing countries.[24] If these negotiations fail, industrial countries, which exchange about 70 percent of internationally traded services among themselves, will probably try to reach a more far-reaching service accord among "like-minded" countries.

Steps Toward Greater Management of Trade Flows

Each little step toward liberalization should also be part of a larger effort to find a better way to manage the trading systems and the world economy. However, rhetoric and action often become confused. For example, recent trade bills introduced in Congress, in order to be tough, threaten to "shoot the United States economy in the foot" unless Japan, Europe, and other countries make their exports less competitive and thus reduce their trade surplus. The United States threatened to impose major duties on European agricultural products, because it felt that American interests were harmed in the way in which Spain and Portugal were integrated into the EEC. But at the last moment an agreement was reached and the tariffs on Brie, wine, and other important products were averted. This was not the case when the United States put new tariffs on Japanese high-technology products during 1987. Although these new tariffs were reduced somewhat after being in place for a short time, the Japanese were offended but became a little more cooperative. Thus United States Administration and the Congress felt righteous, but some important firms such as IBM were hurt.[25] The United States has decided that it can only prevent free riding by others by limiting its own options. This was done by introducing laws that require the United States to retaliate.[26]

Methods for Managing Trade

There are a number of new ways in which countries are trying to control their destinies that are likely to influence the evolution of the trading system in the coming decade.

Increased Tariffs
(Probability: Medium; Confidence: Medium)
Tariffs on individual goods will be raised from time to time for two reasons. First, in the heat of disputes, higher tariffs are likely to be imposed to get other countries to cooperate and to persuade domestic interest groups that the government is working in their interest. In general, among industrial countries, once the disputes pass, these tariffs or threatened tariffs will be removed. Developing countries, however, are more likely to maintain tariffs once they are erected. Second, a few countries may actually try to follow the advice of economists and convert NTBs into transparent tariffs. Despite these two anomalies, the continued push for tariff reductions means that overall, the average tariff level is likely to continue to decline.

More Countervailing Duties and Antidumping Measures
(Probability: Very High; Confidence: High)
The United States feels used. It is also experiencing intense self-doubt about its ability to compete, be productive, and continue to create good jobs in an increasingly global economy.[27] The United States still feels some hegemonic responsibility and usually will not start trade wars, but there is growing support for reciprocity and fair play on the trade playing field. Free riders and cheaters are becoming anathema to United States policymakers, hence vulnerable to swift counterattacks by the United States.[28] Where American industries are injured, the United States is aggressively moving to their defense. So long as the United States trade deficit remains in the stratosphere, this process is likely to continue and even accelerate. Other countries will have to decide how to respond, but it would be surprising if some significant disagreements do not get blown out of proportion.

Fewer Quotas, OMAs, and VERs
(Probability: Medium; Confidence: Medium)

The GATT oversees a shrinking portion of world trade. Perhaps as little as one quarter of all international trade is under GATT "supervision." Agriculture, textiles, apparel, steel, automobiles, fertilizer, chemicals, and other sectors are now beyond the reach of the GATT. (Energy and services have never been covered under GATT.) Remedying this decline is one important goal of the Uruguay Round. Negotiators hope to recapture some lost sectors and extend GATT authority over new ones. There is growing recognition in many countries that, in aggregate, quotas, voluntary export restraints (VERs), orderly marketing arrangements (OMAs), and other mechanisms for managing trade are distorting and fragmenting the trade system. At the same time, these supposedly temporary arrangements swiftly become institutionalized, and domestic interests that benefit fight resolutely to retain them once they are in place. On balance, I expect a slight increase in these actions during the remainder of the 1980s as countries prepare to make concessions at the end of the trade round. In the early 1990s some progress is likely at reducing these practices during the closing phases of the multilateral negotiations. The net result is likely to be a change in the mixture of these barriers but not much change in the relative amount of protection granted to critical sectors by most countries.

More and Higher Subsidies
(Probability: High; Confidence: Medium)

Subsidies go hand in hand with industrial policies being adopted by more and more countries in their efforts to create competitive advantages for their firms. The Subsidies Code fashioned during the Tokyo Round is full of holes. In the race between strengthening the Subsidies Code and the increase in national subsidies, the latter should win, but not by much. Only if the political leadership decides that the issue of subsidies is of great political importance is the balance likely to swing toward the relaxation of subsidies.

Auction Quotas
(Probability: High; Confidence: Medium)

Lots of new ideas come and go. Auction quotas that try to use the market to distribute quotas among producers are the newest economic fad.[29] There is a reasonable chance that Congress and any future Democratic Administration will experiment with auction quotas during the next several years. Ultimately, they are a temporary stopgap and not a permanent solution to trade problems.

"Tit for Tat" Reciprocity
(Probability: High; Confidence: Medium)

"Tit for Tat" is another idea that is receiving considerable attention in policy circles. The Congress is fascinated with the idea of discarding universal application of most-favored-nation treatment as enshrined under Article I of the GATT. Full-scale reciprocity, as envisioned under tit for tat, is unfortunately very difficult to apply in practice.[30] At the same time, it seems almost inevitable that the trading system will be beset by much more conditional MFN in the future. There is danger of fragmentation in this trend, but there is also opportunity for those wishing to liberalize further to do so without being trapped by the need to extend MFN to all other contracting parties.

Bilateral Deals and Multilateral Fragmentation
(Probability: Medium; Confidence: Medium)
Conditional MFN agreements among groups of like-minded countries, particularly in areas like services, could fragment the GATT system. Bilateral accords are also on the rise. In recent years the United States has entered into a series of bilateral investment treaties (BITs) and signed bilateral trade agreements with Israel and Canada. Third countries worry that such deals could have serious consequences for the trading system. In fact, such bilateral and regional deals are already a part of the system. More will occur. They are more likely to provoke progress in multilateral forums than to destroy the system.

Full-Scale Trade War
(Probability: Low; Confidence: High)
We have learned more lessons in the past 50 years than we have forgotten. Global economic interdependence is increasing rapidly and is irreversible. Inevitably, trade and international economic issues will receive more frequent and concentrated high-level political attention than in the past. This in itself minimizes the chances that a miscalculation could blow up into a full-scale economic conflict. We will throw tantrums and have spats, but a full-scale trade war can and almost certainly will be avoided.

NEW MODELS OF TRADE REFORM

So far this chapter has focused on a single dimension, with free trade at one extreme and autarky at the other. In some senses this debate trivializes the real issue. The erosion of barriers separating trade monetary, and investment issues means that a solution that focuses just on trade is inevitably inadequate. The real goal of reform is the management of a world economy that is changing with great rapidity and is increasingly dependent on telecommunications networks instead of transportation infrastructures to carry trade.

This final section explores four models for organizing international trade in our increasingly interdependent world: monopoly, free trade, international vertical integration, and international corporate alliances.[31] The first two models are the traditional trade alternatives. The third and fourth models are related. Both emphasize the role that foreign investment could play in organizing the global market. Although none of these models will ever exist in pure form, they help show how economic and political trends could shape the broad contours of international economic management.

The Monopoly/Cartel Model

Throughout history, free trade was the exception, not the rule, in service sectors. One way to manage the world economy is for designated national monopolies to divide the world and the bulk of business among themselves and to exclude, to the extent possible, interlopers. Often in the past, national monopolies were tied together by an international cartel that legally sanctioned administered prices, divided international revenues, and forbade competition for international traffic. As services became more critical in the world economy, one possibility is for monopolies to try to hold on to the old model.

This seems unlikely. Cartels, especially global cartels, are highly precarious. They disintegrate if members have substantially different discount rates, if there is no dominant member of the group, and if it is difficult to monitor and enforce their arrangements. As times have changed, many key countries have chosen to move toward a more competitive model. The United States, in particular, has aggressively sought loopholes in the international monopoly model. Furthermore, once competition became credible, major players were tempted to start defecting from cartel arrangements and to court new customers with the promise of lower rates. The old monopoly/cartel system is in trouble. Although countries are frequently tempted to revolt against interdependence, it is clear that countries do depend on each other in trade of goods, and they are also increasingly dependent in trade of services.[32]

The continuation of the monopoly/cartel model depends partly on neutralizing the transnational pro-competition coalition of large users, services industries, and certain high-technology firms. (This might happen if corporate bargaining discouraged "end runs" on the monopolists, if labor stiffly supported protectionist policies, and if the service industries were coopted.) Or the old monopoly model might be defended in narrow areas but grudgingly accept competition in new areas to deflect criticism.

The Free Trade Competitive Model

The free trade, competitive model has a long history of application to commodity trade and may be applicable to services as well. Under this model, governments should worry about macroeconomic policy but play a minimal role in shaping individual markets. Each market is ideally a "commodity" market in which subtle differences in labor, capital, and other factors lead to highly specialized trade and competition. The GATT bargaining processes help to strike cooperative bargains covering trade by requiring transparency in trade regulations, nondiscrimination among countries, careful supervision of retaliation against other countreis, and encouraging packages of equivalent concessions rather than item-by-item reciprocity.

The United States government continues to push this model as the best alternative for services as well as goods. It supports the right of private firms to bring their domestic competitive assets to bear in selling abroad. In practical terms, the United States supports allowing service providers to offer their services over international networks and in individual countries. The United States demand for market access, however, raises difficulties for the GATT, because it appears to seek the right to invest as well as trade. As interdependence increases, this model requires governments to relinquish far more control over their own economies than even the United States contemplates. And it is by no means clear that the United States, the United Kingdom, and sometimes Japan can convince the rest of the world of the merits of this approach. Indeed, the more common trend is toward sophisticated efforts to encourage national strength through various industrial policies.[33]

The Direct Foreign Investment Model

But what if governments cannot resolve their disputes over how much competition should be allowed and how it should be managed in the international environment? Firms still have to operate internationally and want to do so as widely and as efficiently as possible. In a world that is changing so rapidly, business executives wonder if existing governments and institutions are capable of bold new action on issues of critical economic importance. If governments cannot agree in the GATT and elsewhere, companies feel they must begin to take matters into their own hands.

Increasingly sophisticated customers demand the luxury of one-stop shopping. They want to be able to use the same equipment (computer terminals or American Express cards) in the same way in every market. In addition, the most lucrative customers require customized goods and services, not the homogenous products favored by national systems. Free traders and monopolists are not very sensitive to these needs. In short, users and providers are thinking globally, but governments are still thinking nationally.

One way firms can proceed is to increase competition without relying on a classics free trade model. They are dreaming of a whole new approach to global competition. They are frustrated by high bargaining costs and by the complexity of providing their products on a global basis. They want to be global companies with the freedom to operate where they choose. As they grope for ways to do this, they are pushing governments into experiments that may ultimately provide an alternative to both monopoly and free trade.

Under this model the operating rights of global firms would be subject to rules set by multilateral and bilateral agreements. The global agreement might assure firms that they could own and operate any facility or service *between* countries while also obligating signatories to offer reciprocal rights to other carriers. The precise terms governing foreign entry *into* domestic markets would be negotiated bilaterally, subject to guidelines of a multilateral agreement. Bilateral bargains might be limited in two ways. First, countries might develop a nondiscriminatory way of limiting the total number of foreign entrants where surplus capacity was an obvious problem. Second, host countries might limit foreign operators' business to certain "gateway" cities. At these gateways, foreign firms could pick up and deposit foreign goods and services.[34]

This model might appeal to large consumers of goods and services and to certain well-situated providers of goods and services. This approach to organizing the world market would also offer some important rewards to governments. Under this model domestic monopolies could protect a part of their domestic markets and at the same time pursue their domestic clients overseas. Countries could implement a domestic industrial policy as long as it did not interfere with the rights of foreign firms to use its own equipment and did not restrict the ability of customers to choose among providers of international goods and services.

The International Corporate Alliance Model

There is probably no firm that would rush into every major market at once if that suddenly became possible. Furthermore, integrated global firms trying to enter even the most desirable markets will confront fierce resistance from those in long-entrenched positions. Inevitably, firms that follow a direct foreign investment model will choose to enter a series of joint ventures to appease local regulators and gain strong local partners. These joint ventures could evolve into international corporate alliances and become the basis for organizing the market.[35]

The international corporate alliance model could emerge if governments recognized (or were forced to recognize) the desirability of substantial competition in all forms of goods and services. But, fearful of changes, governments might still hesitate to permit full competition. Specifically, many governments are convinced that there remain benefits to be derived from economies of scale (and scope), as well as dangers associated with surplus capacity that require continued oversight. Therefore, governments might choose to allow or even encourage consortia to form that represent diverse interests without allowing unlimited competition. Governments might try to force greater efficiency and innovation but assure that a balance of interests were represented. As in Japan, governments might choose to create managed competition that guaranteed major-players representation.

Like the direct foreign investment model, the international corporate alliance model implicitly resolves trade problems by emphasizing the virtues of investment as the key to market entry (although trade is permitted). But under this model, foreign investment takes the form of pools of representative interests implicitly or explicitly approved by governments. Unless companies actively develop significant business partners, they will be left out. To assure balanced representation, the most politically significant ventures will need a large pool of partners.

Over time, the partners should develop broader, international working relationships. Only rarely will relationships be exclusive. The international corporate alliance model places a high premium on developing relationships that can be a continuing source of global advantage in global competition. Firms should seek preferred, not exclusive, partners in markets.

Any international corporate alliance is difficult to maintain over time, because individual firms have many incentives to "shirk" or "defect" from the common effort of the alliance. Instability becomes a particularly acute problem as collaborative ventures move into various commercial projects. However, international alliances can survive if governments' market intervention forces cooperation, or if firms enter arrangements that put them under similar political constraints at home.[36]

The international corporate alliance model is a middle ground between the free trade/competitive model and the monopoly/cartel model. It implicitly recognizes that it is no longer possible for any country to run its regulated domestic market unilaterally. An international agreement is needed to set the terms of domestic regulation and to designate who has a right to compete in major markets. Participation in these international alliances provides firms with an opening wedge into new markets and improves their ability to monitor foreign markets. Therefore, governments are entitled to insist on reciprocity when allowing joint venture partners into their domestic markets. This is one way for governments to assure that their domestic firms receive roughly equivalent treatment in the home countries of investing firms.

NOTES

1. The best history of the Tokyo Round is Gilbert Winham, *International Trade and the Tokyo Round Negotiation* (Princeton, NJ: Princeton University Press, 1986).
2. NTBs can be more effective than tariffs at limiting imports. They often take the form of domestic regulations that are rigged to favor national suppliers. Moreover, tariffs are narrow, affecting only specific products. Restrictions that make it difficult or impossible for foreign firms to obtain domestic transportation, finance, insurance, or telecommunications services can hamper imports of both goods and services.
3. See C. Michael Aho and Jonathan D. Aronson, *Trade Talks: America Better Listen!* (New York: Council on Foreign Relations, 1985), pp. 24–32.
4. See Kenichi Ohmae, *Triad Power: The Coming Shape of Global Competition* (New York: Free Press, 1985).
5. Peter F. Cowhey and Jonathan D. Aronson, *International Corporate Alliances* (Cambridge, MA: Ballinger for Council on Foreign Relations, forthcoming 1989).
6. Fearing that they might lose access to the huge United States market, South Korea and Taiwan have expressed interest in negotiating their own bilateral trade agreements with the United States.
7. Paul Krugman (ed.), *Strategic Trade Policy and the New International Economics* (Cambridge, MA: MIT Press, 1986).
8. The exceptions are rare and take considerable political courage. See for example: Jeffrey Birnbaum and Alan S. Murray, *Showdown at Gucci Gulch: Lawmakers, Lobbyists, and the Unlikely Triumph of Tax Reform* (New York: Random House, 1987).
9. Academics do make a difference. Just as the Laffer curve gained important policy advocates in the early 1980s, Robert Axelrod's argument that "tit for tat" policies lead to beneficial outcomes has generated important supporters among trade policy hands. See his *The Evolution of Cooperation* (New York: Basic Books, 1984).

10. The most famous recent example was the overwhelming House passage of the local content bill aimed at the Japanese auto industry in 1983. House members knew this was a free vote. It was unlikely that the Senate would take up the measure, and the President had promised to veto the measure if it came to his desk. However, a positive vote won credit at home. More recently, in 1986, Senator John Danforth (R, MO) tried to make his displeasure with the Administration's trade policy clear by opposing legislation in the Senate Commerce Committee that was necessary to launch United States–Canadian trade talks. He expected to lose, but discovered to his surprise that he had enough votes to defeat the policy. Ultimately, a deal was worked out behind closed doors for Senator Spark Matsunaga (D, HA) to support the talks, producing a tie vote, which allowed the talks to go forward. In both cases the Congress was more interested in appearing tough than in being tough.

11. This is not always the case. Bankers in the mid-1970s frequently commented that their activities were entirely economic in nature. They disclaimed any influence over politics. In addition, bankers with little knowledge and less respect for history uniformly claimed that it was inconceivable that a sovereign country might default on its external private debts. For a more up-to-date picture see Benjamin Cohen, *In Whose Interest? International Banking and American Foreign Policy* (New Haven, CT: Yale University Press, 1986).

12. The work of Mat McCubbin indicates that, in order to be reelected, legislators prefer to be firemen than policemen. Everybody loves the fireman, who comes to their rescue when a fire breaks out or a cat gets stuck in a tree. But people are wary of the police, who enforce the law.

13. One reason Japan is always so eager to participate in long, drawn-out multilateral negotiations is that they believe that such talks give them a respite from bilateral "Japanese bashing." The Japanese are able to deflect criticism more easily when many countries are involved. Thus, in recent multilateral negotiating rounds, the United States and Europe fight about agriculture; the United States and the developing countries argue about textiles, apparel, and access to United States markets; and the Japanese fade happily into the background.

14. For example, the strong push by the Deutsche Bundepost to protect and even extend its monopoly position in Germany has led some German users (such as the big banks) to begin to work for the opposite result. On the rise of voices for freer trade within the United States even as calls for protection have increased, see I.M. Destler and John S. Odell, *Anti-Protection: Changing Forces in United States Trade Policy* (IIE Policy Analysis No. 21) (Washington, D.C.: Institute for International Economics, 1987).

15. Some economists suggest converting NTBs into tariffs.

16. Japan's NTT was the only PTT to accede to the Government Procurement Code. It did so under extreme pressure from the United States.

17. See for example Stephen Krasner, *Structural Conflict* (Berkeley: University of California Press, 1985).

18. The textile negotiator within USTR holds Ambassadorial rank. His activities are closely monitored and heavily influenced by the textile and apparel industries and their legislative representatives.

19. Raymond F. Mikesell, "The Changing Demand for Industrial Raw Materials," in John W. Sewell and Stuart K. Tucker, eds, *Growth, Exports, and Jobs in a Changing World Economy: Agenda 1988* (Overseas Development Council United States–Third World Policy Perspectives, No. 9) (New Brunswick, NJ: Transaction Bookis, 1988), pp. 139–166.

20. See Jonathan David Aronson and Peter F. Cowhey, "Trade in Services: The Case for Open Markets" (Washington, D.C.: American Enterprise Institute, 1985). For a more critical view see Stephen S. Cohen and John Zysman, *Manufacturing Matters: The Myth of the Post-Industrial Economy* (New York: Basic Books, 1987).
21. The clearest statement of developing country doubts is found in Deepak Nayyar, "International Trade in Services: Implications for Developing Countries," Exim Bank Commencement Day Annual Lecture: 1986 (Bombay: Export–Import Bank of India, 1986). Also see Jagdish Bhagwati, "International Trade in Services and Its Relevance for Economic Development," in Orio Giarini, ed., *The Emerging Service Economy* (New York: Pergamon Press for the Service World Forum Geneva, 1987), pp. 3–34.
22. The focus on development is significant. Part II, "GATT Ministerial Declaration," Punta del Este, Uruguay, Spetember 1986.
23. This agreement is likely to draw heavily on the OECD's "OECD Conceptualization of a GATT Framework for Services Trade," Draft (Paris: OECD, July 11, 1986).
24. See Jonathan D. Aronson, "The Service Industries: Growth, Trade and *Development Prospects, in John W. Sewell and Stuart K. Tucker, eds, Growth Exports, and Jobs in a Changing World Economy: Agenda 1988* (Overseas Development Council United States–Third World Policy Perspectives, No. 9) (New Brunswick, NJ: Transaction Books, 1988), pp. 97–118.
25. With the globalization of production, tough actions often hurt United States firms most. See "High-Tech Tariffs Boomerang on the United States," *Business Week*, Sept. 7, 1987, pp. 26–27.
26. In effect the United States, frustrated that other countries did not believe it would take protectionist actions that hurt its own economy, has resorted to chicken. By demonstrating that the United States is "irrational" and would be willing to risk a trade war if others don't give in, the United States is trying (with some success) to get others to alter their policies. The danger, of course, is that, through a miscalculation, neither side will compromise and a full-scale trade warmight erupt.
27. There is a whole series of books on the decline in United States competitiveness. See, for example, Barry Bluestone and Bennett Harrison, *The Deindustrialization of America* (New York: Basic Books, 1982); Kim B. Clark and Alan M. Kantrow, *Industrial Renaissance: Producing a Competitive Future for America* (New York: Basic Books, 1983); Davis Dyer, Malcolm S. Salter, and Alan M. Webber, *Changing Alliances* (Boston: Harvard Business School Press, 1987); and Cohen and Zysman, *op. cit.*
28. For example, the Reagan Administration has been willing to initiate actions against countries or foreign companies that are perceived to be acting unfairly without waiting for formal complaints from injured parties in the United States. The Republicans, however, want to leave a fair amount of discretion in the hands of the President so that retaliation is not automatic. This issue is at the core of many of the debates over the trade bill, because it speaks directly to implementation.
29. C. Fred Bergsten et al., *Auction Quotas* (Washington, D.C.: Institute for International Economics, 1987).
30. The problems with reciprocity as a guiding principle of trade policies are discussed in Robert O. Keohane, "Reciprocity in International Relations," *International Organization* (Winter 1986), pp. 1–27, and Beth V. Yarbrough and Robert M. Yarbrough, "Reciprocity, Bilateralism and Economic 'Hostages': Self-Enforcing Agreements in International Trade," *International Studies Quarterly* (March 1986), pp. 7–21.

31. For a fuller review of these models with particular reference to services and telecommunications services, see Jonathan D. Aronson and Peter F. Cowhey, *When Countries Talk: International Trade in Telecommunications Services* (Cambridge, MA: Ballinger, 1988).
32. Indeed, even China, the country haled by advocates of this approach, is moving slowly toward a more competitive system domestically and internationally.
33. The most sophisticated argument is found in Stephen S. Cohen and John Zysman, *Manufacturing Matters: The Myth of the Post-Industrial Economy* (New York: Basic Books, 1987).
34. This model is very similar to one in use for international aviation. See Daniel Kasper, *International Trade in Aviation Services* (Cambridge, MA: Ballinger, 1988).
35. This model and its implications are worked out in Peter F. Cowhey and Jonathan D. Aronson, *International Corporate Alliances* (Cambridge, MA: Ballinger for the Council on Foreign Relations, forthcoming, 1989).
36. For example, the British–French alliance to built the Concorde lasted because the two governments controlled procurement and because labor unions in both countries "captured" the effort. See Elliott J. Feldman, *Concorde and Dissent: Explaining High Technology Project Failures in Britain and France* (New York: Cambridge University Press, 1985).

5

A Probabilistic Estimate of International Trade Risk: Quantifications of Trade Policy Outcomes

TAMIR AGMON

CLAS WIHLBORG

The process and the realities of United States trade policy have been shown to create a substantial amount of risk for single industries and corporations at different times. This thesis, as developed in the last three chapters, lacks an important component: a means by which to measure it. In order to estimate the risk associated with a given trade policy, two conditions have to be satisfied: we have to define a measurable outcome, and there must be an operational measure of risk related to that outcome. As we are concerned with corporations, the measured outcome should be related to the value of the corporation under consideration.

In this chapter, Agmon and Wihlborg provide such a measurement. The measurement is based on the rate of protection (RP), assuming a direct relationship between the rate of protection of any given corporation and its cash flow (and, therefore, its value). Different alignments of trade policy will give rise to different sructural risks. These risks are described by means of standard probability distributions that are stylized descriptions of what managers and investors expect to occur.

By organizing the relevant information with regard to the probable outcomes of certain types of trade policies, or the deliberations of trade policies, it is possible to relate it to the various functional responses of a firm to the risk inherent in trade policy. Thus the somewhat formal and abstract presentation below is translated in Part III to a number of more concrete discussions regarding the relationship of international trade risk to issues of organizational structure, marketing policy, operational management, and strategic planning issues of corporations and financial institutions.

Uncertainty about the outcome of United States trade policy, as well as that of many other countries, is a major feature of the international marketplace. This uncertainty is the result of various economic, political, organizational, and even moralistic forces which taken together are creating a trade policy at any given time period. The policy is expressed by tariffs, quantity restraints, and other nontariff barriers.

In order to be able to measure the uncertainty about trade policy, it has to be expressed in terms of probability distribution of the outcome for different products, in different periods. To do that, we need first to define a measurable variable. Explicit and implicit protectionism for each product and for each time period results in a certain rate of protection (RP) that is quantifiable given information about the various types of protective measures. We assume that a probability distribution for the RP of each traded good, service, or factor of production exists. In this case, the shape of this distribution would reflect the various expectations with regard to different policy processes formed by combinations of economic, political, and other forces. By examining the relationship between probability distributions for RP and corporate investment decisions, as well as between distributions and policy processes, we establish a link between the process of trade policymaking and a measurable variable to be used as the proxy for the international trade risk.

Thus, a trade policy is expressed as a whole probability distribution for RP. The probability distribution summarizes a number of aspects of more traditional definitions of trade policy that deal with the values, the goals, the actual legislation, and the specific measures of policy carried out by political bodies like the United States Congress and the Executive branch.

Our preliminary investigation into the probabilistic nature of trade policy and its effects on corporate business decisions opens up a number of interesting and promising avenues of research. Some of these are a calculation of equivalent policies based on a tradeoff between the expected value of the RP and its dispersion measure, the design of investment projects in order to increase the options in managing the political risk associated with trade policies, and the choice between domestic and foreign investments. The analysis can also be used for an evaluation of the effects of anticipated and unanticipated protectionist measures on an industry's productive capacity.

We begin by presenting evidence with regard to the varying nature of United States trade policy. In the following section we show how the probability distributions of RP can be created, given certain assumptions based on the observation of past and present trade policies. Three classes of trade policies are approximated by three types of probability distributions: normal, uniform, and binominal distributions.

THE UNCERTAIN NATURE OF UNITED STATES TRADE POLICY

Since the period following World War I, United States trade policy has been determined by two major forces. One force pulls United States trade policy toward free trade, while the second force pushes the United States toward a protectionist policy.

The term "force" is used here to denote a combination of ideological, economic, and political factors. Various coalitions of interest groups and legislators were formed from time to time, and the result was, and is, high variability in the tendency of the policy between free trade and protectionism. Most of the time the configuration of the overall policy remains balanced, but the incidence of protectionist and free trade measures varies a great deal.

In the ideological dimension, the argument between the free market approach and the protectionistic approach is continuous, and it remains unresolved after more than 200 years. As the self-interests of various industries and groups have changed, so have their lobbying efforts for or against free trade. The attitude of the United States Congress has oscillated between favoring free trade and favoring protectionism for a number of industries, and this process is likely to continue.

The struggle between free trade and protectionism transcends the United States and is becoming an integral part of the international scene. The General Agreement on Tariffs and Trade (GATT), which is the institutional personification of free trade, also houses and administers the Multi-Fiber Agreement (MFA), which is a complex scheme of bilateral quotas and a contradiction to free and multilateral trade. Moreover, in the recent "rounds" meeting in Taupo, New Zealand, a meeting dedicated to the promotion of free trade, the United States trade representative hinted at a possible "trade war" with Japan.

The result of this contradictory and highly variable process is a substantial amount of uncertainty about the industrial incidence of trade policy and, therefore, a substantial amount of risk at the corporate level. The uncertainty exists to some extent with regard to the average RP, across industries and products, but it is more pronounced and more relevant in terms of the RP for particular products or industries.

In a detailed and thorough analysis of United States trade policy since 1930, Canto (1986) records all the major trade actions in the United States during the period 1930–1982. A summary of these actions is presented in Table 5.1. The free trade and the protectionist actions are distributed throughout the period under consideration, and the same process continues for the period 1982–1986.

The oscillating policy creates a substantial amount of political risk. That much is agreed on by most researchers and practitioners in the field. However,

Table 5.1   Free Trade and Protectionist Activities United States, 1930–1982

	Free Trade	Protectionist
Acts of Congress	6	11
Agreements	3	6
Specific intervention	6[a]	26

[a] Expiration or abolition of earlier interventions.
SOURCE: Canto (1986)

political risk in itself cannot be observed and measured. The only way to observe risk is through its effect on some relevant, and observable, variable.

INTERNATIONAL TRADE RISK AND THE DISTRIBUTION OF TRADE POLICY OUTCOMES

We have presented evidence with regard to the inherent uncertainty about the incidence and the execution of trade policy in the United States. In general, the factors affecting trade policy seem to oscillate between two poles, the free trade approach and the protectionistic approach, which have maintained a precarious balance for a very long period, with the first approach dominating in some industries and the second dominating in others. On the aggregate level, whenever one approach seems to have the upper hand, a reversal follows. Therefore, aggregate United States trade policy exhibits a rather stable behavior.

Although the process of reversal can be explained in several ways, including analogies to physical phenomena (Agmon and Khoury, 1988), there is no question that there is substantial variability in the degree of protectionism, particularly where it is applied to a single product or industry.

For the purpose of our model we postulate the following process. Let x be the outcome (RP) of a given trade policy. x is an observed quantity. It includes nontariff barriers for item j, which can be a good, a service, or a factor of production. x_j is measured as percentage points on an ad-valorem basis. Free trade with no tariffs or other restrictions implies $x_j = 0$. On the other extreme, there is a value of x_j such that no trade will occur. Let us define that value as $\bar{x}_j$. The values of RP_j over time are observable. This time series is defined as x_{jt}, $t = 1, 2, \ldots T$, and it describes the changes in the total rate of protection over time for item j.

The risk associated with a given trade policy is estimated by evaluating the probability distribution of x_{jt}, given the information of the time series x_{jt} in the past and any other relevant information about the future. For the following example, we assume that all the information is contained in the time series of historical data. The procedure for the estimation is as follows: Plot the variable x_{jt}, against time t, where $t = 1, \ldots, T$. Thereafter classify the results into one of three categories.

Category 1: x_{jt} lies in most cases between x_{j1} and x_{j2}. There are some observations above x_{j1}, or below x_{j2}. This case is described in Figure 5.1.

Category 2: x_{jt} is spread equally between x_{jmax} and x_{jmin}. This case is described in Figure 5.2.

Category 3: x_{jt} lies close to x_{jmax}, or close to x_{jmin} as in Figure 5.3.

In all cases, RP is adjusted such that he expected value of RP is the same for the distributions.

Category 1 can be described (given the usual inference of a probability distribution based on a time series) by a normal distribution. Category 2 is

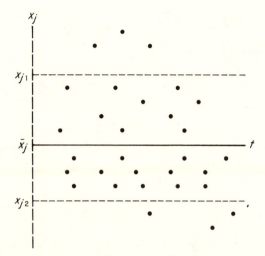

Figure 5.1 A statistical description of a "Consensus" policy.

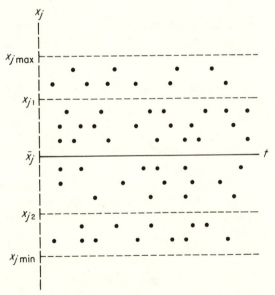

Figure 5.2 A statistical description of a "No-Information" policy.

represented by a uniform distribution that ranges from x_{jmin} to x_{jmax}; category 3 is expressed by a binomial distribution.

Actual policies may now be associated with each of the three probability distribution of RP. Policies may and will vary from one industry to another, and in some cases even among products. The first type of policy is a "consensus" policy. Given a consensus among the decision makers, which may reflect a

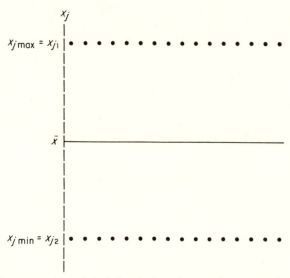

Figure 5.3   A statistical description of an "Either-Or" policy.

broader consensus among various interest groups, a certain policy is deemed most probable by all the actors is the market. This policy is expressed in terms of a compact normal distribution, where most of the weight is around a given expected value of an RP. It is possible that in spite of the consensus, the actual RP at a given time period will fall in one of the two tails of the distribution. In other words, the actual rate of protection will deviate greatly, upward or downward, from the expected rate of protection.

The second type of policy is characterized by almost "no information." There is no consensus, and within some limits every RP is equally likely. Such a policy is an outcome of a feeling of "I don't know what the decision makers may decide. They are capable of anything." This policy is described by, and is consistent with, a uniform distribution between certain limits.

The third case reflects a struggle between two opposing schools of thought, or two opposing interest groups. One group believes in free trade in a certain industry, or for a certain good, and another group believes in protection. We assume that one of the two groups will prevail, but we do not know which one. This process is expressed by a binomial distribution.

The relationship of the underlying policy to the observed time series of x_j is not a unique one. It is possible to relate the observed time series, and the inferred probability distributions, to a different interpretation. We do like to propose, however, that ours is a reasonable explanation, consistent with observed behavior.

The importance of our model is twofold. First, it provides a way to express, in quantitative terms, a well-established feeling that the process by which United States trade policy is formed creates some risk at the corporate level.

Second, it allows one to test the actual behavior of some industries' rates of protection and to examine the question, does international trade risk exist, and if so, where is its impact? These and other related questions are discussed in the rest of the book.

REFERENCES

Agmon, T.; and Khoury, S.J.: "Political Economy of International Diversification: The Case for Partial Integration," Working Paper, USC, April 1988.

Canto, Victor: *The Determinants and Consequences of Trade Restrictions on the United States Economy* (New York: Praeger, 1986).

II

UNDERSTANDING THE RELATIONSHIP BETWEEN THE AGGREGATE CONFIGURATION OF TRADE POLICY AND CORPORATE PERFORMANCE

United States trade policy is a rich tapestry of legislative and regulatory restrictions and policies interwoven with governmental activities which affect tariffs, nontariff barriers, quotas, and foreign exchange rates. These activities are presumably designed to protect United States interests by responding to the United States balance of trade deficits and the effective trade policies of trading partners. The panoply of legislation, administrative action, and market response can be described as a configuration of trade policies.

Changes in the components of this overall configuration affect corporate performance and value. Changes that generate corporate risk can be either prospective or actual and are initiated either at home or abroad. Further, as we have shown earlier, while the aggregate configuration of trade policy is likely to remain stable, this is achieved through a "netting" process whereby positive effects of policy changes in one sector are expected to offset negative effects in another. Thus, the goal of holding protectionism at bay in the aggregate is consistent with and predictive of potentially large changes in policy for individual sectors. The phenomenon of aggregate stability can obscure significant changes in individual, sectoral, and corporate components.

The remaining parts of this book explore the implications of such sector-specific changes for corporate management. In Part II, we look at the fundamental relationships between trade policy changes and corporate response. In Part III, we examine the manifestation of these fundamentals in the actual history of trade policy and corporate response.

In this section, we explore the structure of the relationship between changes in trade policy and corporate performance. We consider from various functional points of view the effects of, responses to, and prescriptions for protecting corporations from trade policy risk. Through this study, we are able to understand important intercorporate relationships better. This process of study also illuminates the determinants of a corporation's ability to respond to changes in trade policy as embodies in changes in quotas, tariffs, barriers to market access, or changes in exchange rates.

Thus, the chapters in this section have important implications for both analytical and managerial activities. By isolating and relating the determinants of corporate sensitivity to changes in trade policy, the materials here can educate the analyst charged with predicting the effect of policy changes on particular companies or investments. Alternatively, these studies of the effects of marketing operations and financial and organizational design decisions on corporate sensitivity to trade policy can be used by managers to improve the probable outcomes of such decisions. While many observers concentrate solely on the initial impact of changes in trade barriers and exchange rates on corporate value, the longer-run effects are critical and deserving of attention. Further, these longer-run effects are not simple, but represent the combined responses of many managers and management groups. In this section, we examine the important management functional groups and the range of responses available to them as they anticipate or experience changes in trade policy.

As we study investment and operating issues as seen by each of the several functional management areas, a common problem emerges—the tradeoff between cost effectiveness and flexibility. In identifying and studying the managerial experience of this tension in each of the functions and for various decisions, we can dramatically simplify comparisons of the alternatives. This simplification leads to improved collection of information about investment and operating prospects and is therefore very useful as a tool for effective decision making.

Study of the cost flexibility tradeoff also gives new insights into the aggregate effect of changes in trade policy on corporate performance. While individual managers or management teams commit to investment or policy, which determines one aspect of the company's ability to respond to trade policy changes, the combined effect of these decisions is an overall sensitivity or ability to respond. An understanding of the history of decisions that yield this sensitivity, and identification of the key determinants of that sensitivity, can be a powerful tool for senior management. On the basis of this understanding, senior management can elect to accept or to alter corporate sensitivity and prepare to manage that exposure.

In sum, corporate adaptability and sensitivity to changes in trade policy are the outcome of a series of decisions by senior management. Corporate adaptability is also an objective of management. Adaptability is addressed below in both guises—as an objective and as a result.

The first chapter of Part II describes the cost/flexibility tradeoff. The tension is almost skeletal in form, when considered as one aspect of the decision to invest in plant, equipment, and/or fixed technology. In this case, the cost/risk tradeoff is an extremely important determinant of the decision outcome when, from the perspective of a particular industry, alternation in effective trade policy is both possible and potent. The authors summarize the dilemma as the need to balance flexibility and cost effectiveness. In their example, that of investing in real, fixed capital, they reason that greater cost efficiency of equipment comes at the expense of that equipment's usefulness in other settings. Equipment that is customized for use in a particular industry or for a specific project has lower resale value than that which is more generally applicable. Therefore, companies or investments that exhibit great "uniqueness" are also likely to represent fairly inflexible technology. Hence, these investments will be very sensitive to any risk, including the risk of changes in trade policy.

The same relationship between cost effectiveness and flexibility is described in Chapter 7, "Organizational Structure and Environmental Change." In this case, however, the capital that is exposed is not plant and equipment but human, or organizational, capital. In this chapter, the contributors describe the many and varied ways in which organizational structure determines the company's response to changes in trade policy and can be altered to improve the response to such changes.

The chapter stresses adaptability as the only actual means of response to a changing environment. The authors contend that to retain adaptability, the organization must recognize change, acknowledge the need to respond, and respond in a manner that is consistent with corporate objectives. In this, corporate adaptability is seen as an objective rather than a result.

The remaining chapters consider the implications of the cost/flexibility tradeoff for short-term asset/liability management, for selecting among the range of responses to volatility in corporate markets, and for the relationship between operations strategies and trade risk. While each chapter addresses guidelines for functional management in these areas, taken together they describe the set of decisions, investments, and policies that determine overall corporate response to trade policy risk.

This overall response to trade policy risk is examined in the section's final chapter. The aggregation of the individual functional responses and the effects of these responses on corporate performance are summarized here by considering the changes in the economic value of the company or investment. Prior decisions, which are represented by human and physical capital in place, determine corporate flexibility in response to change. They also determine cost effectiveness and base-level capital efficiency. Changes in trade policy, real or threatened, provoke many corporate responses. Taken together, these either exacerbate or mitigate the initial effect of the policy change on corporate performance and value. The final chapter of Part II offers a framework for understanding, measuring, and managing this complex set of relationships. With this framework, the subsidiary effects of prior investment and operating decisions can be summarized to describe the aggregate resulting corporate adaptability. The results of this analysis can also be considered as an objective of change.

6

International Trade Risk and the Cost of Flexibility in Capital Investment

TAMIR AGMON

CLAS WIHLBORG

In Chapter 5, "A Probabilistic Estimate of International Trade Risk," Agmon and Wihlborg summarized the effects of trade policy expectations in a probability distribution of the outcomes of a range of policies for different products in different periods. The objective was to "establish a link between the process of trade policy formation and corporate investment behavior." The authors demonstrated that key characteristics of a rich, complex, and dynamic trade policy configuration can be effectively summarized in a statistical distribution that captures information on the likelihood and probable effects of each of many policy scenarios.

This chapter explicitly describes the effects of such trade policy configurations, and their summarization in a probability distribution, on investment value and performance. Implications of this work include technical guidelines for integrating the probability of changes in trade policy into investment analysis and selection. The work also has important implications for investment management, as actual changes in policy alter the strategic and competitive strength of various businesses.

However, the implicit message of this work is even more potent than its explicit insights—namely, the identification of the basic tradeoff to be confronted in the management of effects of trade policy and trade policy risks on corporate assets. By identifying the basic constraints and considerations, the authors provide a simplifying, yet integrating, framework. This framework facilitates investment analysis and the analysis of functional managers' alternatives, which are considered in later chapters.

As the authors show, when prospects for a change in trade policy are high, the value of a prospective or existing investment may be heavily dependent on the project specificity of the capital which represents the investment and its relative efficiency. In this context, the capital may be understood to be plant and equipment and the technology they embody.

In effect, equipment and processes that are designed for a specific corporate use are likely to prove more cost-effective than are those designed for more general use. However, should changes in the trading environment dictate abandonment of the particular technology, the more specialized equipment can be sold only at a discount.

In other words, by committing to an inflexible, albeit low-cost, technology, the corporate investor exposes the company to the risk of future inefficiencies.

Thus the basic tradeoff, as identified and explored in this chapter, is between the cost of capital flexibility and the risk of capital specificity. This tradeoff formalizes the effects of the prices and values of capital equipment, as set in the marketplace, on corporate operations and value. The results affect both the choice of technology as new investments are contemplated and the probability that changes in trade policy will result in the abandonment of incumbent businesses and capital.

The authors identify the components of an investment's capital efficiency and flexibility which sensitize its value to changes in the configuration of trade policy. They also suggest the types of investments and businesses that would become potential divestiture candidates as particular trade policies are enacted, or even seriously debated.

This last point should be heeded by regulators and legislators as well as by corporate executives. Whether a certain trade policy is actually enacted or simply seriously considered, its effects on particular businesses and industries may be both strong and highly predictable. Therefore, for purposes of government policy or corporate investment analysis, one must look beyond the effective rate of protection associated with a particular policy in predicting how that policy will affect the prospects and values of specific businesses.

In Chapter 5 we demonstrated that trade policy creates risk and that the specific international trade risk can be estimated. Moreover, given the nature of trade policy with regard to a certain industry, and in some cases with regard to major product, it is possible to describe the risk in terms of a specific probability distribution.

In this chapter we extend the analysis to corporate investment decisions. We examine a trade policy's effect on corporate decisions to invest in productive capacity in a certain industry.

We assume that the corporation under investigation has decided to supply a foreign market with its products. The corporation can supply the market by exports or by production in the foreign market. In either case, there are two ways of servicing the market—a fully dedicated investment, and a more general investment. We denote the former "rigid" and the latter "flexible." Given this specification, the standard terms of risk and return are expressed as cost effectiveness and flexibility. The first term indicates a minimization of the expected costs of operations, and the second term is related to the dispersion measure of the cost. The more flexible the investment technology, the smaller the dispersion measure of the cost of operating the investment project.

The two competing ways of servicing the foreign market, the "rigid" and the "flexible" investment technologies, are described and analyzed in the following section. The two mutually exclusive projects are then examined against three alternative trade policies, each of which is represented by a probability distribution of the outcomes, the industry-specific rates of protection. The implications of international trade risk on corporate investment decisions are presented and discussed at the end of the chapter.

THE UNCERTAINTY OF TRADE POLICY AND CORPORATE INVESTMENT DECISIONS WITH ABANDONMENT OPTIONS

Investment decisions are a process whereby a corporation commits capital to a specific project. After the capital is committed by creating assets in place, cash flows are generated by these assets (and, in most cases, labor). The basic uncertainty arises from the need to commit these assets prior to the generation of the cash flows. In the event that the cash flows are not up to expectation, the firm has the option to abandon the project. In this case, the firm will lose the difference between the amount of resources devoted to the assets in place, at the first period, and the value of these assets, tangible and intangible, in the abandonment period.

In general, the possibility of abandonment, and the value of the assets in case of abandonment, will affect the choice of the type of capital, or the nature of the assets to be placed by the firm. For example, the firm may employ general or more dedicated rigid assets. The difference in efficiency, assuming that the latter are more efficient than the former, may be balanced by the different abandonment values.[1]

Assume an investment in assets in place that is dedicated to a trade-related activity. Let us say production for exports. Once the investment is completed and the assets are in place, the point of abandonment is affected by the interface between the technological nature of the project, the business risk, and the outcome of trade policy, which represent the international trade risk. We focus first on this last issue. Thereafter, we discuss the choice of investment project.

Consider an exporting firm from a small country that exports to a large country (e.g., the United States). In order to service the market, the firm has to invest in a production facility that is oriented exclusively toward the United States market. The firm can choose one of two technologies—a highly specific, "rigid" technology, or a more general, "flexible" technology. The two technologies are assumed to be identical in their physical output per unit of capital. The flexible equipment is assumed to be less cost-effective, or more expensive per unit of capital. On the other hand, it can be adjusted for other uses. If the firm has to sell the assets to other users, the market value of these assets will be higher than that of the more specific, and initially more cost-effective, assets.

The importing country's trade policy with respect to the product is described by the probability distribution of the rate of protection (RP). The output of the investment project is assumed to be exclusively dedicated to the importing country's market. It follows that the cash flow to be generated by the project, and therefore its value, depends on the relevant RP.

The relationship between project value and trade policy is described within a two-period framework. Investment occurs in period 0. The actual outcome of policy, the actual RP, is known in period 1, before the cash flows accrue to the project. When the RP becomes known, the project can be abandoned or continued.

The expected value of the "rigid" project (V^R) under the assumption that price and quantity are equal to one when RP is zero can be expressed as:

$$V^R = -P_0^R K + \frac{1}{1+r} \int_{x_{min}}^{x^{AR}} (1-ax_1)(1-bx_1)(1-C^R) f(x_1)\, dx_1$$

$$+ \frac{1}{1+r} \int_{x^{AR}}^{x_{max}} P_1^R K f(x_1)\, dx_1 \tag{1}$$

where K = Quantity of capital (equipment) in units in period 0,
P_0^R = price per unit of "rigid" capital (equipment) at time 0,
P_1^R = price per unit of "rigid" capital equipment at time 1,
r = discount rate,
x_{min} = the minimum RP,
x^{AR} = RP at which the rigid project is abandoned,
x_{max} = the maximum RP,
x_1 = RP in period 1,
$f(x_1)$ = the distribution of RP in period 1,
a = elasticity of export prices with respect to RP,
b = elasticity of export quantity with respect to RP, and
C^R = variable input cost per unit of output associated with the rigid project.

In the valuation equation for project R, the first term is the investment, and the second term is the expected value of the cash flow in period 1, if the project is not abandoned. The third term is the expected cash flow if the project is abandoned. A similar expression for the competing, flexible project is presented below with superscripts F:

$$V^F = -P_0^F K + \frac{1}{1+r} \int_{x_{min}}^{x^{AF}} (1-ax_1)(1-bx_1)(1-C^F) f(x_1)\, dx_1$$

$$+ \frac{1}{1+r} \int_{x^{AF}}^{x_{max}} P_1^F K\, dx_1 \tag{2}$$

First we calculate x^{AR} and x^{AF}. These are the RPs at which the rigid and flexible projects respectively will be abandoned (or sold for other purposes). The RP that is the result of trade policy is becoming known at the beginning of period 1.

For the rigid project, this RP is calculated as the minimum value of x, which satisfies the inequality:

$$P_1^R K > (1-ax_1)(1-bx_1)(1-C^R) \tag{3}$$

that is, when the revenues from selling the capital (equipment) exceed the cash flows from the project if continued. We assume that both the price and the quantity elasticities are known—that is, there is no "estimation risk" at the time expected cash flows are evaluated.

For the flexible project, abandonment occurs when x_1 is such that the following inequality will hold:

$$P_1^F K > (1 - ax_1)(1 - bx_1)(1 - C^F) \tag{4}$$

In order to derive simple and explicit solutions, we assume that the firm in question is a price taker in the relevant market. We assume also that world prices are not affected by the RP in the target country ($a = 0$). It follows that the abandonment triggering values of x_1 are

$$x_1^{AR} \geqslant \frac{1}{b}\left(1 - \frac{P_1^R K}{1 - C^R}\right) \quad \text{and} \quad x_1^{AF} \geqslant \frac{1}{b}\left(1 - \frac{P_1^F K}{1 - C^F}\right) \tag{5}$$

respectively. The relative cost of more flexible physical capital to that of more dedicated (rigid) capital for periods 0 and 1 can be defined as

$$p_0 = \frac{P_0^F}{P_0^R} \quad \text{and} \quad p_1 = \frac{P_1^F}{P_1^R}$$

Two more coefficients are defined to highlight the analysis. First, we define "coefficients of project specificity."

$$\alpha^R = \frac{P_1^R}{P_0^R} \quad \text{and} \quad \alpha^F = \frac{P_1^F}{P_0^F}$$

which describe the price at which each type of equipment can be sold, relative to the purchase price. Second, we define a "coefficient of relative project specificity"

$$\gamma = \frac{\alpha^F}{\alpha^R} = \frac{p_1}{p_0}$$

γ is a measure of the relative proportion of "sunk" cost in the rigid and the flexible projects. By assumption $\gamma > 1$, which implies that there are relatively fewer "sunk costs" in the flexible project.

The variable cost of production for the flexible project is assumed to be at least as large as that of the rigid project. This relationship is measured by $\delta = (1 - C^F)/(1 - C^R) \leqslant 1$. Furthermore, we assume, as discussed above, the $P_0 \geqslant 1$. These two conditions imply that either costs of production or costs of equipment are higher for the flexible project.

Given these definitions, we can derive the conditions under which the abandonment triggering value of the RP for the flexible projects will be smaller than that for the rigid project. This condition is

$$x_1^{AF} \leqslant x_1^{AR} \quad \text{if} \quad p_1 \geqslant \delta \text{ or equivalently } \gamma \geqslant \delta/p_0 \tag{6}$$

Equation 6 simply states that the policy under which the flexible project is abandoned, and equipment sold, is less protectionist than the policy under which the rigid project is abandoned, if the resale price of the flexible equipment relative to that of the rigid equipment is larger than the coefficient describing the relative share of revenues remaining after covering variable costs. Alternatively, the condition is stated as the relative project specificity coefficient γ being larger than the ratio between the coefficient for the share of revenues remaining after variable costs (δ) and the coefficient for the relative purchase price (p_0). Since by assumption $\delta \leqslant 1$ and $p_0 \geqslant 1$ and by definition $\gamma \geqslant 1$, the abandonment triggering RPs for the two projects are equal only if they are identical ($\gamma = 1$, $\delta = 1$, $p_0 = 1$). For any differentiation between the projects, the abandonment triggering RP for the flexible project is lower than that of the rigid project. It follows that specific protectionist policies will have a greater impact on the productive capacity in an exporting industry if the productive capacity is flexible than if it is rigid ($\gamma > 1$).

In period 0 the management does not know what the relevant RP is going to be. What they do know is the distribution of RP at period 1, which is denoted by $f(x_1)$.

Following the earlier discussion of international trade risk (see Chapter 5), we examine three alternatives cases: a normal distribution, a uniform distribution, and a binomial distribution. These distributions of policy outcomes reflect the policies, as was shown in the preceding section.

The parameters of the distributions are as follows: (1) the normal distribution has a mean $\bar{x}_1$ and a variance $\sigma^{2N} = \sigma^2$; (2) the uniform distribution has also a mean $\bar{x}_1$, and the variance σ^{2U} is equal to $(n\sigma)^2/2$, where n is the number of standard deviations from $\bar{x}_1$ to x^U_{min} and x^U_{max}—the minimum and maximum RPs with uniform distribution; (3) the binomial distribution also has a mean value of $\bar{x}$, and its variance is equal to $\sigma^{2B} = (n\sigma)^2$, where n is the number of standard deviations from $\bar{x}_1$ to x^B_{min} and x^B_{max}, where x^B_{min} and x^B_{max} are the two possible values of x_1 under the assumption of binomial distribution. The probability that each of the extreme values of RP will be realized is .5.

We calculated earlier the trade policies at which abandonment occurs. It is now a simple task to derive the probabilities, evaluated at time 0, (π^U, π^B, and π^N, respectively) that abandonment occurs under different trade policy distributions. There probabilities are important for the choice of project as can be seen in Eqs. 1 and 2. Table 6.1 shows these probabilities for each project based on Eq. 5 and incorporating definitions for project specificity of the rigid project (α^R), the relative project-specificity coefficient (γ), the relative cost of flexible and rigid equipment in period 0 (p_0), and the coefficient for the relative variable costs of production (δ). Note that the price of flexible equipment in period 1 is $P^F_1 \equiv P^R_0 \alpha^R p_0 \gamma$.

We analyze next how the probability of abandonment of a specific project depends on the shape of the probability distribution of trade policy. We compare normal, uniform, and binomial distributions with *identical* mean ($\bar{x}_1$) and variance (σ). These parameters imply certain values of the maximum and minimum RPs under uniform and binomial distributions, respectively. These values are then inserted into the expressions in Table 6.1. With information about the policies at which abandonment occurs (X^{AR}_1 and X^{AF}_1, respectively),

Table 6.1 Probabilities of Abandonment

	Rigid	Flexible
Normal	$\pi^{NR} = \displaystyle\int_{x^{AR}}^{\infty} f(x_1)\,dx_1$ $x_1^{AR} = \dfrac{1}{b}\left(1 - \dfrac{P_0^R \alpha^R K}{1 - C^R}\right)$	$\pi^{NF} = \displaystyle\int_{x^{AF}}^{\infty} f(x_1)\,dx_1$ $x_1^{AF} = \dfrac{1}{b}\left(1 - \dfrac{P_0^R \alpha^R p_0 \gamma K}{\delta(1 - C^R)}\right)$
Uniform	$\Pi^{UR} = \dfrac{x_{max}^U - \dfrac{1}{b}\left(1 - \dfrac{P_0^R \alpha^R K}{1 - C^R}\right)}{x_{max}^U - x_{min}^U}$	$\Pi^{UF} = \dfrac{x_{max}^U - \dfrac{1}{b}\left(1 - \dfrac{P_0^R \alpha^R p_0 \gamma K}{\delta(1 - C^R)}\right)}{x_{max}^U - x_{min}^U}$
Binomial	$\Pi^{BR} = .5 \quad \text{if} \quad x_{max}^B \geq \dfrac{1}{b}\left(1 - \dfrac{P_0^R \alpha^R K}{1 - C^R}\right)$ $\phantom{\Pi^{BR} = }0 \quad \text{if} \quad x_{max}^B < \dfrac{1}{b}\Big($	$\Pi^{BF} = .5 \quad \text{if} \quad x_{max}^B \geq \dfrac{1}{b}\left(1 - \dfrac{P_0^R \alpha^R p_0 \gamma K}{\delta(1 - C^R)}\right)$ $\phantom{\Pi^{BF} = }0 \quad \text{if} \quad x_{max}^B < \dfrac{1}{b}\Big($

Table 6.2   Ranking of Probability Distributions in Terms of Probability of Abandonment (π) for different Abandonment Levels of Policy (x_1^A)

Level of policy at which abandonment occurs	Ranking of distributions
$\bar{x}_1 \leqslant x^A \leqslant \bar{x}_1 + .8\sigma$	$\pi^N < \pi^U < \pi^B (= .5)$
$\bar{x}_1 + .8\sigma < x^A < \bar{x} + \sigma$	$\pi^U < \pi^N < \pi^B (= .5)$
$\bar{x}_1 + \sigma \leqslant x^A < \bar{x}_1 + \sigma \cdot 2^{\frac{1}{2}}$	$\pi^B (= 0) < \pi^U < \pi^N$
$\bar{x}_1 + \sigma \cdot 2^{\frac{1}{2}} \leqslant x^A < \infty$	$\pi^B = \pi^U (= 0) < \pi^N$

we can rank the distributions for each project in terms of probability of abandonment.

Under our assumptions about the mean and variance of all three probability distributions, and implicitly about maximum and minimum RPs, Table 6.2 can be constructed. It shows how the probability of abandonment depends on the shape of the distributions for different exogenous values of the policy at which abandonment occurs. In other words, given parameters characterizing the projects and therefore given the RPs at which abandonment occurs, the probabilities of abandonment for each probability distribution are calculated.

Table 6.2 shows that, as the policy level at which abandonment occurs increases, the ranking of distributions changes. If abandonment occurs at very low levels of protectionism, the normal distribution has the lowest probability of abandonment and the binomial has the highest. At somewhat higher levels of the RP at which abandonment occurs, the uniform distribution becomes the one with the lowest probability up to a point where the binomial obtains the lowest probability of abandonment. If abandonment occurs only with extremely protectionist policies, the normal distribution is the only one for which there is a positive probability of abandonment.

The ranking of Table 6.2 is derived under the assumption that the RP at which abandonment occurs is exogenous. In Eq. 6 and in Table 6.1, we showed that abandonment depends on the choice of capital equipment. Thus, the probability of abandonment is partly under the firm's control. The final question we wish to address is whether the rankings of distributions in terms of probability of abandonment influence the rankings of the two projects under different trade policy distributions. The answer to this question is yes, since a relatively high probability of abandonment for a given x^A in Table 6.2 implies that the value of the abandonment option increases. We showed in Eq. 6 that the probability of abandonment for the flexible project is always higher than the probability for the rigid project. Thus, for any given δ, p_0, and p_1, a higher probability of abandonment of the rigid project for a specific RP distribution in Table 6.2 implies that the relative attractiveness of the flexible project increases. For example, the table shows that for low levels of x^A—the abandonment level of RP—the binominal distribution is associated with the highest probability of abandonment. The abandonment option is most valuable for this distribution, and this option has a relatively larger weight in the value of the flexible project. Similarly, for high levels of X^A for the rigid project, the normal distribution is associated with the highest probability of abandonment. Therefore, under these circumstances the flexible project becomes relatively more attractive. This reasoning implies that if only very high RPs will cause abandonment of the rigid project, then the flexible project is most attractive when trade policy is characterized by a normal distribution.

It can be noted that it is only the relative attractiveness of the projects that is influenced by the RP distribution in the way described earlier. The absolute ranking of the projects may or may not be influenced by the RP distribution. This ranking depends not only on the probability of abandonment associated with each distribution but also on the actual values of δ, p_0, and p_1, which also influence the probability of abandonment. Without exploring the absolute ranking of the projects in detail, it can be seen that increasing $\gamma = p_1 p_0$ (given δ) increases the attractiveness of the flexible projects for two reasons. First, the relative value of the flexible equipment at abandonment increases, and second, the probability of abandonment increases as shown in Eq. 6. However, increasing δ (given γ) lowers the cash flows from the flexible project in operation, but this loss to the value of the project is partly or fully offset by the increased probability of abandonment.[3]

IMPLICATIONS FOR INVESTMENT DECISIONS, TRADE POLICY, AND EXTENSIONS

We have analyzed how the shape of the probability distribution for trade policy in an importing country influences the exporting firm's choice of capital equipment. Relating the shape of probability distributions to policy process, we conclude, for example, that if the policy process tends to create oscillations of policy between free trade and protectionism (binomial trade policy distribution), then flexible projects tend to be favored over rigid projects, when project cash flows are very sensitive to trade policy (abandonment at low levels of protection). In this case, the abandonment may take the form of shifting sales to a different market, or to shifting production to a different product.

This conclusion holds only to a lesser extent if the policy process is characterized by "consensus" (normal trade policy distribution). On the other hand, in this case, project choice may be influenced even if cash flows are not very sensitive to protectionism and even if abandonment would not occur under the expected consensus policy.

In order to draw exact conclusions with respect to project choice, it is necessary to evaluate not only project characteristics and the expected trade policy, but also the variance of the protectionist policies and the shape of the probability distribution for these policies. All these aspects of protectionist policies may be viewed as trade policy.[4]

Our analysis has implications for trade policy as well. For example, it follows that *anticipated* protectionist policy measures would have a *greater* impact on exports from another country than unanticipated measures. The reason is that a firm anticipating such measures would tend to invest in more "flexible" capital equipment, and, therefore, it would be more likely to abandon the project.

Different industries are characterized by different degrees of project specificity in their capital equipment. Unanticipated trade policy would be more effective in terms of reducing production capacity for exports in the short run in an industry with relatively flexible equipment. The abandonment option is more likely to be used in such an industry. Unanticipated protectionism may accordingly be less effective in an industry characterized by advanced technology and high product differentiation, since equipment would be specialized and "rigid." Anticipated protectionism may be more effective, however, in such an industry if it is very costly to build flexible equipment that could provide an abandonment option for the exporter.

An obvious extension of this analysis is to derive the exact conditions under which the flexible project will be favored over the rigid project. The choice will depend on the relative degree of firm specificity of equipment, the relative variable costs of production, the relative costs of flexible and rigid equipment, and the shape of the probability distribution of trade policy. The exact conditions become somewhat complex when the firm chooses to abandon different types of equipment or shift production and sales at different levels of protection. The investment decision is further complicated if the size of each project is variable.

We assumed in the above analysis that the firm knows the impact on its exports of each policy in the importing country. In reality there is uncertainty about the magnitude of the quantity effect as well as the price effect of trade policy. In the words of Brown et al. (1984), there is "estimation risk," which may influence the choice of equipment. To solve the investment problem under this type of risk, it is necessary to develop a scenario analysis. Only after a long period of observing trade policies and export sales is it possible to know with reasonable certainty the price and quantity effects of protectionism.

Another extension of the analysis presented here is to apply it to industries with different cost structures and different degrees of firm specificity of equipment. It may also be applied to countries with different policy processes and corresponding differences in shapes of trade policy distributions.

A more complete analysis of investment decisions and trade policy should take into account that many firms may have the choice of placing the capital equipment in the importing country. We would expect, therefore, that there would be a higher proportion of multinational firms in industries characterized by high costs of flexible investments. In essence, the firm using highly project-specific technology is able to create flexibility by being multinational. Investment choice for potentially multinational firms would depend not only on the relative costs of flexible and rigid equipment, relative production costs in the two countries, the policies of both origin and host countries. The choice will also depend on the costs of relocation. For multinational firms, one should evaluate both the abandonment option and the "relocation option."

NOTES

1. The term "abandonment value" is used here as in Brealey and Myers (1984).
2. In general, we can express the conditions under which the variances of the uniform and the binomial distributions, σ^{2U} and σ^{2B}, exceed the variance of the normal distribution. These conditions are

$$\sigma^{2U} > \sigma \quad \text{if} \quad n^{U} > 2^{\frac{1}{2}}$$

$$\sigma^{2B} > \sigma \quad \text{if} \quad n^{B} > 1$$

and

$$\sigma^{2B} > \sigma^{2U} \quad \text{if} \quad n^{B} > n^{U} 2^{\frac{1}{2}}$$

3. It should be noted that a positive present value implies that there is imperfect competition in some markets. In our case markets for capital equipment must be characterized as imperfect, since the firm is assumed to be a price taker. The firm may decide to continue the project even if the actual trade policy, in the form of RP, reduces the cash flows in period 1. Abandonment will follow if its present value is higher than the continuation of the project. We ignore here the question "who will benefit from the reduced present value to the exporting firm, if the project will not be abandoned."
4. Compare this analysis with the one presented and discussed by Finger et al. (1982).

REFERENCES

Agmon, T.; and Khoury, S.J.: "Political Economy of International Diversification: The Case for Partial Integration," working paper, July 1987, USC.

Aronson, J.: "Possible Trades Policies in the 1990's: An Overview," mimeo, September 1987, USC.

Brealey, R.; and Myers, S.: *Principle of Corporate Finance*, 2d Ed. (New York: McGraw-Hill, 1984).

Bawa, V.; Brown, S.B.; and Klein, R.W.: *Estimation of Risk and Optimal Portfolio Choices* (New York: North Holland, 1979).

Canto, Victor: *The Determinants and Consequences of Trade Restriction on the United States Economy* (New York: Praeger, 1986).

Finger, J.M.; Hall, H. Keith; and Nelson, D.R.: "The Political Economy of Administered Protection," *The American Economic Review*, June (1982), pp. 452–465.

Odell, J.; and Willett, T.D.: "Influences on United States Trade Policies: Experiences and Outlook," mineo, April 1987, USC.

7

Organizational Structure
and Environmental Change

THOMAS G. CUMMINGS

MARIA NATHAN

In the previous chapter, Agmon and Wihlborg identified cost effectiveness and flexibility of capital equipment and processes as the primary determinants of an investment's sensitivity to changes in the configuration of United States trade policy. Further, they demonstrated that investment choices that resulted in greater cost effectiveness are likely to be more restrictive in use, thereby constraining attempts to respond to trade policy revisions.

Their argument derived from and emphasized the role of this cost/risk tradeoff in decisions to invest in plant and equipment capital. However, the argument can also be productively applied to human capital, management processes and organization. This is the application presented here by Cummings and Nathan.

The authors begin with the joint premise that the possibility of changes in trade policy is a major source of corporate risk and that this risk can be managed effectively through the design of organizational structures that will respond effectively to change. As a result, organizations simultaneously shape and are shaped by uncertainty in the environment.

How should senior corporate management structure the organization in order to exert influence and promote effective adaptation to policy? First, account for the nature of the environment. Second, understand the nature of environmental influences on corporate organizational structure. Finally, outline and analyze alternative organizational structures and change existing structures to improve adaptability to the specific environment and uncertainties faced by the organization.

Cummings and Nathan offer powerful guidelines for this process of analysis and redesign. They present a system for organizing information about the essential aspects of the environment and its uncertainty. This conceptual structure accounts for several types and sources of risk including changes in the configuration of trade policy.

Corporate organizational structures evolve in response to environmental uncertainties as they attempt to translate information about the environment into strategies and decisions that yield effective performance. This chapter characterizes various types of corporate organizations and assesses the effectiveness of each type in recognizing and responding to environmental change. Effectiveness demands a response that is oriented simultaneously to internal (corporate) and external (market) opportunities and constraints. Finally, the authors address issues that arise in the application of concepts to redesign and organizational change. They highlight the particularly important distinction between incremental and strategic changes and offer useful insights for managing each.

Organizations are open systems that exist in environmental contexts (Katz and Kahn, 1978). Environments provide organizations with necessary resources, information, and legitimacy, and consequently organizations must create and maintain effective relationships with suitable environments in order to survive and prosper. Because organizations are dependent on environments, they can structure themselves to satisfy external constraints and contingencies and to take advantage of external opportunities. Organizations can also shape environments and move them in favorable directions through such devices as political lobbying and vertical integration (Pfeffer and Salancik, 1978).

Trade policies can be a significant part of the environment of both domestic and multinational corporations. They can influence the competitive structure of an industry as well as access to foreign goods and markets. For example, protectionist policies can help to insulate troubled industries, such as steel and automobiles, from competitive pressures by decoupling them from hostile environments. Conversely, policies favoring free trade can increase competition among firms, linking them more tightly to their environment.

In examining how organizations structure themselves to adapt to and influence trade policies, it is difficult, if not impossible, to disentangle the effects of trade policies from the effects of a myriad of other environmental elements, such as government regulations, economic conditions, industry composition, technological innovation, and culture. These environmental elements can place a diversity of demands on organizations, and organizational structures represent cumulative responses to the combination of those different pressures. Rather than attempting to identify organizational effects for each environmental element separately, organization theorists have tended to develop summary measures of the environment and to relate those measures to different organizational structures (Lawrence and Lorsch, 1967; Duncan, 1972; Mintzberg, 1979). For example, the interaction of different environmental elements facing an organization can be summarized in terms of environmental dimensions such as complexity and stability, and those dimensions in turn can influence how organizations are structured.

A major underlying premise is that trade policies are an important major source of environmental complexity and change facing corporations. There is considerable speculation about the future direction of United States trade policy along a continuum from protectionism to free trade. It is suggested here that while the predominant form which United States trade policy will take over the next 5 to 10 years is unknown, an organization can intelligently position itself for whichever policy occurs by developing various structures for coping with uncertainty. These structures can enable the organization to interrelate effectively with its environment despite this element of uncertainty. Because organizations need to structure themselves to manage their environments, this chapter explores how organizations can design structures responsive to environmental complexity and change. The paper first describes the concept of organizational environment and then presents a model explaining how environments can influence the choice of organizational structures. From this background, alternative structures for managing environmental complexity and change are discussed. Finally, processes for designing and changing such structures are presented.

ORGANIZATIONAL ENVIRONMENTS

Organizational environments consist of everything outside of organizations that can affect, either directly or indirectly, organizational performance and outcomes. This might include external agents such as suppliers, customers, regulators, and competitors as well as economic political, and cultural forces within the wider society and global context. This general definition, however, is too broad to explain how the environment specifically influences organizations. Clearer understanding of this relationship requires examination at different environmental levels. Further insight is also gained by analyzing the various dimensions of environments.

ENVIRONMENTAL LEVELS

Following the lead of Pfeffer and Salancik (1978), organizational environments can be categorized into three levels. The highest level, called the contextual environment, consists of the totality of external forces that can influence an organization *indirectly* by virtue of impacting the external agents and organizations with which the organization directly interacts. This indirect environment comprises a network of interconnected agents and organizations that are related to each other and the organization through the organization's transactions. Members of the network can indirectly influence an organization by impacting other organizations directly interacting with it. For example, an organization may have difficulty obtaining raw materials from a supplier because the supplier is embroiled in a labor dispute with a national union, a lawsuit with a government regulator, and a boycott from a consumer advocacy group. These members of the organization's contextual environment can affect the organization without having any direct connection to it.

The next lower level, the transactional environment, consists of the individuals and organizations that interact directly with an organization. It is through these direct relationships that organizations and environments influence each other. Although the transactional environment and the contextual environment operating through it can affect organizations, these environments do not determine organizational actions. The environment must be perceived before it can influence behavior. Organizational members must actively observe, register, and make sense out of the environment before it can affect their decisions and actions. Because observation and attention require action, Weick (1979) referred to this perceptual process as "enactment." Consequently, the lowest environmental level is called the enacted environment, the organization's perception and representation of its environment. The enacted environment is inextricably linked to the other environments. It is created out of the stimuli provided by the transactional environment, and those transactions can be influenced by the contextual environment. Only the enacted environment determines organizational *actions*, although the other environmental levels may affect the *outcomes* of those action.

ENVIRONMENTAL DIMENSIONS

In explaining how the three levels of environment affect organizations, researchers characterize environments along a number of dimensions. These dimensions can be used to determine the nature of the environmental demands facing organizations and the degree to which organizations need to be responsive to those demands.

At least two major perspectives provide knowledge about environmental dimensions. One approach views environments as information flows and suggests that organizations need to process information in order to relate effectively to their environments (Lawrence and Lorsch, 1967; Galbraith, 1977; Weick, 1979). The key feature of the environment affecting information processing is information uncertainty, or the degree to which environmental information is equivocal. Organizations tend to structure themselves to remove equivocality from their environmental transactions. The second perspective views environments as consisting of resources for which organizations compete (Aldrich, 1972; Pfeffer, 1972; Hannan and Freeman, 1977, 1984). The primary dimensions of the environment is resource dependence, or the degree to which an organization must rely on other organizations for resources. From this approach, organizational structures are aimed at managing critical sources of environmental dependence. We will first examine environmental characteristics contributing to organizational uncertainty and dependence and then combine the two perspectives into a more comprehensive view of organizational environments.

Information Uncertainty

Researchers have identified at least two key dimensions that determine the amount of environmental uncertainty organizations can experience (Burns and

Stalker, 1967; Duncan, 1972). The first characteristic refers to the amount of stability or change occurring in the environment. Environments can be characterized as falling along a continuum from stable to dynamic. Stable environments change either very little or in a predictable manner. They hold few surprises for organizations, because their future states are readily anticipated. Dynamic environments, on the other hand, shift abruptly and unpredictably. Their changes are not patterned, and organizations cannot forecast future states or plan responses in advance.

The second dimension is complexity, or the number of external elements that can affect an organization. Environments can vary along a continuum from simple to complex. Simple environments have few parts influencing organizations. They are relatively easy to interact with, because organizations can focus on a limited set of environmental demands. Complex environments have a diverse number of elements, and the elements themselves can be richly jointed. Such complexity can pose problems, because organizations may not have the diversity of responses needed to attend to the full range of external demands.

The two characteristics are interrelated and contribute to the amount of information uncertainty organizations can experience. Environments that are relatively stable and simple are highly certain. Because they change predictably and have few parts or elements, organizations typically have few difficulties coping with them. Information processing is rather straightforward, as there is little need to make adaptive changes or to have diverse responses. As the environmental characteristics become more dynamic and complex, organizational environments become more uncertain. However, highly uncertain environments pose severe problems for organizations. Because the environment changes unpredictably and has many elements, organizations must make rapid adaptive responses to a diverse set of external demands. This requires considerable information processing to remove equivocality from the environment.

Resource Dependence

Researchers have examined organizational dependence on environments in terms of interorganizational power (Benson, 1975; Pfeffer and Salancik, 1978). They argue that organizations seek power over other organizations that control critical resources. Following Emerson's (1962) work on power relationships, power is considered a relational concept having to do with dependence between two or more actors or organizations. The more dependent an organization is on other organizations, the more power others have over it. Organizations are dependent on other organizations to the extent that other organizations control critical resources that are not easily obtained elsewhere. Consequently, two dimensions—resource criticality and availability—determine the extent to which an organization is dependent on other organizations. Organizations seek to manage their dependencies so that they can gain access to critical resources.

They avoid becoming dependent on other organizations while making others dependent on them.

Integration of the Two Perspectives

These two environmental dimensions—information uncertainty and resource dependence—influence organizational transactions with the environment. Taken together, these characteristics explain the degree to which organizations are constrained by their environments and consequently how responsive they must be to external demands (Aldrich, 1979). Organizations have the most freedom from environmental demands when information uncertainty and resource dependence are both low. In this situation, organizations do not need to be very responsive to their environments. They can make choices and behave relatively independent of their context. As information uncertainty and resource dependence become higher, however, organizations are more constrained and must be more responsive to external demands. They must accurately perceive the environment and respond to it appropriately. Under these conditions, the environment can be expected to have maximal influence on organizational outcomes. Whether such environments impact organizational decision making and subsequent actions depends, of course, on how accurately organizations perceive them (Meyer, 1982).

A MODEL OF ENVIRONMENTAL EFFECTS

So far, we have described organizational environments and identified dimensions that influence organizations. This section provides a model explaining how organizations translate knowledge of environments into strategic choices about structure.

There has been considerable debate in organization theory about the role of environments in structuring organizations (Astley and Van de Ven, 1983; Hrebniak and Joyce, 1985). Attempts to explain variation in organizational structures have taken two conflicting paths. One approach, called strategic choice, argues that organizations can change their structures to adapt to external demands (Chandler, 1962; Child, 1972). Managers are seen as playing a key role in enacting the environment and making requisite choices about structure. The competing approach, called population ecology, proposes that organizations are severely limited in making structural changes, and variations in structure across organizations can be explained by the forces of environmental selection (Hannan and Freeman, 1977, 1984; Pfeffer and Salancik, 1978; Aldrich, 1979). Organization structures that have a relative advantage in acquiring resources from the environment are selected for survival. Managers are viewed as highly constrained in making adaptive responses to the environment. For example, they may misperceive the environment and make inappropriate choices; organization culture and tradition may reinforce existing structures and serve as barriers to strategic change; economic and institutional forces may limit the range of structure considered feasible or legitimate (Meyer and Rowan, 1977).

Based on the work of McKelvey (1982), these conflicting perspectives can be synthesized into a model of organizational effects. The model proposes that organizational environments pose certain informational and resource problems for organizations, and organizational members can choose structures to try to resolve them. Depending on the characteristics of the environment, members are more or less constrained in making strategic choices and having to respond to external demands. This model includes three components: (1) environmental problems, (2) enactment processes, and (3) strategic choices about technology and structure. Although the elements are presented sequentially, in reality they do not form a linear causal chain but mutually interact with each other. The components are described here.

Environmental Problems

Environments can be seen as posing certain problems for organizations to solve if they are to acquire the information and resources needed to function. Depending on environmental characteristics such as those shown in Figure 7.2, organizations may experience a diversity of problems in trying to respond to environments. Dynamic and complex environments, for example, have high amounts of information uncertainty, and organizations may have problems understanding external demands and generating appropriate and timely responses. Similarly, when other organizations control critical resources that are not readily available elsewhere, organizations have high resource dependence and may need to be highly responsive to the demands of those powerful others. Satisfying those demands may severely limit an organization's autonomy.

Enactment Processes

Organizations must perceive and make sense out of their environments before they can choose to respond to them (Weick, 1979). Environments present organizations with a diversity of equivocal stimuli, and organizations must work on that material to extract meaning from it. This enactment process involves attending to certain aspects of the environment while neglecting others. Because it is not possible to attend to things that have not yet occurred, organizations always enact environments of the past (Schutz, 1967). Thus, knowledge of the environment that guides decisions about organizational structures is retrospective.

Organizations enact their environments through information systems and boundary-spanning units specializing in particular parts or aspects of environments (Leifer and Huber, 1977; Pfeffer and Salancik, 1978). Information systems include measuring devices such as accounting practices and reports and statistics that are regularly collected and transmitted through the organization. Because of time and resource constraints, information systems only attend to limited aspects of environments. They focus attention on those environmental forces the organization believes are important. Boundary-spanning units, such as sales, purchasing, and customer relations, relate the organization to parts of the environment. These units generally have special skills and knowledge to monitor the environment and to assign meaning to stimuli. They reduce uncertainty for the organization by translating equivocal material into meaningful representations that guide decision making.

Although organizational decisions and behaviors are determined by the enacted environment, organizational outcomes can be affected by parts of the environment that are ignored or overlooked. Pfeffer and Salancik (1978) identified several problems in environmental enactment that can render organizational responses ineffective. Organizations may incorrectly identify external dependencies, including groups they are dependent on and demands from them. They can also encounter problems reconciling conflicting demands from powerful sources and changing perceptions rooted in past commitments. These kinds of enactment problems can result in organizational structures that are inappropriate to the demands of the transactional environment.

Strategic Choices About Technology and Structure

The third component of this model of environmental effects is strategic choice. Based on enacted environments, organizations make strategic choices to respond to external opportunities and demands. These choices fall into two general categories: those relating to technology and those pertaining to structure.

Technology

Choices about technology involve the most immediate response to the environment and concern how the organization will transform inputs into outputs. Structural choices are responses to problems posed by the technology and include how to operate the technology and relate it to the environment. Because the enacted environment provides input materials, such as information and resources, to the technology, it determines the nature of the technological activities needed to convert the inputs into products and services (Perrow, 1970). When environments are relatively certain, input materials are generally well understood and predictable, and consequently technological activities can be standardized and routinized. Rather, technical activities require high amounts of complex information processing and decision making to discover how to convert the ambiguous materials into outputs valued by the environment.

Structure

Choices about technology pose two kinds of structural problems: how to structure organizations to operate the technology effectively and efficiently, and how to relate the technology to the environment (Pugh, 1966; Thompson, 1967; Scott, 1981). Consequently, structural choices are oriented both *internally* to the organization's technology and *externally* toward the wider environment. Decisions about internal structures for operating the technology include dividing tasks and assigning them to organizational units, coordinating work across the units, and planning and controlling task activities. Internal structures are generally designed to match technological conditions of routines and interdependence with themselves and are determined by enacted environments (Mintzberg, 1979; Scott, 1981). Relatively certain environments allow routinized technologies, and bureaucratic structures are most efficient for operating them. Conversely, uncertain environments do not permit routine technologies, and internal structures need to be more flexible to respond to such ambiguity.

Choices about external structures for relating the technology to the environment involve approaches for buffering the technology from external disturbances and for bridging the organization to external sources of information and resources (Scott, 1981). These may include creating appropriate boundary-spanning units to manage exchanges and scan the environment (Thompson, 1967), forming alliances with other organizations to jointly manage information or resources (Leblebici and Salancik, 1982), and manipulating the environment in favored directions. External structures are generally intended to be responsive to environments and thus are designed to fit external conditions. Organizations may attempt, however, to change environments to fit organizational structures.

Although we have been discussing structural choices as though they were rationally planned, they can result from informal processes, such as accidental variations and spontaneous discoveries (McKelvey, 1982). Indeed, structural solutions to environmental and technological problems are frequently unplanned. Organizations can accidentally improve structures and can devise solutions without consciously attending to them. Thus, structural choices are rooted in both planned and unplanned processes, though their prevalence may vary considerably across situations and time periods.

STRUCTURAL CHOICES FOR COMPLEX AND CHANGING ENVIRONMENTS

Structural-choice theories identify a variety of structures to respond to different environmental conditions (Galbraith, 1977; Tushman and Nadler, 1978; Mintzberg, 1979). Because this paper is concerned with structural responses to environmental complexity and change, only those structures suited to these contexts will be reviewed. A major premise underlying structural choices is that organizational structures are effective to the degree they fit environmental conditions. In this view, fit means that structures facilitate the information processing necessary to remove enough equivocality from environmental inputs to perform technological activities efficiently and to manage critical sources of external dependence. In general, structures must have the requisite variety and flexibility of responses to match the variety and stability of environmental conditions. When environments are complex with many elements, structures must be equally complex to attend to those different parts. Similarly, when environments are dynamic with unpredictable forces, structures must be equally flexible to respond to those changes.

Internal Structures

Internal structures are concerned with operating the organization's technology. They help to organize and control task activities so organizations can efficiently transform raw materials of information and resources into products and services valued by the environment. This includes organizing tasks into appropriate groups or departments, coordinating relationships among the units, and planning and controlling task performance. Internal structures can be characterized along at least four design features (Fredrickson, 1984; Miller and Friesen, 1984):

1. Formalization. The degree to which structures emphasize a clear hierarchy of authority and standard rules and procedures.
2. Centralization. The extent to which power and control are concentrated at the top of the managerial hierarchy.
3. Differentiation. The degree to which organizations are divided into units that are designed differently.
4. Integration. The extent to which relationships among units are coordinated.

These design elements can be combined into different structures which, depending on the environment, can vary in effectiveness. When environments are complex and dynamic, organizations need to choose technologies capable of working with input materials that are not easily understood or predictable. The technologies must be able to process considerable information to learn enough about raw materials to convert them efficiently into useful outputs. Internal structures for operating such technologies must be complex and flexible enough to facilitate high levels of information processing and innovation. They should have low amounts of formalization and centralization so that those closest to the work flow have the discretion to develop new methods and make decisions as the circumstances demand. The structures should be differentiated into many groups or departments, each oriented toward a different part of the technology. These functional groups should have different designs, each geared to the technical demands of its task activities. The departments should include specialists with high levels of expertise for solving complex and uncertain technical problems. Integration among the groups should be high so the different technological activities can be coordinated. This should include coordinating mechanisms that facilitate mutual interaction among specialists, including liaisons, task forces, special integrator roles, and product or project teams integrating across the functional departments.

Mintzberg (1979) referred to such organic, matrix structures as "adhocracies" which are capable of coordinating experts drawn from different functional departments into integrated market-based project or product teams.

Adhocracies are highly innovative and can process considerable information to respond to complex and changing conditions. They take one of two forms. The operating adhocracy innovates and solves problems for other organizations. It tends to work under contract and applies teams of multispecialists to solve clients' problems. Examples of operating adhocracies include construction firms, advertising agencies, and consulting firms. The administrative adhocracy performs work for itself and, in contrast to the operating adhocracy, separates its technological component from its administrative and staff parts. The technological or operating core is designed mechanistically for routinized forms of work, while administrators and staff specialists are formed into an organic structure promoting flexible interaction on ad hoc projects. In order to keep the two structures separate so each can perform its respective kind of work, administrative adhocracies can operate the technological part as a separate organization or contract it out to other organizations. Examples of administrative adhocracies include oil companies, high-technology firms, and the National Aeronautics and Space Administration. In examining the evolution of organizational structures for multinational corporations, researchers have observed a movement toward adhocracies as such firms encountered a diversity of dynamic global environments (Stopford and Wells, 1972; Davidson and Haspeslagh, 1982; Robock and Simmonds, 1983). When faced with a complex and dynamic array of environments, multinationals tended to combine different structures, often superimposing matrix structures on global, centralized structures.

External Structures

External structures guide an organization's efforts to adapt to and change its environment. They help to buffer the organization's technology from external disruptions and to bridge it to sources of information and resources. External structures generally organize the work of administrators and staff specialists who are responsible, at the institutional level of the firm, for setting corporate strategy and managing the environment, and at the managerial level, for translating strategy into operational goals and procedures. There are at least four broad categories of external structures: (1) scanning units for mapping the environment; (2) diversification for loosening dependencies and coping with conflicting demands; (3) collective structures for negotiating a more manageable environment; and (4) manipulative structures for modifying the environment in favorable directions.

Scanning Units
Organizations must have the capacity to monitor and make sense out of their environments if they are to choose responses for managing them successfully. When environments are complex and dynamic, organizations need to gather a diversity of information in order to comprehend external demands and opportunities. For example, they must attend to segmented labor markets, changing laws and regulations, rapid scientific developments, emergent

economic policies, shifts in customer and supplier behaviors, and various competitive pressures. Organizations tend to establish special units for scanning particular aspects or parts of the environment, such as market research, public relations, and strategic planning departments. These units generally include specialists with expertise limited to a particular segment of the environment. As environments become more complex, organizations need to elaborate their external structures, adding new staff and support units to deal with diverse parts of the environment (Pfeffer and Salancik, 1978; Scott, 1981). They must match environmental complexity with structural complexity.

Pfeffer and Salancik (1978) suggested that diverse scanning units can produce necessary information about complex environments. However, organizations may have difficulty integrating the diverse information into a comprehensive, long-range view of external conditions needed to choose strategic responses to it. Problems in using environmental information typically arise from the sheer magnitude and diversity of information generated by specialized scanning units. Administrators who need the information to choose strategic responses can become overloaded with informational reports; they can have problems understanding and trusting the staff specialists who collected the information; they can have troubles integrating the information that tends to be widely dispersed throughout the organization. Pfeffer and Salancik (1978) suggested that organizations can resolve these issues by bringing together the various sources of scanning expertise in a structured format which facilitates integrated use of information for strategic planning and decision making. They identified techniques, such as the Delphi (Linstone and Turoff, 1975) and Nominal Group Technique (Delbecq et al., 1975), for gathering and integrating information from diverse specialists, and gaining commitment to forecasts, plans, and decisions about environmental responses.

Diversification

Organizations must manage external dependencies if they are to acquire the resources and information needed to function effectively. When environments are complex and dynamic, organizations tend to experience a diversity of external demands from numerous groups and organizations interested in the organization's resources. These external dependencies can reduce the organization's discretion to adapt to changing conditions; they can place conflicting demands on organizations that are difficult to reconcile (Pfeffer and Salancik, 1978). Organizations can resolve these dependency issues through diversification, performing a variety of activities in a diversity of environments. Diversification enables organizations to loosen dependencies on others, because it provides multiple sources for acquiring inputs and disposing of outputs. Organizations gain control over environments by having alternative sources of information and resources.

Diversification can also help organizations respond to conflicting demands. It disperses dependencies across numerous environmental groups and organizations, thus reducing the impact of failing to respond to any given demand. Moreover, if the diversified units of the organizations are loosely coupled to each other, it may be possible to respond to conflicting demands simultaneously. Each organizational unit can respond to a particular demand, and so long as the units are not tightly coordinated, their separate responses do not have to be consistent with each other (Pfeffer and Salancik, 1978). Loose coupling among organizational subunits, as found in multidivisional structures (Chandler, 1962), can also provide a more sensitive mechanism for detecting variations in the environment and for encouraging opportunistic adaptation to local conditions (Weick, 1979). Allowing subunits to adapt independently to local environments can increase the stability of the overall organization by localizing external disturbances and not letting them affect other parts of the organization.

Collective Structures
In addition to managing dependencies through diversification, organizations can cope with problems of environmental dependence and uncertainty through increased coordination with other organizations (Pfeffer and Salancik, 1978; Aldrich, 1979). Increasing coordination with other organizations can enable the interacting organizations to control their interdependencies, thus reducing uncertainty through the mutual exchange of commitments (Thompson, 1967). In essence, each party surrenders some power or control to others in exchange for commitments about future transaction. Researchers have examined a variety of collective structures for coordinating transactions among organizations, including bargaining, contracting, coopting, joint ventures, and federations (Kochan, 1975; Palmer, 1983). Because these different collective structures vary in the amount of autonomy organizations need to surrender to gain commitments from others, organizations tend to choose structures minimizing control costs. They generally start with less costly structures, such as bargaining and contracting; as the environment becomes more complex and dynamic, they may be forced to choose more costly structures, such as joint ventures and federations, to reduce uncertainty to more manageable levels.

Cummings (1984) has described the growing use of joint ventures, coalitions, and federations to manage environmental uncertainty and to perform tasks that are too complicated and costly for single organizations to undertake. He called these collective structures "transorganizational systems," which are groups of organizations that have joined together for a common purpose. Such systems have traditionally been used in the public sector to coordinate public services. Their use is growing rapidly in the private sector as a means for sharing resources for large-scale research and development, for reducing risks for innovation, for applying multiorganization expertise to complex problems and tasks, and for overcoming barriers to entry into foreign markets. For example, joint ventures among firms from different countries are increasingly being used to cope with potentially restrictive trade barriers. A growing number of high-technology firms in the United States are forming research consortia to gain the resources needed to undertake significant research and development. Similarly, an increasing number of defense contractors are forming strategic alliances to bid on and potentially undertake large government projects. Cummings (1984) suggested that a major barrier to the growth of transorganizational systems is organizational drive for autonomy. This "rugged individualism" often prevents the surrender of control necessary to form collaborative relationships with other organizations. Ouchi (1984) argued that such problems can be overcome in the United States by enacting federal laws, economic policies, and national advisory councils promoting coordination among organizations. He cited Japanese industrial and economic policies as promoting the kinds of transorganizational collaboration needed to respond to complex and dynamic global environments.

Manipulative Structures

This final type of external structure involves attempts by organizations to change or modify their environments. Aldrich (1979) argued that organizations prefer to manipulate the environment because they can generally gain control over external elements without having to sacrifice their autonomy. For example, they can engage in political activity to influence government laws and regulations; seek government regulation to control entry to industries; gain legitimacy in the wider society by appearing to conform to valued social norms; and acquire control over raw material or markets by vertical and horizontal integration (Meyer and Rowan, 1977; Pfeffer and Salancik, 1978; Aldrich, 1979; Harrigan, 1985). Although the range of manipulative structures is almost limitless, organizations tend to be highly selective in choosing such approaches. The structures can be costly to enact, and because many of them appear aggressive to others, they may evoke countervailing actions by powerful others, such as the government, competitors, and various interest groups.

DESIGNING AND CHANGING ORGANIZATIONAL STRUCTURES

We have identified a variety of internal and external structures for coping with complex and dynamic environments. The structures have been described statically, as though once implemented, they require little modification or change. A more dynamic perspective is needed, however, to understand the process by which environments design and redesign their structures as the circumstances demand. Designing organizational structures can be considered an ongoing process of generating structural variations or innovations, learning whether they are successful, and modifying them if necessary (Cummings and Mohrman, 1987). This requires considerable experimentation and learning as organizations continually learn, unlearn, and relearn how to structure themselves (Hedberg, et al., 1976).

When environments are complex and changing, organizations must have the capacity to redesign themselves almost continuously. They must be able to detect environmental changes and modify their structures accordingly. Because organizational responses to the environment must be timely and include commitment to change, structural design cannot be relegated to external experts. Rather, it must be part of the normal functioning of the organization, a process called *self-design* (Hedberg et al., 1976; Weick, 1977; Cummings and Mohrman, 1987). Self-design requires organizations to be proficient at two kinds of organizational change: incremental change and strategic change.

Incremental Change

This type of change involves incremental improvements to existing organizational structures. It requires detecting and correcting errors in how current structures are being enacted (Argyris and Schon, 1978). When deviations from desired structures are discovered, organizations must learn the causes of the error and devise appropriate solutions. This may result in fine-tuning the structures to make them operate better, or adjusting them to better fit environmental conditions (Tushman et al., 1986).

Incremental change is oriented to improving the status quo and is the most prevalent form of self-design occurring in organizations. Because it makes the organization's existing structures more effective without fundamentally changing them, it includes the myriad of minor structural adjustments organizations make daily almost as a matter of course. For example, organizations may refine policies and methods, hire and train personnel better suited to existing structures, and modify reward systems to support and reinforce certain structures. Incremental change is appropriate when structures are relatively adaptive to external conditions, and organizations want to make them even better. It requires good problem-solving skills so organizational members can correctly identify sources of structural error and devise appropriate modifications. Norms promoting open exchange of information among members can facilitate gathering and integrating the diversity of information applicable to incremental change.

Strategic Change

This type of change involves fundamental reorientations of organizational structures, drastically altering them to fit current or anticipated environmental shifts (Nadler and Tushman, 1986, in press). Tushman et al. (1986) pointed out that strategic change is discontinuous, requiring abrupt and often revolutionary changes throughout the organization. It typically occurs in response to or in anticipation of major environmental shifts caused by such factors as deregulation, technological innovation, and sharp discontinuities in legal, political, and market conditions. Such drastic changes can render existing organizational structures obsolete or maladaptive to external conditions. Organizations may fail to recognize the need for strategic change, however, because past successes tend to reinforce existing structures and environmental enactments (Hedberg et al., 1976). When faced with abrupt environmental shifts, organizations either may fail to detect them or respond by doggedly adhering to existing structures.

The growing literature on strategic change suggests that organizations may overcome these inertial tendencies through strong executive leadership and corporate values challenging the status quo (Hedberg et al., 1976; Nystrom et al., 1976; Nadler and Tushman, 1986; Tichy and Devanna, 1986; Mohrman et al., in press). Strategic change must be initiated and directed by corporate executives. These leaders must create a vision of desired structural changes and energize and enable organizational members to move rapidly in that direction (Nadler and Tushman, in press). They must, for example, articulate the need for and direction of strategic change, and express personal commitment and support for it. Executives must also clarify the kinds of behaviors needed to implement the changes, and create measurement and reward systems to reinforce the new behaviors. Because existing executives are often committed to the status quo and lack the energy and talent for strategic change, organizations may have to bring in outsiders to manage the change program. Externally recruited executives can bring different skills and a fresh approach to organizations; they are not constrained by prior commitments and can strongly promote strategic changes (Tushman et al., 1986).

In addition to strong executive leadership, corporate values challenging existing structures and response can promote strategic change. Hedberg et al. (1976) argued that organizations need a healthy balance between values promoting stability and those promoting change. When organizations have too much inertia, they tend to ignore environmental shifts and respond too slowly if at all. Conversely, when organizations are too change-oriented, they tend to respond too quickly to external changes that are relatively unimportant. Hedberg and his colleagues suggested that organizational stability derives from values favoring consensus, contentment, affluence, faith, consistency, and rationality. These values promote the status quo. The authors argued that organizations need to challenge these values if they are to undertake strategic change. For example, they must strive for minimal consensus, often introducing dissension to enable conflicts to be genuinely resolved. They must seek to minimize contentment with existing structures, becoming more sensitive to signals of maladaption to the environment. Organizations need to strive for minimal affluence, reducing slack resources that tend to insulate them from environmental changes. They must have minimum faith in long-range plans and forecasts, keeping ready to replace plans to adapt to environmental shifts. Organizations need to minimize consistency, striving to break with precedents if the circumstances demand. They must minimize rationality, questioning established models of reality and presumed facts.

CONCLUSION

Organizations must create and maintain transactions with suitable environments to survive and grow. They can structure themselves to adapt to and shape environments in favored directions. Choices about organizational structures are determined by the nature of the environment—the degree to which information about it is uncertain and organizations are dependent on others for critical resources. When faced with high levels of information uncertainty and resource dependence, organizations are heavily constrained by environments and must be responsive to them. Structural choices must facilitate the information processing necessary to understand environmental inputs to they can be converted into valued outputs and to manage key sources of external dependence.

Organizations can choose internal structures for operating their core technology and external structures for relating the technology to the environment. These structures must have the requisite variety and flexibility of responses to match external conditions. When environments are complex and dynamic, structures must be equally complex and flexible to respond to them. Internal structures satisfying these requirements include organic, matrix structures or adhocracies, with low levels of formalization and centralization and high levels of differentiation and integration. External structures fitting these conditions include scanning units for mapping the environment, diversification for loosening dependencies and coping with conflicting demands, collective structures for negotiating more manageable environments, and manipulative structures for changing the environment in favorable directions.

Organizations' ability to design and modify structures relies on proficiency in two kinds of change. Incremental change involves making structures more effective and requires good problem-solving and information-processing skills. Strategic change involves radically transforming structures and requires strong executive leadership and corporate values that challenge the status quo. Organizations must manage these two kinds of change if they are to operate effectively and respond to changing environments. This requires knowledge about environments, how they impact structural choices, and the range of alternative structures responsive to changing conditions. Hopefully, this contribution is a step toward providing that understanding.

REFERENCES

Aldrich, H.: "Technology and Organization Structure: A Re-Examination of the Findings of the Aston Group." *Administrative Science Quarterly*, 17 (1972), pp. 26–43.

Aldrich, H.: *Organizations and Environments* (Englewood Cliffs, NJ: Prentice-Hall, 1979).

Argyris, C.; and Schon, D.: *Organizational Learning* (Reading, MA: Addison-Wesley, 1978).

Astley, W.; and Van de Ven, A.: "Central Perspectives and Debates in Organization Theory." *Administrative Science Quarterly*, 28 (1983), pp. 245–273.

Benson, J.: "The Interorganizational Network as a Political Economy," *Administrative Science Quarterly*, 20 (1975), pp. 229–249.

Burns, T.; and Stalker, G.: *The Management of Innnovation* (London: Tavistock, 1967).

Chandler, A.: *Strategy and Structure* (Cambridge, MA: MIT Press, 1962).

Child, J.: "Organization Structure and Strategies of Control: A Replication of the Aston

Studies." *Administrative Science Quarterly*, 17 (1972), pp. 163–172.

Cummings, T.: "Transorganizational Development," in B. Staw, and L. Cummings, eds, *Research in Organizational Behavior*, Vol. 6 (Greenwich, CT: JAI Press), 1984, pp. 367–422.

Cummings, T.; and Mohrman, S.: "Self-Designing Organizations: Toward Implementing Quality-of-Work-Life Innovations," in W. Woodman, and W. Pasmore, eds, *Research in Organizational Change and Development*, Vol. 1 (Greenwich, CT: JAI Press, 1987).

Davidson, W.; and Haspeslagh, P.: "Shaping a Global Product Organization," *Harvard Business Review*, 60 (1982), pp. 125–132.

Delbecq, A.; Van de Ven, A.; and Gustafson, D.: *Group Techniques for Program Planning* (Glenview, Il: Scott, Foresman, 1975).

Duncan, R.: "Characteristics of Organizational Environments and Perceived Uncertainty," *Administrative Science Quarterly*, 17 (1972), pp. 313–327.

Emerson, R.: "Power-Dependence Relations," *American Sociological Review*, 27 (1962), pp. 31–41.

Fredrickson, J.: "The Effect of Structure on the Strategic Decision Process," *Academy of Management Proceedings* (1984), pp. 12–16.

Galbraith, J.: *Organization Design* (Reading, MA: Addison-Wesley, 1977).

Hannan, M.; and Freeman, J.: "The Population Ecology of Organizations," *American Journal of Sociology*, 82 (1972), pp. 929–964.

Hannan, M.; and Freeman, J.: "Structural Inertia and Organizational Change," *American Sociological Review*, 49 (1984), pp. 149–164.

Harrigan, K.: "Vertical Integration and Corporate Strategy," *Academy of Management Journal*, 28 (1985), pp. 397–425.

Hedberg, B.; Nystrom, P.; and Starbuck, W.: "Camping on Seesaws: Prescriptions for a Self-Designing Organization," *Administrative Science Quarterly*, 21 (1976), pp. 41–65.

Hrebniak, L.; and Joyce, W.: "Organizational Adaptation: Strategic Choice and Environmental Determinism," *Administrative Science Quarterly*, 30 (1985), pp. 336–349.

Katz, D.; and Kahn, R.: *The Social Psychology of Organizations*, 2d Ed. (New York: John Wiley, 1978).

Kochan, T.: "Determinants of the Power of Boundary Units in an Interorganizational Bargaining Relation," Administrative Science Quarterly, 20 (1975), pp. 434–452.

Lawrence, P.; and Lorsch, J.: *Organizations and Environments* (Boston: Division of Research, Graduate School of Business Administration, Harvard University, 1967).

Leifer, R.; and Huber, G.: "Relations Among Perceived Environmental Uncertainty, Organization Structure, and Boundary-Spanning Behavior," *Administrative Science Quarterly*, 22 (1977), pp. 235–247.

Linstone, H.; and Turoff, M.: *The Delphi Method: Techniques and Applications* (Reading, MA: Addison-Wesley, 1975).

McKelvey, W.: *Organizational Systematics: Taxonomy, Evolution, and Classification* (Berkeley: University of California Press, 1982).

Meyer, A.: "Adapting to Environmental Jolts," *Administrative Science Quarterly*, 27 (1982), pp. 515–537.

Meyer, J.; and Rowan, B.: "Institutionalized Organizations: Formal Structure as Myth and Ceremony," *American Journal of Sociology*, 83 (1977), pp. 440–463.

Miller, D.; and Friesen, P.: *Organizations: A Quantum View* (Englewood Cliffs, NJ: Prentice-Hall, 1984).

Mintzberg, H.: *The Structuring of Organizations: A Synthesis of Research* (Englewood Cliffs, NJ: Prentice-Hall, 1979).

Mohrman, A.; Lawler, E. III; Ledford, G.; Mohrman, S.; Mitroff, I.; and Cummings, T.: eds, *Large-Scale Organization Change* (San Francisco: Jossey-Bass, in press).

Nadler, D.; and Tushman, M.: *Strategic Organization Change* (Homewood, IL: Scott, Foresman, 1986).

Nadler, D.; and Tushman, M.: "Leadership and Organizational Change: Beyond the Magical Leader," in M. Mohrman, E. Lawler III, G. Ledford, S. Mohrman, I. Mitroff, and T. Cummings, eds, *Large-Scale Organization Change*. San Francisco: Jossey-Bass, in press).

Nystrom, P.; Hedberg, B.; and Starbuck, W.: "Interacting Processes as Organization Designs," in R. Kilmann, L. Pondy, and D. Slevin, eds, *The Management of Organization Design*, Vol. 1 (New York: North-Holland, 1976, pp. 209–230).

Ouchi, W.: *The M-Form Society: How American Teamwork Can Recapture the Competitive Edge* (Reading, MA: Addison-Wesley, 1984).

Palmer, D.: "Broken Ties: Interlocking Directorates and Intercorporate Coordination," *Administrative Science Quarterly*, 28 (1983), pp. 40–55.

Perrow, C.: *Organizational Analysis: A Sociological View* (Belmont, CA: Brooks/Cole, 1970).

Pfeffer, J.: "Mergers as a Response to Organizational Interdependence," *Administrative Science Quarterly*, 19 (1972), pp. 382–394.

Pfeffer, J.; and Salancik, G.: *The External Control of Organizations: A Resource Dependence Perspective* (New York: Harper and Row, 1978).

Pugh, D.: "Modern Organization Theory: A Psychological and Sociological Study," *Psychological Bulletin*, 66 (1966), pp. 235–251.

Robock, S.; and Simmonds, K.: *International Business and Multinational Enterprises*, 3d Ed. (Homewood, II: Irwin, 1983).

Schutz, A.: *The Phenomonology of the Social World* (Evanston, II: Northwestern University Press, 1967).

Scott, W.: *Organizations: Rational, Natural, and Open Systems* (Englewood Cliffs, NJ: Prentice-Hall, 1981).

Stopford, J.; and Wells, L. Jr.: *Managing the Multinational Enterprise* (New York: Basic Books, 1972).

Thompson, J.: *Organizations in Action* (New York: McGraw-Hill, 1967).

Tichy, N.; and Devanna, M.: *The Transformational Leader* (New York: John Wiley, 1986).

Tushman, M.; and Nadler, D.: "Information Processing as an Integrative Concept in Organizational Design," *Academy of Management Review*, 3 (1978), pp. 613–624.

Tushman, M.; Newman, W.; and Romanelli, E.: "Convergence and Upheaval: Managing the Unsteady Pace of Organizational Evolution," *California Management Review*, 29 (1986), pp. 29–44.

Weick, K.: "Organization Design: Organizations as Self-Designing Systems," *Organizational Dynamics*, 6 (1977), pp. 30–46.

Weick, K.: *The Social Psychology of Organizing*, 2d Ed. (New York: Random House, 1979).

8

Strategic Planning for Possible Changes in Trade Policy

REUVEN HORESH

In the preceding chapters, Agmon and Wihlborg review the commitment of corporate investment to fixed capital equipment and the consequent effect of that decision on corporate costs and flexibility, and Cummings and Nathan consider the nature of organizational design and restructure and their effects on cost and flexibility dimensions. In "Strategic Planning for Possible Changes in Trade Policy," Reuven Horesh addresses the question of corporate flexibility—the capacity to respond to change in policy—from the perspective of companies based in Israel. This historical experience of firms in a small, trade-oriented country, from which he draws the illustration of his message, has two important distinguishing characteristics.

First, the Israeli government, like many of its size and circumstance, is extremely activist with regard to industrial and economic policy management. Second, because of the extremely close relationship between government and business, corporate management and performance are strongly affected by government action. Horesh provides many examples of the means by which such business and economic policy enforcement is affected.

Horesh asserts that the most important objective of corporate management in such settings is to protect the corporate capacity for long-range planning and performance results. In other words, opportunities for business investment, corporate operations, and planning must all be shielded from the intense effects of shifts in government policy.

This chapter introduces and highlights as an important protective device, the strategic structure and management of the firm's short-term, financial asset/liability portfolio. This portfolio, and the trade credit, inventory, and short-term financing policies that substantially determine the portfolio balance, must provide at least partial protection from sometimes dramatic policy shifts. In many cases, portfolio management can provide significant protection.

The chapter reviews the structure of policy in each area and delineates those elements that determine both cost and value, and the degree to which the structure of the portfolio enhances or restricts the company's flexibility. This review, and the description of the experiences of Israeli firms in these regards, has very useful implications for this important aspect of managing corporate flexibility in response to changes in the configuration of trade policy.

The growing interest in strategic planning has produced a large number of attempts to come up with an accurate and comprehensive definition of this activity. Therefore, the definitions vary with respect to scope and emphasis. Most of them, if not all refer to the key elements of where the firm wants to be, how to get there, and how to deal with surprises—both favorable and unfavorable—that may occur while the firm is on its way toward the target.

Clearly, the amount of effort to be invested in the preparation for such surprises and in maintaining the potential to deal with them as they come should be a positive function of the likelihood of their appearance and their impact on the economics of the firm. Surprises are of different natures, to mention only a few: technological, customers' needs and tastes, increased or decreased competition, and macroeconomic changes, both domestic and international.

One may argue that most of these changes should not be regarded as surprises because they can be forecast through a carefully planned monitoring process. For example, technological changes usually follow a logistic curve with parameters that can be estimated by a combination of time series and cross-sectional analyses. Needs and taste changes usually follow a diffusion process and as such can be extrapolated from some observed trends.

However, even if this claim is justified and the argument becomes a matter of "value of information," much less can be said in favor of reducing the macroeconomic surprise issue to a pure cost-of-information consideration. Although macroeconomic variables in general follow a certain evolutionary process driven by the continuous struggle of the markets for an equilibrium state, they are bound to experience sudden changes, both in trend and magnitude, due to the interventions and actions of governments and other powerful central forces. These actions are often motivated by short-term and/or less than general welfare goals, and as such are as hard to predict as any other political move.

Hence, the more a government is involved in trying to fix the economic variables, the more chances are that the business unit that operates in this economy will be faced with sudden and unexpected changes in vital variables such as nominal and/or real interest rates, exchange rates, relative prices of both inputs and outputs, and availability of funds for both short-term and long-term uses.

Following those arguments we suggest that the higher the level of involvement of the regime in the economy, the more changes in macroeconomic variables fall into the category of "surprises." Thus, the effort to predict them is harder, more costly, and less accurate with regard to its results.

THE ISRAELI CASE

One of the unique characteristics of the Israeli economy is the strong government intervention in a wide scope of economic variables. The role of the government is played mostly through controlling the different costs of financing business activities, prices of other inputs, prices of outputs, availability of credits, and exchange rates.

A variety of instruments have been designed to help control the relative prices of both inputs and outputs, such that the ever changing economic goals will be obtained. Sometimes, the prime goal is to improve the trade balance while paying the toll of increased inflation. In other times, when foreign currency reserves are satisfactory, curbing inflation will become the main goal.

An overview of the Israeli industrial policy focus that was included in a recent comprehensive study—*Export Struggle for Israel*, presented to the government of Israel and to the Economic Task Force, by J.I.M. Telesis and Dr. S. Tilles in February 1987—demonstrates the extensiveness and the dynamic nature of the government involvement in the economy (Table 8.1). Every stage was characterized by a complex network of subsidies and controls, some direct and some indirect, some new and some leftover from a previous stage.

1984 Price Freeze

In the 12 months ending October 1984, the inflation rate in Israel was 465 percent, reaching a record monthly rate of 24 percent in October 1984,

Table 8.1 Historic Orientation of Israel's Industrial Policy

	Main Driving Force	Policy Focus
1948–55	Agriculture and infrastructure Economic self-sufficiency Immigrants' employment	Import licenses Government investment in agriculture and infrastructure
1956–65	Emphasis on industrial import substitution	Very activist policy to develop industry
1966–73	Self-sufficiency in defense	Capital subsidies and guarantees Tariffs
1973–84	Export: Through international integration Emphasis on short-term economic crisis control: Balance of payments and Inflation	Free trade agreements Exchange rate insurance Liberalization of foreign exchange controls
1985	Inflation control	Macroeconomic focus Reduction in direct industrial assistance Attempts to free capital market

which amounts to 1265 percent annual inflation. Recognizing that the situation was getting out of control, the government of Israel ordered a drastic noncompromising price freeze for all goods and services bought and sold in the domestic market.

Although one should expect some kind of a sharp measure to be taken by a government facing runaway inflation, most business units and the economy as a whole were caught by surprise, totally unprepared with respect to almost every business aspect.

One explanation for the "business as usual" atmosphere prior to the price freeze act was the very elaborate linkage mechanism that was uniquely applied to the Israeli economy and the near indifference of both the business sector and the household sector to the frequent sharp price changes of goods and services, including labor. As a matter of fact, some prices were adjusted daily—following the changes in the Israeli shekel–United States dollar exchange rate. Linking the prices to the dollar rather than the CPI avoided the 1 month delay in adjusting prices to cost and hence reduced the uncertainty with regard to profitability and, very important for our further discussion, the real interest rate.

1985 Package Deal

In spite of the price freeze of October 1984, the price level increased in the following months, although at a much slower rate than prior to the act. The period of November 1984 to June 1985 measured an inflation of 103 percent amounting to an annual rate of 190 percent with a price level increase of 15 percent in June 1985 amounting to an annual rate of 535 percent. We will not analyze here the conflicting message of a "price freeze" and "high inflation." Some of the reasons for the inconsistency came from political sources, some came from institutional sources, and some are just a result of failing to control the markets.

At this stage, the government, which managed to gain almost a political consensus, acted much more comprehensively than in October 1984 and applied a "package deal," which involved an agreement between all the economic sectors to curb inflation. Among other actions, the Israeli shekel/United States dollar exchange rate was frozen as well as other prices, whereas the price freeze of 1984 had been applied to domestic trade only.

SOME MANAGERIAL MODELS

In the following discussion we will describe briefly some managerial models that can be used to determine the desired level of some business variables. These variables were chosen because they can be used to demonstrate our strategic arguments, owing to their sensitivity to the two economic acts of 1984 and 1985. However, by no means are they the only ones that are affected by such acts.

Inventory

A typical production cycle will be supported by three types of inventories: (1) raw materials, (2) products in process, and (3) finished goods. The level of each inventory will be determined to minimize the cost of holding the inventory and will involve knowledge (or at least estimation) of the periodical demand for the item, cost of carrying (including the cost of the tied-up capital), cost of ordering, cost of shortage, and delivery time.

A well-known conceptual approach to the inventory level determines the economic order quantity (EOQ, which is the highest inventory level) to be a nonlinear function of the demand, the carrying cost, and the ordering cost:

$$2D\,Co\,EOQ = Cs$$

where D is the demand per period, Co is the fixed (and only) ordering cost, and Cs is the carrying cost per unit per period. Once the inventory level is determined, all the variable cost components associated with its management, except for the cost of the tied-up capital, can be added to the price, which in turn will be used as a basis for the cost of inventory financing.

Credits

The term "credit" in this analysis describes the formation of a commitment by or to the firm caused by the time difference between the purchase (or sale) of inputs (or outputs) and the payment (or receipt) of cash. If payment for inputs is required t4 days after purchasing and collection of cash for outputs occur t5 days after sale, the total (simple) cost of credit financing is

$$C2 = -M + L\left(\frac{rt_4}{365}\right) + (M + L)(1 + M)\left(\frac{rt_5}{365}\right)$$

where r is the same in C1, A is the profit margin, and it is assumed that all inputs offer the same credit terms.

Financing Cost

We recall that the nominal interest rate (i.e., the rate that is actually charged) is related to the real rate (i.e., the rate that determines the real compensation for differing consumption from the present to the future, and the expected change in the price level, which determines the compensation for the loss (or gain) in the purchasing power of both the principle and the real rate charged to it. The nominal rate can be written as

$$i = (1 + r)(1 + E\dot{P}) - 1$$

where r is the real rate and $E\dot{P}$ is the expected change in the price level.

In reality, the only observed variable of the three above is i (the nominal interest rate). Hence one of the other two has to be assumed in order to determine the second. Obviously, this creates an uncertain situation with respect to both the required real rate and the expected inflation.

In other words, the true real rate in the ex post sense is a random variable which can be expressed as

$$r = \frac{1+i}{1+\dot{P}} - 1$$

where $\dot{P}$ is the true (ex post) recorded change in the price level. The uncertainty regarding the real rate should be noted with respect to our further discussion.

Inventory Financing

We recall that the cost of inventory financing over the production cycle T is

$$M\left(\frac{rT}{365}\right) + L\left(r\frac{(2^{t^2} + t^3)}{365}\right)$$

The question is which rate (r) should be used to determine the cost of inventory financing, the nominal or the real rate?

If a unit of output is selling for Po today, it will sell for $Pox(1 + Po, t)$ at time t. Selling the output is really selling the inputs plus a profit, which really means that the inputs are selling at a price which includes the compensation for the price change $\dot{P}$.

It is clear that although the nominal cost of funds that were used to finance the inventories was i, a partial compensation is obtained by the linkage of output prices (and hence the input prices) to the price level in the economy. As a conclusion, the only financing cost that is charged to the basic cost figure is related to the real component of the nominal cost, and r in our C1 equation is the real rate. It should be noted that using the nominal rate i in an inflationary economy will constitute a double counting of the inflation, hence a too high cost figure which in turn will cause a too high selling price, hence a less competitive position.

Credit Financing

In practice, the cash cycle of a production process is different from the real cycle. The difference is due to credit terms that are granted to customers on the selling end and enjoyed by the producer on the purchasing end. It has been shown above that the cost of financing the credit is

$$C2 = -(M+L)\frac{rt^4}{365} + (M+L)(1+A)\frac{rt^5}{365}$$

where t^4 is the number of credit days (assumed to be equal for all inputs) granted by the suppliers, t^5 is the number of credit days granted to (all) the customers, A is the profit margin, and r is the interest rate.

The question is which interest rate should be used here, and the answer is quite simple; granting the credit should be considered as a simple monetary transaction. Rather than paying (or receiving cash on a certain day, an obligation is made to transfer the cash as a later date. If the supplier needs the cash on the day of trade, he can get a loan, paying the lender an interest rate that reflects both the real compensation and the expected inflation—namely, the nominal rate.

To conclude the discussion of the financing cost, some observations will be in order:

1. In order to figure the cost of financing credits, the future interest rate should be predicted. This in turn requires the prediction of the rate of price change in the future. This is not the case in figuring the cost of inventory financing, where only the real rate is used.
2. While in a price stability period, inventory financing will account for most of the financing cost, an inflationary situation will increase the portion of the credit financing.

Effect of Foreign Currency Transaction

It may be argued that the case of foreign currency transaction, both on the purchasing and selling ends, does not fall in the domain of across the board price change. This argument follows the observations regarding the frequent changes in trade terms for firms involved in international activities.

However, if the economic theory is employed, or more specifically the purchasing power parity (PPP) approach, one should expect a zero real devaluation of the base currency, which is used in the cost calculation, against all the foreign currencies involved in both purchasing some (or all) inputs and/or selling some (or all) outputs.

A zero real devaluation will be achieved if the nominal devaluation is affected by both the inflations in base counting and the foreign one such that:

$$1 + d_{1,2}^n = \frac{1 + \dot{P}_1}{1 + \dot{P}_1}$$

where $d_{1,2}^n$ denotes the nominal devaluation of the currency of country 1 against this of country 2, and $\dot{P}_1$, $\dot{P}_2$ are the inflation rates in countries 1 and 2, respectively.

If this is the case, no adjustment is required to account for changes in exchange rates, and the costing calculation is reduced to the "one-country across-the-board price change" case. It should be noted, however, that any deviation from the zero real devaluation implies a relative price change.

It has been argued that if a zero real devaluation exists, the relative purchasing power of the different currencies is maintained. However, if for any reason, intended or unintended, the exchange rate does not follow the PPP pattern, its changes will become a major source of changes in the relative prices of inputs and outputs when expressed in the domestic currency. Expectations as to the future real changes in the exchange rates should hence be taken into account in the costing process.

Given the above explanatory models, it follows that a profit-maximizing firm must carefully consider and employ three important parameters: (1) the real interest rate, vital for determining the inventory levels of raw materials, goods in process, and finished goods, (2) the nominal rate to determine the type of credits to be accepted from suppliers or granted to customers relative to a *can* basis trading; and (3) the "real" change in the exchange rates to determine the relative prices of domestic and imported inputs and those of domestic and exported outputs, such that an optimal mix of inputs and outputs will be employed.

EXPECTATION AND SURPRISES

In a typical business environment, changes in the decision-making inputs are relatively slow and follow a clear pattern. Indeed, changes in the direction and in the rate of changes may also be experienced; however, they will allow ample time for the managers to adjust their business practice without suffering major actual and/or opportunity losses.

Moreover, in most cases it is quite satisfactory just to observe the variables directly and act according to their observed values. What we are really saying is that in such a "normal and calm" situation, a computer can manage many aspects of the business provided the optimization models built into it make sense.

The situation is completely different in a turbulent environment, where the rates of change of business-related variables change wildly and frequently with respect to both magnitude and direction. Here, failing to adjust business practices promptly may be very costly, and the chance of being able to do it is very slim. The only possible solution to this situation involves the ability to predict the changes in the business-related variables by analyzing their underlying economic forces, a skill not too many people share.

1984 AND 1985 SURPRISES AND THEIR EFFECTS ON SOME VARIABLES

We will analyze the effects of the price freeze of 1985 on the real interest rates, the alternative cash basis price, and the relative import/export price of an imaginary firm (Table 8.2).

Needless to say, such adjustments require time and effort. For example, it will take at least 1 month to reduce a 4 month inventory level to a 3 month inventory level. Meanwhile a sizable penalty will be imposed on the firm that is now financing its inventory at 17 percent real rate per month rather than the 3.2 percent prior to the act.

It is important to note, however, that an increase in the export portion of the output allocation that was appropriate in October 1984 became quite harmful in June 1985, when the exchange rate was frozen strictly (until January 1987, when a 10 percent devaluation was applied). Although domestic prices did increase at a slow pace, the relative prices of domestically sold outputs to the exported outputs clearly increased, calling for lowering the export activity level.

Table 8.2   Effects of Israel's 1985 Prize Freeze on an Imaginary Firm

	Prior to Freeze	One Month After Freeze
Monthly nominal rate	28%	17%
Price increase	24%	0%
Real rate	3.2%	17%
Cash basis price (I.S.)	100	109
1 month credit price (I.S.)	128	128
Exchange rate (I.S.)	517	586
Price (United States $)	0.193	0.193
Price United States $ (I.S.)	100	113.1
Relative price United States $/I.S.	1/1	113.1 = 1.038

The required adjustments indicated by the data in Table 8.2 are (1) reduce inventories; (2) export less; and (3) export more.

THE STRATEGIC LESSON

In an economy where government is significantly involved in the economic scene, we do expect sharp changes in the domestic economy as well as in the foreign trade sector. These changes are expressed by unanticipated changes in the rate of inflation and in the exchange rate. Such changes are hard to predict, hard to follow, and hard to adjust to in terms of financial management. However, failing to recognize the need to adjust may cause heavy losses.

Hence, business strategists should understand and consider the long-run goals of the government Temporary losses should be tolerated to allow managers to plan ahead rather than react fearfully. Long-run performance should be evaluated, and ample liquid reserves should be set aside when profit is produce, rather than following the temptation to grow too fast. Business cycles should be managed very carefully, because their appearance is quite erratic, and, last but not least, the strategic portfolio of the firm should be heavily affected by the politically related considerations. The government may implement drastic changes due to political factors. The corporation should design its portfolio of financial activities to reflect this eventuality.

9

Protectionism and Marketing Strategies for United States Firms

WESLEY J. JOHNSTON

While the title of this chapter suggests a very narrow focus, Johnston's approach is far-reaching. In fact, like the other chapters in this book that relate to functional areas, Johnston defines the marketing function quite broadly. In essence, he examines the interrelationship between government protectionism and corporate competitiveness, with more limited, traditional marketing techniques providing only a few of the many options available for corporate action.

Johnston's recognition of the bilateral nature of the government/corporate interface in this area is an interesting contribution to the study of the effects of protectionism and the protectionist threat. He outlines the two-way nature of the relationships as government protectionist policy attempts to preserve the competitiveness of United States companies. Companies can respond with actions that capitalize on the protection and undertake strategic investment designed to eventually increase their competitive power, or they can use the protectionist umbrella as a defense against forces calling for competitive response. When companies or industries effectively select the latter, the initial protection becomes the vehicle by which further protection is required and sought. Thus, the two-way street becomes a vicious cycle.

Johnston describes this cycle and the strategic choices, at both government and corporate levels, that lead to cyclical behavior. The chapter also lists the broad range of corporate responses that can serve to break the cycle. These include changes in production strategy, corporate joint ventures and other structuring strategies, refocusing, and repositioning. As suggested above, these strategies reach beyond the traditional function of marketing management and might be considered strategies for a broader management function—management of competitiveness. The chapter not only describes the generic forms of these strategies but explores examples of their use in two industries—telecommunications and textiles.

The common element to the strategies is that their success, and their ultimate objective, is reflected in competitive success. This objective depends, of course, on the effects of protectionism and the responsive corporate actions on the relationship between the company and its customers.

If protectionists merely mean that under their system men will have to sweat and labour more, I grant their case.... The protectionist has to prove not merely that he has made work, but that he has increased the national income.... Is there anything that a tariff could do, which an earthquake could not do better?

—John M. Keynes,
The Nation and Athenaeum,
December 1, 1923

Since the end of World War II, the United States has tended to pursue policies that encouraged freer trade and investment flows. This was accomplished through establishment of and participation in the General Agreement on Tariffs and Trade (GATT), the International Monetary Fund (IMF), the World Bank, and other international institutions. In the first three decades of the postwar era, world trade increased dramatically. Given the high levels of protectionism and the worldwide depression of the 1930s, followed by the disruption of the war, some continued increase in international trade was inevitable. What actually happened was unexpected: trade increased sevenfold, tariffs were reduced, the European Economic Community was established, numerous new nations became industrialized, and, in spite of periodic recessions, trade increased steadily from 1945 until the oil embargo of the mid-1970s. Critical to much of the economic progress in Asia during recent years has been the openness of the United States market. The United States has been the major market for Japan and the newly industrialized countries (NICs). On a worldwide basis, the United States takes over 60 percent of the developing countries' exports.

More recently the trend has been less positive, and worldwide trade growth has actually plateaued since 1980 (Jefferson 1985). In recent years, many countries have turned to policies that protect domestic industry and distort international trade because of slower economic growth, increasingly difficult adjustment problems in some established industries, and a perceived need in many industrial countries to pursue national policies to assure the growth of emerging high-technology industries. During this period, there have been some disturbing events in the United States economy that have caused some to question the ability of United States firms to compete under the previously established framework of lower tariffs and freer trade. Prestowitz (1986, pp. 15–16) provides an enlightening review of this period:

The inability to compete first surfaced in the garment industry; United States wages were $3 per hour, compared with $3 per day in Asia. Various protective measures were negotiated to ease the situation, but eventually United States economists and the public at large came to accept that this older industry should gradually decline here and grow in the less developed countries.

Later, the steel industry came under attack. This was a little harder to accept, since steel had long been seen as the core of any industrial economy. On the other hand, it was a "smokestack" industry that could be criticized as suffering from rigid, arrogant management, and intransigent, grasping unions. At about the same time, the consumer electronics industry began to feel pressure and started to move offshore. This movement resulted in a number of acrimonious trade disputes, but it was argued that these were commodity products and not really the advanced technology that is the true forte of the United States. In the late 1970s the auto industry came under the gun, but it was still possible to argue that this was another "smokestack" industry bedeviled by poor management and blind unions.

Over the past five years, however, as we have seen industries such as semiconductor equipment and telecommunications begin to crumble and fall, it has become obvious that even the highest of high tech is in difficulty.

Given these wrenching structural changes in the patterns of production in the United States economy, the question facing policymakers in the federal government has become how best to ease this adjustment. Since structural change is believed to be essential to economic development, the importance of appropriate adjustment policies is obvious. Underlying this concern are the following statistics:

1. The United States has recorded a trade surplus in only 1 year since 1970, and in 1986 the trade deficit reached a record high of $169.8 billion.
2. For the first time since 1914, the United States is a debtor nation. And not only a debtor nation but the largest. Interest on the debt was $150 billion in 1986.
3. Between 1971 and 1982, real average disposable income and earnings for nonagricultural workers in the United States fell by about 12 percent.
4. According to the Bureau of Labor Statistics, 2.3 million manufacturing jobs have disappeared in the United States since 1980.
5. According to the Commerce Department, the United States has lost market share in nine of 10 high-technology industries since 1960. The office computing and accounting machine industry is the exception.

These figures and the fears related to the United States' ability to compete in the international marketplace have created a political sensitivity to trade legislation. During the 99th Congress, more than 300 "international trade" bills were introduced. In the 100th Congress, an omnibus trade package was created and was passed by the full House in April 1987. This intense push for trade legislation, together with an Administration that reluctantly asserted leadership in setting trade policy, indicates that past United States trade policy has come into question and that some form of increased protectionism may be forthcoming. This chapter examines just what form this protectionism may take and how United States firms should react with respect to marketing strategies under various levels and forms of protectionism.

PROTECTIONISM AND STRUCTURAL ADJUSTMENT

"Structural change" constitutes an integral part of United States economic development. The shift of productive resources from sectors with lower productivity, such as agriculture, to sectors with much higher levels of productivity, such as manufacturing, has been the driving force behind the economic advances recorded since World War II. Behind this broad shift lay structural changes of a more micro nature in the composition of industrial output. Light industries such as textile and apparel gave way to heavy industries based on iron and steel, transportation equipment, and chemicals and eventually to increasingly knowledge-intensive activities such as telecommunication and data processing. Structural change also took place at an even more disaggregated level—within industries. In the case of some industries, survival strategies often represented shifts toward higher value-added activities. The textile and apparel industries, for instance, developed a variety of man-made fibers through technical research and development.

Structural change results from the interaction of a complex set of forces. The cause may be underlying trends in productivity, technological innovation, or demand patterns and trade flows. Shifts in the competitiveness of industries within national boundaries, brought about by government policies and actions, can also lead to structural change.

> Although structural change can come about in a variety of ways, its desirability is never really in doubt.... Structural change is the *sine qua non* of economic growth and development, and the absence of appropriate structural adjustment manifests itself in a long-term disequilibrium (UNCTAD Secretariat, 1982, p. 2).

That structural change is not synonymous with "structural adjustment" may not be immediately apparent. The term "adjustment" indicates that change may include private and social costs that are not easily absorbed. For instance, workers may have to be retrained and/or redeployed to new lines of activity, declining sectors may face a sharp reduction in profit levels, many individual firms may be eliminated from the industry, and so on. Such costs can be high when the level of economic activity may already be low owing to a recession or when the mobility of labor and capital is obstructed by structural rigidities. Structural change may also encounter resistance from those with vested interests in the prevailing structures. Structural adjustment policies, then, allow the structural change to take place in a more socially desirable manner by minimizing the social costs involved in such change. Structural adjustment can be defined as "the transformation of national patterns of production and factor allocation in a socially optimal way in order to accommodate shifts in comparative advantage as revealed by unhindered trade flows" (UNCTAD Secretariat, 1982, p. 2).

Protectionsim is one means of achieving a controlled structural change and is therefore one form of structural adjustment policy. Motivations for protectionism usually result from one or more of the following five reasons:

1. To collect revenue
2. To protect infant industries
3. To address balance-of-payments difficulties
4. To protect strategic industries
5. To prevent "market disruption" in domestic industries

In the United States, record trade deficits, Japan's resistance to eliminating trade barriers to United States goods and services, the steady decline of manufacturing jobs, and a steep drop in agricultural exports have created a strong protectionist movement. Whether protectionism is the best approach to solving the dilemma facing the United States is not within the scope of this chapter. The issue here is that a number of protectionist measures have been proposed and are being considered by the Congress. If passed, they will affect the environment of United States firms which are also trying to adjust their marketing strategies to improve competitiveness.

FORMS OF PROTECTION

The heightened interest in making United States firms more competitive and the intense push for trade legislation have inspired hundreds of proposed bills in Congress. These trade proposals make more sense when they are grouped into five broad categories:

Legislation Aimed at Specific Countries

These bills are aimed at a specific country or countries that are believed to practice unfair trade practices. The most prominent was a scheme to levy a 25 percent customs surcharge on imports from any country whose exports to the United States exceeded its imports from the United States by 65 percent. A country could earn exemption from the surcharge in any year in which it reduced its trade surplus by 10 percentage points. Although the measure was primarily aimed at Japan (as is much of this type of legislation, because Japan is viewed as the country most responsible for United States trade problems), it would also have affected Korea, Taiwan, and Brazil.

Another measure would have required the President to retaliate within 90 days against unfair trading practices by imposing countervailing duties, quotas, or embargoes on specific imports. These actions would be similar to those the Administration actually imposed on Japanese imports when it was recently determined that Japanese semiconductor firms were "dumping" semiconductors in the global marketplace.

Industry Safety Nets

Rather than disciplining an export nation, this type of legislation is aimed at protecting specific industries. This type of protectionism is not new. The textile industry has long been protected by a fairly high level of tariffs covering a large portion of the products and imposed against all suppliers. In addition, quantitative restrictions are imposed on most of the leading foreign exporters. The 1985 Textile and Apparel Trade Enforcement Act would have reduced existing textile import quotas by roughly 20 percent, rolling them back to 1980 levels. A bill has also been introduced that would bar Japanese telecommunications exports to the United States unless the Japanese government opens its markets to competing American equipment. Legislators have introduced many other industry-specific proposals, ranging from higher duties on European roses to a quota on Chilean copper.

The most recent thought on industry-specific trade quotas is that perhaps they should be auctioned. Since the United States sets quotas on imports of a variety of products, such as steel, automobiles, textiles, and sugar, the general effect is to push the price of these products above the world market price. For foreign exporters this makes the United States an unusually profitable market. Normally, quotas are negotiated with each exporting country, and then its government decides which companies get to sell to the United States and how much. This policy presents a bonanza either to the foreign firms that receive the import rights or to foreign officials if they are corrupt and choose to sell these rights. The auctioning of import quotas would allow the United States government to sell the rights to import quotas to the highest bidders and keep any fees. This new policy of allocation of quotas could generate $5 billion to 10 billion per year based on the current level and volume of quota restricted goods.

Stricter Enforcement of Existing Laws

The current Administration does not favor legislation and has vetoed a number of bills that have passed the full House and Senate, including the 1985 Textile and Apparel Trade Enforcement Act. The Administration believes that it can deal with the trade problem by intensifying enforcement of existing laws. Action has already been taken under Section 301 of the Trade Act to force greater market access for United States products. The first complaints covered restrictions on United States tobacco products in Japan, insurance in Korea, and computers in Brazil. Other actions in the form of improving the enforcement of existing laws include the Customs Service with respect to copyright and trademark violations by United States trading partners, most notably Taiwan, and improving the speed of investigating complaints from domestic industries regarding unfair practices of foreign competitors.

Countersubsidization

In an attempt to offset the advantages foreign exporters receive from their governments, this form of trade support would allow the United States government to increase its own export subsidies. Basically, this would be done through interest rates and perhaps taxes. The Administration has subsidized some agricultural exports in an attempt to match European Economic Community practices. In addition, $300 million was added to a "war chest" to allow the Export-Import Bank to match or beat competitors' subsidies. The United States Department of Agriculture implemented a plan that provided incentives for foreign purchases of United States agricultural goods by giving them free grain from government stockpiles. This plan was a major irritant to several allies also whose economies are agriculturally based, especially Australia. Another proposal, which would affect Canada and Mexico, is to impose countervailing duties against foreign goods such as wood products and petrochemicals manufactured with subsidized natural resources.

Marketing Sharing

This form of trade proposal has been referred to as the "new" protectionism. This new protectionism comes in many forms and guises. The most important policy tools used to implement market sharing are voluntary export restraints (VERs) and orderly marketing agreements (OMAs). These bilateral arrangements attempt to bias consumption in the United States in favor of domestic producers. Attempts at marketing sharing such as VERs and OMAs have three basic characteristics:

1. Negotiated agreements between an importing and exporting country
2. Quantitative limits based on the type of good and not on its price
3. Selective restrictions applied to a limited number of producers

The Multi-Fiber Arrangement (MFA) is probably the best known of market sharing agreements. For over a decade (the first bilateral agreements for textiles actually began in 1961), nations that produce textile fibers have regulated shares of the world market through the MFA.

The steel and automobile industries have recently seen voluntary export agreements. In 1984, the United States negotiated agreements with Japan, the European Economic Community, and Third World steel producers to voluntarily limit the penetration of steel imports into each other's markets. In the automobile industry, Japan and the United States have had an agreement for over 4 years limiting the number of Japanese automobiles that will be exported to the United States.

Recently the United States and Israel have agreed to establish a free trade zone, which gives each an advantage over third parties in the other's markets. A new free trade agreement was just signed by the United States and Canada, the United States' largest trading partner. The Administration favors this approach to trade policy and says it will attempt to reach other regional and bilateral pacts if a new negotiating round of GATT is not convened. Some international economists believe these agreements could lead to a cartelization of many markets.

To summarize this plethora of trade proposals and actions, it seems fair to view United States foreign trade policy, like that of most other countries, as facing in opposite directions. On the one hand, it advocates free trade and pushes for trade liberalization. For example, tariffs have been reduced substantially across the board. On the other hand, as the lowering of tariffs and other circumstances have led to a perceived inability to compete by some industries, the free trade policy is challenged, and attempts are made to reverse it and prevent potential "disruptions." Tariffs have been lowered to the point that they are no longer perceived by many observers as the dominant barriers to trade. Indeed, even in the textile and apparel industry, where post–Tokyo Round GATT reductions left tariffs above 10 percent foreign exporters continue to make major inroads into the United States market. Other nontariff barriers, however, have risen as tariffs have been reduced. These trade-distorting practices can be used to reduce imports and/or promote exports.

Table 9.1   Tariffs and Other Trade-Distorting Practices

Practices affecting producer *and* consumer prices

  Revenue-generating practices
    Tariffs
    Variables levies
    Excessive fees or charges for service (e.g., parts)
    Import deposits
    Tariff quotas
    Auction quotas
    Arbitrary customs valuation
    Discriminatory applications of excise taxes

  Nonrevenue-generating practices
    Nonauction quotas, orderly marketing agreements, and other quantitative restraints
    Discriminatory government procurement
    Excessive import documentation costs and delays
    Arbitrary application of product standards
    States trading
    Split exchange rates
    Performance requirements on foreign investors
    Countertrade and offset agreement

Practices affecting producer prices only

  Direct industry subsidies
    Direct cash grants
    Tax credits, special tax arrangements
    Benefits-in-kind

  Preferential access to credit
    Concession rates
    Loan guarantees and insurance programs

  State ownership or equity participation at less than competitive rates of profit

  Export-specific subsidies
    Subsidized export credit
    Government-financed export promotion
    Tied aid to less developed countries
    Loan guarantees for foreign investment
    Tax incentives

SOURCE: Adapted from Morici et al. (1983).

They also have varying effects on producer and consumer prices, as categorized in Table 9.1. From a managerial perspective, a number of questions remain. To what level of protectionism will legislation and the Administration lead the United States economy? What forms of legislation/trade policy will be most prevalent? What implications does the variety of pending protectionist legislation have for corporate managers' marketing strategies?

WHAT'S A MANAGER TO DO?

In a recent advertisement of Allen-Edmonds Shoe Corporation, the following points are made:

Keep your shoes to yourself. That's the clear message the Japanese government has given Allen-Edmonds and other United States shoe manufacturers. Tough licensing, even tougher tariffs and various other obstacles are making it nearly impossible to do business in Japan.

There is a market for our shoes there.... But the duty makes them terribly expensive. Fact is, United States shoes sold in Japan are taxed up to 60 percent higher than Japanese shoes sold in this country.

Don't misunderstand. We're not looking for help or sympathy....

The point is, a company—even a small one like our own—can't wait for political solutions to unfair trade barriers. Manufacturers must initiate action in a friendly but firm manner (Allen-Edmonds Shoe Corporation, Port Washington, WI, 1986).

Many managers doubt the ability of the United States to act in a meaningful way with a revised trade policy. In addition, they are skeptical as to whether legislation would really work.

Government cannot legislate success.... America's ability to compete lies primarily within the private sector (John Young, President of Hewlett-Packard Co. and Director of Presidential Commission on Industrial Competitiveness, 1985).

The high level of protectionist-oriented legislative action coupled with United States managements' efforts to be competitive, even though skeptical about the government's ability to help, raises the most critical of questions: How can the United States government and corporations meet the increasing challenge of foreign competition? To this question, four potential response strategies have been proposed (Kotler et al., 1985).

The strategic respones available to business and government can be classified along two lines: (1) whether the public or private sector undertakes the response, and (2) whether the response is competitive or cooperative in nature. These dimensions permit a two-by-two classification scheme for strategic responses, as indicated in Table 9.2.

Actions taken by the United States government and firms need not be

Table 9.2   Potential Strategic Responses to the Challenge of Foreign Competition

Public	Private
Competitive	
Providing direct financial aid to industry	Improving quality and service
Enforcing antitrust laws	Lowering costs
Imposing higher tariffs, quotas, bans	Increasing aggressive stance
Etc.	
Cooperative	
Reducing mutual trade barriers	Licensing companies in other Nations
Arranging joint foreign aid to developing countries	Entering joint ventures with other companies (horizontal and vertical)
Etc.	Using the other nations trading companies and banks
	Pursuing mergers and acquisitions

SOURCE: Adapted from Kotler et al. (1985), p. 218.

mutually exclusive. That is, both the government and individual firms' managements may act. The actions may also comprise a number of steps both competitive and cooperative. What should be done, who has the ability to influence the issue, and how action can proceed remain difficult questions and create a need for dialogue between the government and private enterprise to coordinate activities. Lobbying action on the part of the individual firms and industries can increase the government's awareness of sector-specific problems. Section 301 of the Trade Act also establishes a complaint process for firms that feel unfair trade practices exist. Finally, special commissions such as the one the President established to examine industrial competitiveness can also improve the dialogue between the private sector and the government. Some issues and possible solutions have already been identified (Windham et al., 1985).

Three of the most viable strategies that have been evolving are these:

1. Protection—through increased tariffs and/or other nontariff barriers, as previously discussed
2. Offshore facilities—moving manufacturing and/or sales offices offshore to gain cost and/or other competitive advantages; forming joint ventures to gain access to restricted markets
3. Refocusing and repositioning—downscaling management, production facilities, and so on concentration on market segments (niches) where a competitive edge can be gained (i.e., through advanced technology and/or R&D)

The issue of protectionism meets with a mixed audience. For one, a geographical split develops between parts of the United States that have significant trade with foreign countries in agriculture and manufacturing industries, such as aerospace, and other states that have lost manufacturing jobs in such industries as steel, textiles, and automobiles. Another problem with protectionism is that it affects industries differentially depending on their position with respect to the value-added stream. Firms that are downstream, such as semiconductors and textiles, may be protected at the expense of manufacturers further upstream who are required to pay prices above the world market for materials and components, such as telecommunications and clothing retailers. These national differences with respect to the acceptance of protectionism are perhaps what lead Congressmen to propose numerous bills aimed at protecting firms and industries within their states while the Administration, looking to the best interests of the nation as a whole, disfavors such legislation. Although the impact of protectionist legislation would not affect most industries as it did the steel industry, some disruption of normal markets would probably occur. Protectionism is also questionable with respect to whether it leads to laziness and a failure to develop adequate competitive capabilities as in the steel and perhaps automobile industries. Finally, the result of any protectionist action could, but there is debate as to whether it would, prompt action by United States trading partners who have trade agreements with the United States allowing for reprisals if the United States erects trade barriers.

A second strategy is to move facilities and/or operations offshore. This strategy, if viewed in a broad perspective, also includes joint ventures, licensing, contract management, and contract manufacturing. However, it is leading to what some observers are calling the "hollowing of the corporation"; that is, as manufacturing facilities leave the United States, only service-oriented jobs remain. Whether this is a problem or not remains uncertain. The United States has become a service-oriented economy (as of 1980), with more people employed in the service sector than in manufacturing or agriculture. Another observation on hollowed-out corporations is that only about 5 percent of the total value added is lost if the manufacturing is done offshore. The argument normally presented against allowing the trend toward offshore manufacturing to continue is the weakening of national security. It is believed that a strong manufacturing sector is necessary for national security reasons. A trend that can reverse the emigration of United States manufacturing jobs and facilities is automation. The key question is whether highly automated United States plants can be as productive as less automated, lower wage rate, foreign facilities. If not, the government would need to protect them with legislation support them through tax policy or other subsidies.

In some industries, moving offshore is overdue. In the textile industry, economies of scale are available in cases where demand for a particular product in the United States market is relatively small and production costs are high. Producing the product offshore would allow the company to gain economies of scale, thus lowering overall costs.

In the telecommunications industry the choices are not so clear. With respect to semiconductors, the trend has been to custom-designed products and away from mass-produced, commodity-type products. If the trend remains this way, United States manufacturers can continue to be competitive in the technology-intensive, labor-insensitive, custom-designed semiconductor market segments. Another issue will be the success of the research consortia recently formed under the auspices of the government and allowed by recent changes in the antitrust laws. Ventures such as M.C.C. in Austin, Texas, and Semetech will attempt to leapfrog the next generation in semiconductor technology. If successful, they should give United States firms a medium-range advantage in technology.

In the PBX and switching products market, the United States is the most competitive at the high end, where computer-integrated large systems are used. This advantage seems to be slowly eroding, however. The United States and Japanese telecommunications markets are the only deregulated, non-government-controlled or -owned ones in the world. The Japanese market has slowly begun to open up but is still highly protected compared to the United States market. This is a major irritant to United States manufacturers trying to sell equipment to Japan. A counterpoint is made, however, that a high level of competition is necessary to stay technologically current in this market, and thus the structure of the United States market is really an advantage to United States firms. In the market for receiving instruments the United States is no longer competitive, and most of these plants have moved offshore to manufacture receivers.

Repositioning and refocusing involve both industry actions (e.g., industrial renaissance) and governmental/industrial cooperative activities. In the textile industry, after 6 years of suffering from rugged import competition, overcapacity, and diving profits, many textile companies were severely weakened. The industry adjusted, however, by refocusing. Companies emerged as leaner, more profitable operations aimed at staying competitive by targeting market niches and keeping overheads low. Refocusing by pulling back to selected sectors of business, targeting strong market areas, and an attitude of "sell where the imports are weakest" enabled many textiles firms to survive. No longer are United States textile makers trying to sell in all product categories. Firms are emphasizing styling, modern distribution systems, and upscale, service-oriented marketing strategies. Changes in production strategies have also been made. Making fabrics for fashion garments that require short production runs and just-in-time delivery coupled with computer-aided design and computer-aided manufacturing (CAD/CAM) systems has permitted United States apparel manufacturers to stay competitive in some markets.

In the telecommunications industry, government efforts and persistent activity have permitted a handful of United States firms to penetrate foreign markets. The United States government started market-oriented, sector-selective discussions, known as the MOSS Talks, with Japan in January 1985. These negotiations cover the telecommunications, medical equipment, and pharmaceutical, electronics, and forest product industries. Essential equivalency of equipment was achieved in the telecommunications area, and most problems have been substantially resolved. A number of United States firms have sold equipment to Japan.

Northern Telecom Ltd.'s United States unit won a $250 million contract to supply digital telephone switching systems to Nippon Telegraph and Telephone Public Corporation. Other smaller sales have been made by United States firms, but often only with unusually high levels of effort. For instance, one firm relates the following:

> It took a lot of convincing on that day and many that followed to win the first sale. We had to persuade NTT that our system of "intelligent" multiplexing was the only one that could deliver the speed and savings it sought for its customers. We also had to show that no Japanese company in NTT's family of suppliers could provide the same technology.
>
> NTT came up with more questions almost daily. We had a standing rule that every question would be answered within eight hours. NTT figuratively took our company apart to find out how we engineered products, guaranteed quality, and met delivery schedules. Most important, at the critical time of the first installation, Japan Pirex had the know-how to make changes on the spot to handle any problems that arose (Alexander, 1986, p. 113).

Thus, for some industries it will take both concerted government action and a commitment to an industrial renaissance to survive. Two points seem to be clear here:

1. United States industry can and must work together with the government to achieve policies that do not damage the overall strength and competitiveness of the economy.

2. United States industry, as well as individual companies, can and must become more competitive while developing long-range solutions to United States industrial problems.

CONCLUSION

The end results of the debate over protectionism are nowhere in sight. Whether the government will act, and in what way, is unclear. Meanwhile, management must continue to make competitive decisions daily. There are ways to coordinate government policy and management action. Most important to this effort will be a conceptual view to structure the various alternatives available to both. Viewing both public and private strategies as competitive or cooperative seems to be fruitful. The three most likely actions seem to be (1) public competitiveness in the form of tariffs and other barriers; (2) private cooperativeness in the form of locating facilities offshore; and (3) a combination of public cooperativeness and private competitiveness in the form of repositioning and/or refocusing. The textile and apparel and telecommunications industries provide examples of how each of these strategies can actually be implemented.

REFERENCES

Alexander, Thomas: "How We Sold Japan's Toughest Customer," *Fortune* (Jan. 20, 1986), pp. 113–14.

Jefferson, E.G.: "Building a New Consensus on Trade," *Columbia Journal of World Business*, XX, Winter (1985), pp. 9–11.

Kotler, Philip; Fahey, Liam; and Jatusripitak, S.: *The New Competition* (Englewood Cliffs, NJ: Prentice Hall, 1985).

Morici, Peter; and Megna, Laura L.: United States Economic Policies Afficting Industrial Trade (Washington, D.C.: National Planning Association, 1983, p. 6).

Prestowitz, Clyde V. Jr.: "Our Asian Myopia," *New Management*, 4 (2) (1986), pp. 15–20.

United Nations Conference on Trade and Development: "Protectionism and Structural Adjustment in the World Economy," New York: UNCTAD Secretariat, (1982).

Windham, Robert G.; Ozanne, Marq R.; and Jones, Joseph L.: "The Hand Tool Industry," in Catherine Stirling and John N. Yochelson, eds, *Under Pressure: United States Industry and the Challenges of Structural Adjustment* (London: Westview Press, 1985, pp. 31–61).

10

International Trade and Protection
in Financial Services

INGO WALTER

This chapter offers two unique insights regarding the nature of protectionism and the many ways in which both protectionist and competitive forces affect corporate performance. The singularity of the chapter's contribution derives from the distinct perspective of the author, who considers protectionism not from the perspective of a manufacturer but from that of a service organization. Further, the chapter studies the effects of protectionist actions by foreign government on the competitive positions of United States companies abroad rather than examining the United States government's policies.

This chapter contributes to, and expands upon, preceding chapters in several ways. First, the description of the progress of growth and foreign direct investment in the financial services industry is woven around a straightforward, conceptual model. This model is quite consistent with the frameworks that support analysis in other chapters.

The model characterizes products, markets, and customers to arrive at a definition of the determinants of market structure and competitive advantage. With this framework, Walter is able to study the effects on the system and the participants when restrictions on market access are unevenly applied.

With this approach the chapter redefines the nature of protectionism. Here protectionism is seen as a set of actions that limit access to markets. In other words, protectionism may be more broadly defined as inequality of competitive opportunity. This last result also defines the conditions under which the free trade objective is achieved—equal access to markets for all competitors. This conceptualization of the nature of protectionism is extremely useful as one extends beyond consideration of the bilateral effects of protectionism to consider its broader impact.

By deriving this framework and describing the nature of the key relationships in the services sector, Walter offers a valuable service: the translation of terminology, concepts, and results from the more fully explored manufacturing sector into the realm of the service industries. Because of the literal explosion of service-sector economic activity and the increasing delivery and investment of service-sector technologies across national borders, this translation becomes an important contribution to the study of the more general economic impact of protectionism.

The chapter contributes to a conceptual understanding of protectionism in one additional way. It adds yet another set to the list of instruments by which government can pursue protectionist objectives. This set is that of regulation and imposition of both entry and operating barriers.

Finally, the chapter is peppered with data that describe the effective results of protectionist policies on corporate and national competitive positions in the industry. Professor Walter shows that where the policies of protectionism in this area are applied indirectly, through regulatory limitations and barriers, the effective results are dramatic.

The growing role of the services sector in the economies of the major industrial countries has triggered a rapid increase in market interpretation with respect to specific service industries such as insurance, banking, law, and accounting. This chapter examines the international financial services industry, broadly defined with reference to the determinants of market structure, competitive advantage at the sectoral level, and the role played by distortions of international market access. The chapter concludes by identifying a set of bench marks that could be taken to represent necessary conditions for equality of international competitive opportunity in this sector and hence serve as objectives for international trade negotiation in the Uruguay Round under the auspices of the GATT.

INTERNATIONAL COMPETITIVE STRUCTURE

There are three core dimensions that define the world market for financial services (Walter, 1987):

1. Client (C dimension)
2. Arena (A dimension)
3. Product (P dimension)

Firms in the financial services industry have an unusually broad range of choice with respect to each of these dimensions, and different combinations yield different strategic and competitive profiles. Table 10.1 depicts these dimensions in the form of a matrix comprising C × A × P cells. Each cell has a distinctive internal competitive structure, based on fundamental economic as well as public-policy-related considerations.

Largely as a result of technological change and deregulation, financial institutions confront expanded potential access to each of the dimensions in the C–A–P opportunity set. Financial deregulation, in particular, has had a key influence in terms of (1) accessibility of geographical arenas, (2) accessibility of individual client groups by players originating in different sectors of the financial services business, and (3) substitutability among financial products in meeting personal, corporate, or government financial needs.

Table 10.1   International Financial Services Activity Matrix (C-A-P) Model

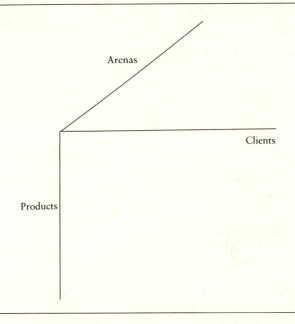

First, client groups served by firms in the financial services industry may be segmented according to attributes such as currency and timing requirements, liquidity and maturity needs, risk levels, industry categories, overall service level requirements, and price sensitivity. Effective market definition and segmentation in the financial services industry involves identifying coherent client groups that embody relative uniformity with respect to each of these variables.

Second, the international market for financial services can be divided into various on shore and offshore arenas with respect to geographic location. Each is characterized by different risk/return profiles, levels of financial efficiency, regulatory conditions, client needs, and other variables. The arena dimension of the C–A–P matrix in Table 10.1 can be taken into the analysis at the global, regional, national, subregional and location-specific levels, although the national level is unique because of the significance of regulatory and monetary policies.

Geographic interpenetration of financial institutions with respect to various domestic and offshore arenas has become very significant indeed (see Table 10.2). For example, in 1950, only seven American banks had activities abroad, with 95 branches. By 1970, there were 79 banks with 536 branches, and by 1984, there were about 150 banks with over 1000 branches that booked assets in excess of $337 billion. This actually understates the degree of internationalization by United States banks, since forms of involvement other than branches are not captured in the data. Nor do the data capture the growing involvement abroad by United States investment banks, brokerage

Table 10.2 Foreign Banking, Presence, by Host
Country

Country	1970	1980	1985
United States*	50	579	783
United Kingdom	95	214	336
Germany*	77	213	287
France*	58	122	147
Switzerland	97	99	119
Japan*	38	85	112
Luxembourg*	23	96	106
Belgium	26	51	58
Canada	0	0	58
Netherlands	23	39	44
Italy	4	26	40

The data are not fully comparable. Except for countries denoted (*),
the data count foreign banking institutions or families operating
through branches or majority-owned subsidiaries (branches only
for Italy).

* Data count banking offices (branches only for Japan), so that
  foreign organizations represented by more than one entity are
  double-counted. At the end of June 1985, total represented
  foreign organizations numbered 350 in the United States, 95 in
  Germany, and 76 in Japan.

SOURCE: Bank for International Settlements, as reported in Morgan
  Guaranty, World Financial Markets, Nov.–Dec. 1986.

houses, and other types of financial services firms. According to a study by
Morgan Guaranty (1986), foreign banks had 577 branches, agencies, and
subsidiaries in the United States in 1986, booking $411 billion in deposits
(13 percent of the United States total) and $110 billion in business loans
(22 percent of the total United States market and 50 percent of the New York
City market). In dollar-denominated acceptance financing, they took
33 percent of the United States market. Japanese banks alone captured a
40 percent share of foreign bank assets in the United States and an 80 percent
share of foreign banks' dollar-denominated acceptances. Meanwhile, the 30
Japanese banks in London held over 25 percent of all banking assets booked in
the United Kingdom in 1986.

The reasons for the rapid growth in the activities of financial institutions in
various onshore and offshore arenas lie primarily in the nature of the services
provided. It is often imperative for a financial institution to be physically close
to the client in order to do business effectively. While a certain amount of a
business can certainly be done through correspondent relationships and travel,
the increasingly complex nature of financial services and client needs has
enhanced the importance of reliable "direct connect" relationships.

Third is the product dimension. Financial services offered in the global
market have expanded dramatically. With a clear requirement for product
differentiation in the marketplace, firms in the industry have created new
instruments and techniques tailored to the needs of their clients. Financial

institutions produce five more or less distinct "primary" products that are sold to clients. Essentially, all financial services that are traded internationally, including the most complex innovations, can be broken down into one or more of these "primary" categories, which are (1) credit products, (2) financial engineering products, (3) risk management products, (4) market access products, and (5) arbitrage/positioning. This classification of international financial services can be broken down still further into some 50 more or less distinct financial services that are made available to individual client segments in various market arenas (Walter, 1987).

Competitive Cell Structure

Clearly, the competitive structure of each C–A–P cell in Table 10.1 is a major determinant of the returns a financial institution may be able to obtain from it—earning that in turn must be adjusted for the risks involved. Each cell has imbedded in it a certain value quotient potentially available to all players, and its allocation depends on at least four sets of factors.

First, depositors and purchasers of securities issued by financial institutions demand returns commensurate with the perceived level of risk. This depends heavily on the credit rating of the individual institution. To the extent that it is perceived as being less credit worthy owing to the quality of its assets or its exposure to other types of risk, its market power is eroded as bondholders and depositors demand higher yields for the funds they supply. The more financially sophisticated and the less subject to regulation the suppliers of funds, the more capable they are of exploiting available alternatives.

Second, borrowers and other purchasers of financial services naturally seek to attain the highest level of value added at lowest cost. The more successful they are, the narrower the margins, and the lower the rents available to the financial institution in a specific C–A–P cell. Especially in international wholesale markets, buyers of financial services are sought after by a large number of institutions competing fiercely for their business. Client groups such as multinational corporations and high-net-worth individuals have significantly more monopsony power than other client groups for whom competition is less intense. The market power of buyers of financial services can be expected to differ in all three dimensions of the C–A–P matrix—from one client group to another, from one product category to another, and across different arenas.

Third, product substitutes available to clients in a given cell clearly increase the price elasticity of demand, which in turn determines the price—volume vectors that are accessible to the financial institution and, consequently, the overall level of returns. The closer the substitutability among financial services, the higher the price elasticity of demand and the lower the level of returns that are available within a given C–A–P cell. One would expect the degree of product substitutability to differ from one client group to the next and across different arenas.

The most important factor relating to product substitutes in financial services is information and technology content, so the creation of product substitutes has become one of the most important and pervasive effects of financial innovation. Successful innovations that an institution introduces into a given cell are those embodying a low degree of product substitutability over a relatively long duration.

The fourth determinant of potential C–A–P cell profitability is competitive structure, conventionally measured using concentration ratios based on the number of firms, distribution of market share among firms, and similar criteria. The durability of cell-specific returns is based mainly on the ability of new players to enter the cell and the development of substitute products over time.

Normally, the addition of players to a particular C–A–P cell would be expected to reduce market concentration, increase the degree of competition, and lead to an erosion of profit margins as well as a more rapid pace of financial innovation. If the new players are from the same basic strategic groups as existing players (e.g., one more investment bank joining a number of other investment banks competing in a given cell), the expected outcome would be quite different from a case where the new player comes from a completely different strategic perspective (e.g., the finance affiliate of a major oil company penetrating the same market cell for investment banking services in London). This is because of potential diversification benefits, scope for cross-subsidization and staying power, and incremental horizontal or vertical integration gains that the player from a "foreign" strategic group may be able to capture.

Natural Barriers to Entry and Contestable Markets

The higher the barriers to entry, the lower the threat of the players' reducing the level of returns available in each C–A–P cell. Natural barriers to entry include capital adequacy, human resources, financial technologies, economies of scope, and economies of scale. They also include "contracting costs" avoided by virtue of a close relationship between a financial institution and its client, which in turn is related to the avoidance of opportunistic behavior by either party.

Not least, the competititve structure of each cell depends on the degree of potential competition. This represents as application of the "contestable markets" concept, which suggests that the existence of potential entrants causes existing players to act as if those entrants were already active in the market. Profit margins, product quality, and the degree of innovation in a given cell may thus exhibit characteristics of intense competition, even though the degree of market concentration is, in fact, quite high.

Cell Linkages

Financial institutions will want to allocate available resources to those C–A–P cells in Table 10.1 promising to throw off the highest risk-adjusted returns. Consequently, they will have to appropriately allocate costs, returns, and risks across cells. But beyond this, the economics of supplying financial services internationally is jointly subject to economies of scale and economies of scope. The existence of both types of economies have strategic implications for competitors in the industry. Economies of scale suggest an emphasis on deepening activities within a cell, or across cells in the P dimension. Economies of scope suggest an emphasis on broadening activities across cells—that is, a player can produce a given level of output in a given cell more cheaply or effectively than institutions that are less active across multiple cells. This depends importantly on the benefits and costs of linking cells together in a coherent web.

The gains from linkages among C–A–P cells depend on the possibility that an institution competing in one cell can move into another cell and perform in that second cell more effectively than a competitor lacking a presence in the first cell. The existence of economies of scope and scale is a critical factor driving institutional strategy. Where scale economies dominate, the objective is to maximize throughput of the product within a given C–A–P cell configuration, driving for market penetration. Where scope economies dominate, the drive is toward aggressive cell proliferation.

Client-driven linkages exist when a financial institution serving a particular client or client group can, as a result, supply financial services either to the same client or to another client in the same group more efficiently in the same or different arenas. With respect to a particular client, this linkage is part of the value of the "relationship." With respect to a particular client segment, it will clearly be easier for an institution to engage in business with a new client in the same segment than move to another client segment. It is possible that client linkages will decline as market segmentation in financial services becomes more intense.

Arena-driven linkages are important when an institution can service a particular client or supply a particular service more efficiently in one arena as a result of having an active presence in another arena. The presence of nonfinancial multinational corporate clients in the same set of arenas as their financial institutions is one important form such linkages can take. By competing across a large number of arenas, a financial institution also has the possibility of decreasing the overall level of risk to which it is exposed, thereby potentially increasing its overall risk-adjusted rate of return.

Product-driven linkages are important when an institution can supply a particular financial service in a more competitive manner because it is already producing the same or a similar financial service in different client or arena dimensions. Product specializations would appear to depend on the degree of uniformity of the resource inputs required, as well as on information and technology commonalities. Thus, certain types of skills embodied in human resources may be applied across different clients and arenas at relatively low marginal cost within a given product category, as may certain types of information about the environment, markets, or client needs.

The performance of a firm in the international financial services industry clearly depends on the static and dynamic characteristics of the individual

Table 10.3 Alignment of Competitive and Product Dimensions in International Financial Services

Financial Services	Competitive Resources[a]						
	1	2	3	4	5	6	7
Funding	+				+++	+	
Lending	+++	+++	++				
Financing	+++	+++	++				++
Credit activities	+	++	++		++	++	
Trading	+++	+++	+++		++		
Broking	++	++	+++	++		+	
Advisory services		+++	+++		+	++	+++
Asset management services		+++	+++		+	+++	+
Underwriting	+++	++	++		++	+++	+++
Distribution			+	+++			
Payment activities			+++		+++		
Insurance services	+++	++	++				
International trade services		++	++		++	+	

Key: + + +, principal factor; + +, important factor; +, contributing factor.

[a] 1. Adequacy of capital base; 2. quality of human capital; 3. information; 4. placing power; 5. technology; 6. innovative capability; 7. franchise.

C–A–P cells to which it is able to gain access, the costs and risks of serving those cells, and the competitive resources it is able to bring to bear, as outlined in Table 10.3.

Price Discrimination and Predation

In penetrating a particular cell or set of cells, it may be to the advantage of a particular player to "buy into" the market by cross-subsidizing financial services supplied in that cell from returns derived in other cells. This may make sense if the cell characteristics are expected to change in future periods, so that an unprofitable presence today is expected to lead to a profitable presence tomorrow. It may also make sense if a player's behavior in buying market share has the potential of driving out or discouraging competitors and fundamentally altering the structure of the cell in its favor. And it may make sense if the assessed horizontal, vertical, or lateral linkages (see next section) are sufficiently positive to justify cutthroat pricing.

Predatory behavior in financial services is no different from predation in markets for goods. The institution "dumps" (or threatens to dump), forcing out competitors either as a result of their limited staying power in the face of the dumping or as result of its effects on competitor expectations regarding future profitability. Once competitors have been driven from the market, the institution takes advantage of the reduced degree of competition to widen margins and extract excess returns. It may also be possible for an institution with significant market power to keep potential competitors out of attractive

C–A–P cells through explicit or implied threats of predatory behavior. It can make it clear to prospective entrants that it will respond very aggressively to incursions, and that they face a long and difficult road to profitability. In this way, new competitors may be discouraged, and cell structure can be kept more monopolistic than would otherwise be the case.

INTERNATIONAL TRADE IN FINANCIAL SERVICES

To a significant degree, international trade in services tends to differ from international trade in goods in terms of the linkages that exist between the producer and the consumer, or user, of the product. In merchandise trade, goods are manufactured in one country and marketed in another, either through independent arm's-length business relationships or through local agents or affiliates of the manufacturer. In trade in services, either the consumer has to be physically transported to the product (as in tourism) or the service has to be taken to the consumer via some kind of direct contact, which often involves an established presence on the part of the supplier in the importing country. Perhaps to a lesser degree this also occurs in trade in manufactures through foreign direct investment, especially where product, process, management, and marketing "know-how"—as well as an after-sales service— are important characteristics of the "product" that is being bought and sold. But the "direct concent" mechanism remains much more important in the case of services. In the absence of foreign direct investment and the establishment abroad of branches or other types of affiliates, international trade in financial services, to the extent that it has evolved today, is virtually unthinkable (for a contrary view, see Grubel, 1987).

A loan by a London-based bank to a private borrower in Malaysia clearly fits the definition of a financial service produced by residents of one country and sold to the residents of another. But without some physical presence in the service-importing country to provide contact with the customer and facilitate credit evaluation, such a transaction—while not impossible—would be extraordinarily difficult or would have to be handled through participation in a loan syndication. But even here, the lead manager(s) would have to have close borrower contact. Similarly, confirmation of an export letter of credit by a New York bank requires little more than a correspondent relationship with a bank in the importing country.

Yet such arm's-length transactions in the provision of financial services are certainly not of the highest order in terms of value added. Of much greater interest are transactions that require some form of foreign direct investment in order to work, ranging from a low-level presence, such as a representative office, through successively higher levels of involvement in the form of agencies, subsidiaries, consortia, joint ventures, and full branches in the host country. The more complex and sophisticated the financial product, the greater tends to be the importance of such investment. The need for establishing this presence thus defines the types of competitive distortions that may be applied in this sector and raises the issue of protection and market access conditions for countries that have different competitive advantage and dissadvantage profiles with respect to the financial service industry.

POLITICAL ECONOMY OF PROTECTION IN FINANCIAL SERVICES

The political economy of protection has been extensively developed in the literature. Several models have been suggested, most of which involve rent-seeking behavior on the part of market participants. Firms, labor unions, or other groups find that it makes more sense to devote substantial resources to lobbying for government protection than it does to devote comparable resources to adapting to changes in the marketplace. In essence, the expected risk-adjusted net present value of returns from lobbying, at the margin, are deemed to be higher than comparable returns from adjustment. Lobbying takes the case out of the economic marketplace and into the political marketplace, where those seeking protection are exposed to counterarguments by other groups (such as consumers and exporters fearing retaliation) under established political rules of the game. In the financial services industry, the typical argument is that the country is already "overbanked" and needs no additional players.

Protection-oriented interests generally seek to bolster their argumentation in several ways. First, they can argue that the activities to be protected have significant external benefits for the national economy or society. The "national defense" argument is typical of this reasoning, basically designed to maintain uneconomic (at free-market prices) levels of output as insurance against a future political or military eventuality. High-technology industries, agriculture, and import-sensitive industries employing large numbers of low-skill, disadvantaged labor are among those interests frequently making use of this argument.

Second, protectionists can use the adjustment-equity argument. Few people can challenge the notion that economic adjustment creates costs that, barring government intervention, those directly affected are forced to assume. At the same time, society as a whole obtains significant static and dynamic gains from economic adjustment. This asymmetry in costs and benefits can be related to political norms of equity or fairness, to make the case that some of the gains should be siphoned off through taxation and allocation to support those that are injured. Many find considerable social justice in this argument. Its problems lie in actually implementing temporary protection or subsidization in such a way that it promotes rather than retards structural adjustment and avoids robbing people of the incentive to adjust to new competitive realities (the "moral hazard" argument in this context).

Third, protectionists can use the "infant industry" argument that free trade will, by exposing an industry to world-class competition prematurely, prevent an industry that is fully capable of eventually competing internationally without government help from ever reaching that stage of development.

Fourth, the argument may be raised that the real world is far from the perfectly competitive market—that there are economies of scale and economies of scope involved that require a certain firm size in order to attain their full potential. This, it is argued, can only be achieved through government assistance and perhaps some form of "industrial targeting" to maximize the gains from international trade and production obtained by the nation.

All of these arguments in support of basic rent-seeking interests at the sectoral level must then be effectively marshaled and converted into political influence. Economic interests, in other words, must be translated into political power. This depends on the ability of an industry to claim that it is in some way "critical"—for example, in terms of the level of employment and the availability of alternative opportunities for those employed, or the degree of regional concentration of the industry—and the ability to form political coalitions with other interest—groups.

Finally, if protectionist interests seem unlikely to survive such argumentation and political counterpressures in open "high-road" debate, they may have access to "low-road" protection through administrative measures such as discriminatory health and safety requirements, government procurement, licensing and other forms of quantitative controls, and similar nontariff barriers to market access.

How do these political issues relate to protectionism in the financial services industry? It is clear that the normal rent-seeking drive for protectionism applies here. Financial services firms are highly sensitive to competition in various dimensions of their activities where natural entry barriers are limited. This is certainly more true in the wholesale and capital markets end of the business than it is in the retail side (dependent on a large number of outlets), although even here there is ample scope for entry by foreign players. Market penetration by foreign-based competitors thus threatens to erode indigenous players' returns and raises the classic set of rent-seeking motivations.

Given the economic interests involved, it can be argued that banks and other financial institutions are in an excellent position to convert them into political power. They are often exceedingly well connected politically, and their lobbying power can be awesome on critical issues. In some cases, the financial institutions themselves are government owned and may thus have direct access to the levers of protection. They can form powerful coalitions by engaging their clients at both the wholesale and retail levels on their behalf.

Moreover, protection in financial services is likely to come through the regulatory process, and to the extent that financial institutions have co-opted the regulators to their mutual benefit, access to the vehicles of protection is facilitated.

Besides applying restrictions to foreign-based players, regulators may tolerate a certain amount of anticompetitive, cartel-like behavior on the part of domestic institutions. Foreign players that become troublesome may be stepped on by concerted action on the part of domestic institutions, and the competitive consequences overlooked by the authorities. In marshaling their arguments, however, financial institutions are on very much weaker ground than manufacturing firms.

First, they cannot argue convincingly that there will be significant job losses and adjustment costs as a result of market penetration by foreign financial institutions, since these will tend to absorb roughly the same number of employees with roughly the same skill content. Indeed, it is possible that participation by foreign firms could lead to significant employment gains in the domestic financial services sector.

Second, a substantial share of financial services are sold to producers of other goods and services in the national economy rather than to ultimate consumers. Shielding from import competition, therefore, has a high effective protection content—that is, protection of financial institutions raises costs to large numbers of firms in other industries that are themselves exposed to international competition and thus erodes their competitive performance. Interests indirectly affected in this manner can be expected to resist protectionism in the financial services sector, alongside consumers whose welfare is directly affected through credit costs, deposit rates, and the cost and quality of other financial services.

On the other hand, financial institutions may be able to use the externalities and infant-industry arguments in support of their cause. As an integral part of the national payments systems, the banking and financial services industry is a source of significant external benefits for society at large. The same is true of its safekeeping function, its role in financial intermediation, and its role as a "transmission belt" for monetary policy. It is therefore often argued that financial services represent a "public good" whose private costs and returns do not accurately reflect the social costs and returns.

Whether financial institutions are domestically or foreign owned, economists would argue, has nothing to do with any of these issues. Nondiscriminatory regulation can assure that financial institutions continue to throw off the full range of external benefits in most cases, and in problem cases (e.g., maintenance of rural bank branches) targeted government subsidies can take care of maintaining external benefits—perhaps better than cross-subsidization by protected domestic financial institutions. In short, the public-good characteristics of the industry can be maintained while at the same time achieving the static and dynamic gains associated with increased competition.

The infant-industry argument, on the other hand, may be more difficult to deal with in a political context. On the one hand, domestic financial institutions are never really "infants" in the classic sense, since all countries have had them for decades—in many developing countries arising out of colonial institutions. On the other hand, we have emphasized that many dimensions of the financial services industry today are relatively knowledge and technology intensive, with scale economies also giving a competitive edge in certain areas. Hence it is possible, even likely, that domestic financial institutions in many countries are economically "retarded," rather than "infant," and would indeed have a difficult time competing with outsiders capable of importing know-how at very low marginal cost.

Yet retarded financial sectors can have a severely adverse impact on the process of economic development by supplying substandard channels of savings into investment, inefficient payment mechanisms and high transaction costs, discouraging economic activity and possibly encouraging capital flight. Competition from foreign-based financial institutions, perhaps in partnership with local interests and using primarily local human resources, can give such institutions a run for their money and create large potential allocational and dynamic gains for the economy as a whole.

Such argumentation notwithstanding, the infant-industry case remains a powerful force in the political context, especially when combined with the assertion that inroads by foreign-based institutions would somehow lead to an erosion of national sovereignity. Countries like Singapore, which now has some of the most sophisticated banks in Asia, continue to restrict the onshore business of foreign banks in order to shield 25-year-old "infants."

BARRIERS TO MARKET ACCESS

Previous studies by the United States Treasury (1979), the OECD (1983), and Walter (1985b) have undertaken extensive surveys of the restrictions that are imposed on foreign-based banks and other firms in the financial services industry, and data on specific barriers have been updated periodically by the Office of the United States Special Trade Representative (STR) and its counterparts in other governments as part of a program of submissions to the GATT secretariat. Unlike tariffs and other barriers that impede merchandise trade, those affecting international trade in financial services tend to change continually, making inventories of such barriers obsolete very quickly. This, combined with extraordinary difficulties in measuring the restrictive effects of barriers on value added in financial services, has made empirical research in this area virtually nonexistent.

There are basically two types of barriers to market penetration in the financials service sector—entry barriers and operating barriers. Both types, to a large extent, operate as paraquantitative restrictions to markets by limiting access to all or certain segments of the market, although some act as paratariffs by making market access more costly than it would otherwise be.

Barriers to Entry

Entry barriers inhibit foreign-based firms in the financial services industry in servicing the needs of domestic clients. As noted in Walter (1985b), they range from complete embargo (including visa denial to foreign bankers) and limiting foreign presence to representative offices only (with no banking powers) to restrictions on the forms a foreign presence can take and limits on foreign equity positions in local financial institutions. As with other quantitative restrictions of international trade, entry barriers can be either global or selective.

Global measures apply equally to all foreign-based institutions, while selective measures apply differently depending on the specific foreign institution involved or its home country. Global entry barriers may prohibit a foreign presence entirely (embargo) or limit foreign presence to certain forms of involvement in the domestic financial system ab initio.

Selective measures may permit differential entry for institutions from different home countries, based on considerations of banking reciprocity or general reciprocity in bilateral trade relations. They may also allow entry by institutions singled out on the basis of "desirability" criteria such as past or potential future contributions to the development of the national financial system.

Selectivity in entry into domestic financial services markets is heavily based on reciprocity considerations. Domestic financial institutions, in developed countries as well as in developing countries, usually find it necessary or desirable to establish a presence abroad. This may involve foreign countries with intensive trade, investment, or migration links; locations of major significance for foreign-currency funding requirements; or a necessary presence in the important financial financial centers of the world. Domestic institutions thus face an inherent conflict between their interest in accessing foreign markets for financial services and their desire to keep foreign-based players out of domestic markets. This assessment, and the domestic lobbying activity that results, obviously depends on the stakes involved in each case, as well as the probability that the foreign government will demand reciprocity (and that its own institutions will lobby for it).

It should also be noted in this context that foreign-based institutions that are already in a particular market, either because they were grandfathered at the time entry barriers were imposed or because they have achieved entry in some other manner, will have an unambitions incentive to resist further opening of the market to foreign players. They have no reciprocity incentive with respect to their home country or third countries, and unless they perceive significant external benefits from additional entrants, they have every reason to resist additional, potentially powerful competition.

Distortions of Operating Conditions

Once in a particular market, foreign-based financial institutions generally become fully subject to domestic monetary-policy, supervisory, and regulatory controls. At this point there are three possibilities: (1) domestic controls, in law or in administrative practice, fall less seriously on foreign players than on their domestic competitors; (2) the nominal incidence of regulation is identical for both; or (3) foreign players are subjected to more restrictive regulation than their local competitors.

The first option seems to be a relatively rare occurrence. Probably the most important case in point involved foreign banks in the United States prior to the passage of the International Banking Act (IBA) of 1978. Foreign-based institutions were exempt from membership in the Federal Reserve system, from the McFadden Act restrictions on branching across state lines, and from Glass–Steagall prohibitions against an institution's involvement in both commercial and investment banking. The IBA eliminated this discrimination in favor of foreign players, except that institutions already involved in both commercial and investment banking—and those already having branches in multiple states—were grandfathered. This created tension that has become more important with the continued securitization of financial flows in the United States. Certain developing countries, such as India, require that local banks become actively involved in providing financial services to clients in rural agriculture, a requirement that does not bear on foreign-based institutions. But except for a few such anomalies, usually based on historical reciprocity considerations, preferential treatment is not likely to be encountered.

The second case applied in many OECD countries and a number of developing countries. Foreign institutions here are subject to precisely the same nominal operating constraints as are domestic institutions. This applies to reserve requirements, asset ratios, lending limits, exposure constraints, capital adequacy, banking powers, access to funding sources and central bank lending, and so on. Despite nondiscrimination de jure, the incidence of such measures may in fact fall more heavily on newcomers or on foreign players that are forced to enter the market through affiliates rather than branches, thus being relatively poorly capitalized. These are essentially unintentional operating barriers and can either directly limit market access or raise the cost of doing business.

The third case involves the explicit use of operating barriers to restrict the competitive positioning of foreign-based institutions after they have achieved access. The measures range from restrictions on expatriate employment, number and location of offices, client groups that may be served, types of business that may be handled (including trust business, lead management in securities underwriting, and retail deposit taking), mandatory linkage of allowable business to institutional transactions, and the like. Most are paraquantitative restrictions in that they place positive limits on the nature and scope of activities. Some, however, may be paratariffs, as in the case of funding restrictions that raise the cost of funds in the local market relative to domestic competitors.

National Treatment and Equality of Competitive Opportunity

Given the structure of entry barriers and distortions of operating conditions, it would appear that "national treatment" is the substantive equivalent of free trade in a highly regulated industry such as financial services—an industry whose sensitivity to systemic problems will assure that it will continue to be subject to regulatory controls. This is not necessarily the case, however. As we have noted, even nominal national treatment can have differential effects on domestic and foreign-based institutions because of their different starting positions and operating characteristics. What is really required is "equality of competitive opportunity," in the sense of a level playing field. This is an extraordinarily difficult concept to define, much less to deliver, in the case of an industry as complex as financial services. But as a goal, it is the equivalent of free institutional trade as applied to this sector.

Competitive Distortions and Global Competitive Performance

Returning to the basic C–A–P model, reproduced in Table 10.4, how do competitive distortions affect the individual cells in the matrix and, therefore, the formulation and execution of institutional strategies? This can be discussed in terms of entry barriers, operating restrictions that affect access to client groups (tape A), and operating restrictions affecting the ability to supply the market with specific products (tape B).

First and most obvious, entry barriers restrict the movement of financial services firms in the lateral "arena" dimension of the matrix. A firm that is blocked out of a particular national market faces a restricted lateral opportunity set that excludes the relevant tranche of client and product cells. To the extent it is the outcome of protectionist political activity, the entry barrier will itself create supernormal returns in some or all of the cells in the tranche. It may, of course, have this effect even if there is no protectionist intent. Foreign-based institutions already in the market will, as noted earlier, tend to have a vested interest in keeping others out. Windows of opportunity, created by countries relaxing entry barriers, tend to be taken advantage of by

Table 10.4 Trade Barriers in the International Financial Services Activity Matrix

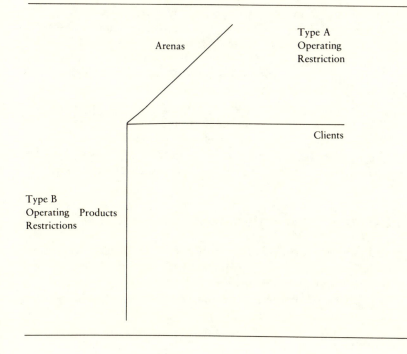

institutions envisioning potential supernormal returns in some of the previously inaccessible cells.

Second, firms that are allowed into a particular market only through travel or representative offices may nevertheless be able to access particular client/product cells in that tranche, securing business and returns by transferring the actual transaction to a different arena—for example, one of the Euromarket functional or booking centers in the institution's home country. This option applies primarily to the wholesale and private banking components of the client and product dimensions. Correspondent relationships with local banks are probably the only alternative for sharing in the returns associated with the blocked cells in product dimensions having to do with international trade, foreign exchange, syndications, and other wholesale transactions.

The story becomes more complicated in the case of operating restrictions. The firm now has access, in one form or another, to the arena tranche but is constrained either in the depth of service it can supply to a particular cell (e.g., lending limits, staffing limits, restrictions on physical location) or in the feasible set of cells within the tranche (e.g., limits on services foreign banks are allowed to supply and the client groups they are allowed to serve). These limits may severely reduce profitability associated with the arena concerned.

To the extent that horizontal integration is important in the international financial services industry, despite the presence of barriers and other competitive distortions affecting a given arena tranche, supernormal returns may still be obtained in unaffected cells. Even a limited scope for transactions with the local affiliate of a multinational enterprise may generate business with that company elsewhere in the world. For example, the value of a physical presence of any sort in an otherwise restricted market may thus support competitive positioning elsewhere in the institution's international structure. Obviously, the value of these linkages is very difficult to assess.

The strategic implications of barriers to trade in financial services thus seem clear. They reduce the feasibility set within the C–A–P matrix. They place a premium on windows of opportunity. They increase the importance of horizontal linkages and the assessment of their value. And they raise the importance of lobbying activity to open up markets where cells having potentially supernormal returns are blocked or restricted and to keep them that way when barriers to competition are the source of such excess returns.

TRADE LIBERALIZATION AND INTERNATIONAL FINANCIAL SERVICES

In a very real sense, the growth of international trade in financial services has already proceeded very far indeed. Beginning with the removal of exchange controls by many industrial countries in the 1960s and the simultaneous overseas expansion by American commercial banks following their multinational corporate clients into Europe, continuing into today's intense market interpenetration by financial (and indeed nonfinancial) institutions of all types, the expansion of international trade in financial services appears to have been rapid indeed. A critical factor in this respect has been the offshore markets, which make it clear to countries how costly distortions can be for the national economy and how lagging liberalization and deregulation can impair both a country's chance of maintaining a role as a financial center *and* its institutions' chances of becoming world-class competitors. One could thus argue that international trade in financial services has, in fact, been one of the few really bright spots on the trade policy scene—all without formal trade negotiations or the involvement of the GATT.

This would seriously overstate the case, however, since such a conclusion would be largely (though not entirely) limited to the OECD group of countries. In much of the rest of the world, the ability of foreign-based players to supply financial services remains severely restricted. Even in the OECD countries, there continue to be significant restrictions with respect to specific forms of involvement, client groups, and products that bear differentially on foreign-based institutions. Nevertheless, the direction of change has definitely centered on liberalization, and the pace of change has been impressive indeed.

As noted earlier, equality of competitive opportunity is the standard by which market access must be measured with respect to the international financial services industry. This can be viewed as comprising the following components:

1. Freedom to establish branches, agencies subsidiaries, representative offices, or other affiliates within a national market on a basis identical to that applying to locally owned financial institutions. Referring once again to the C–A–P matrix reproduced in Table 10.4, this freedom of establishment is critical to competitive equality in serving the client and product cells lying within a national arena and maximizing the positive linkage effects to cells in the rest of the matrix. National antitrust and other policies relating to establishment would bear on foreign players identically to domestic players.
2. Regulatory symmetry, insofar as possible, with respect to domestic and foreign competitors. This includes the incidence of prudential controls such as capital requirements, asset ratios, lending limits, and reserve requirements. It also involves equality of access to the domestic securities markets, including lead-managing local-currency issues in the local and offshore markets, as well as equal access to the national payments clearing system, money markets, central bank discount facilities, and trust and investment businesses.
3. Freedom to import critical resources, including travel and resettlement of professional staff, subscriptions of capital in the case of certain nonbranch affiliates, data processing, and telecommunication equipment on the same basis as local firms. Included is equality of access to transborder communication and data transmission.
4. Symmetry with respect to the application of exchange controls, if any, as between foreign and local players. This bears on capital outflows such as foreign borrowing in the local markets and local investments abroad as well as remittances of earnings.
5. Equality of access to domestic client groups, financial institutions, and product markets, including branching privileges equal to those of local firms and the right to purchase shares in local financial institutions consistent with domestic laws regarding competition.

Together, these elements provide a consistent set of bench marks for equality of competitive opportunity, which, as noted, is the equivalent of liberal trade in the financial services sector. This does not mean that foreign-based financial institutions should be able to avoid the effects of national tax, prudential, and monetary control policies, and it is clear that the implementation of a truly level playing field is made vastly more complicated because of these considerations.

The challenge for the multilateral trade negotiations begun in 1987 will be to devise a coherent approach for moving in directions that reflect these bench marks. Whether the GATT is up to this task, at a time when many of its tenets are honored as much in the breach as in observance, remains to be seem.

REFERENCES

Aliber, Robert Z.: "International Banking: A Survey," *Journal of Money, Credit and Banking* (Nov. 1984).

Bailey, Elizabeth E.; and Friedlander, Ann F.: "Market Structure and Multiproduct Industries," *Journal of Economic Literature* (Sept. 1982).

Bank for International Settlements: *Recent Innovations in International Banking* (Basel: Bank for International Settlements, 1986).

Channon, Derek F.: *Bank Strategic Management and Marketing* (New York: John Wiley, and Jonathan D. Aaronson 1986).

Cowhey, Peter F.: *Trade in Services: A Case for Open Markets* (Washington, D.C.: American Enterprise Institute, 1984).

Crane, Dwight B.; and Hayes, Samuel L. III: "The New Competition in World Banking," *Harvard Business Review* (July–Aug. 1982).

Cohen, Michael; and Morante, Thomas: "Elimination of Nontariff Barriers to Trade in Services: Recommendations for Future Negotiation," *International Law Journal* Georgetown University Law Center (1981).

Cooper, Kerry; and Fraser, Donald R.: *Bank Deregulation and the New Competition in Financial Services* (Cambridge, MA: Ballinger, 1986).

Corbet, High: "Prospect of Negotiations on Barriers to International Trade in Services," *Pacific Community* (April 1977).

Davis, Stephen I.: *Excellence in Banking* (London: Macmillan, 1985).

Diebold, William; and Stalson, Helena: "Negotiating Issues in International Service Transactions," in William R. Cline, ed., *Trade Policy in the 1980s* (Washington, D.C.: Institute for International Economics, 1983).

Dunning, John H.: *International Production and the Multinational Enterprise* (London: Allen and Unwin, 1981).

Fieleke, Norman S.: "The Growth of United States Banking Abroad: An Analytical Survey," in *Key Issues in International Banking* (Boston: Federal Reserve Bank of Boston, 1977).

Galbraith, Craig S.; and Kay, Neil M.: "Towards a Theory of the Multinational Firm," *Journal of Economic Behavior and Organization* (March 1986).

General Agreement on Tariffs and Trade: *Articles of Agreement* (Geneva: GATT, 1984).

General Agreement on Tariffs and Trade: *The Scope, Limits and Function of the GATT Legal System* (Geneva: GATT, 1985).

Gladwin, Thomas N.; and Walter, Ingo: *Multinationals Under Fire* (New York: John Wiley, 1980).

Goldberg, Ellen S., et al.: *Off-Balance-Sheet Activities of Banks: Managing the Risk-Reward Tradeoffs* (Philadelphia: Robert Morris Associates, 1983).

Gray, H. Peter; and Gray, Jean M.: "The Multinational Bank: A Financial MNC?" *Journal of Banking and Finance* (March 1982).

Grubel, Herbert G.: "A Theory of Multinational Banking," *Banca Nazioale del Lavoro Quarterly Review* (Dec. 1977).

Grubel, Herbert G.: "There is No International Trade In Services," *American Economic Review, Papers and Proceedings* (March 1987).

Hindley, Brian; and Smith, Alasdair: "Comparative Advantage and Trade in Services," *World Economy* (June 1984).

Kallberg, Jarl S.; and Saunders, Anthony: *Direct Sources of Competitiveness in Banking Services* (New York: Salomon Brothers Center for the Study of Financial Institutions, 1986; mimeo).

Ladreit de Larrechere, Guy: *The Legal Framework for International Trade* (Geneva: General Agreement on Tariffs and Trade, 1984).

Letiche, J.M.: "Dependent Monetary Systems and Economic Development, in W. Sellekaerts, ed., *Economic Development and Planning* (London: Macmillan, 1974).

Leutwiler, Fritz, et al.: *Trade Policies for a Better Future* (Geneva: General Agreement on Tariffs and Trade, 1985).

Neu, C.R.: "International Trade in Banking Services," paper presented at NBER/CEPS Conference on European-United States Trade Relations, Brussels (June 1986; mimeo).

Organization for Economic Cooperation and Development: *Trade in Services in Banking* (Paris: OECD, 1983).

Panzar, John C.; and Willig, Robert D.: "Economies of Scope," *American Economic Review* (May 1981).

Pastre, Olivier: *Multinationals: Banking and Firm Relationships.* (Greenwich, CT: JAI Press, 1981a).

Pastre, Olivier: "International Bank-Industry Relations: An Empirical Assessment." *Journal of Banking and Finance* (March 1981b).

Pecchioli, R.M. *Internationalization of Banking* (Paris: OECD, 1983).

Porter, Michael E.: *Competitive Strategy* (New York: Free Press, 1980).

Sagari, Sylvia B.: "The Financial Services Industry: An International Perspective." Doctoral dissertation, School of Business Administration, New York University (1986).

Tschoegl, Adrain E.: *The Regulation of Foreign Banks: Policy Formation Outside the United States* (New York: Salomon Brothers Center for the Study of Financial Institutions, New York University, 1981).

Tschoegl, Adrain E.: "Foreign Bank Entry into Japan and California," in Allen M. Rugman, ed., *New Theories of the Multinational Enterprise* (London: Croom Helm, 1982).

Tschoegl, Adrain E.: "Size, Growth and Transnationality Among the World's Largest Banks," *Journal of Business*, 56, No. 2 (1983).

Tugendhat, Christopher: "Opening-up Europe's Financial Sector," *The Banker* (Jan. 1985).

United States Department of the Treasury: *Report to the Congress on Foreign Government Treatment of United States Banking Organizations* (Washington, D.C.: Department of the Treasury, 1979; updated in 1984).

United States Office of the Comptroller of the Currency: *Foreign Acquisition of United States Banks* (Washington, D.C.: United States Government Printing Office, 1982).

Walter, Ingo: *Secret Money* (London: Allen and Unwin, 1985a).

Walter, Ingo, ed.: *Deregulating Wall Street* (New York: John Wiley, 1985b).

Walter, Ingo: *Global Competition in Financial Services: Market Structure, Protection and Trade Liberalization* (Cambridge, MA: Ballinger for the American Enterprise Institute, 1987).

Walter, Ingo; and Gray, H. Peter: "Protectionism in International Banking," *Journal of Banking and Finance* (Dec. 1983).

Yannopoulos, George N.: "The Growth of Transnational Banking," in Mark Casson, ed., *The Growth of International Business* (London: Allen and Unwin, 1983).

11

Impact of Trade Policies
on Multinational Operations:
Strategy and Performance

WILLIAM H. DAVIDSON

In this chapter Davidson adds to the list of factors that determine the relative sensitivity of a corporation's performance to actual or anticipated changes in the trade policy configuration. He demonstrates that the firm's operating strategy is an important determinant of that sensitivity. Further, the nature of the relationship is a function of the cost/flexibility tradeoff described by Agmon and Wihlborg in Chapter 6.

As it applies to operating strategy, the cost/flexibility tradeoff is most clearly seen as the distinctive difference between two extremes. At one extreme, cost effectiveness is maximized under a structure that emphasizes sourcing from a single location. Such a strategy, however, clearly increases corporate vulnerability to protectionist action. At the other extreme, scale economies diminish with production strategies that call for dispersion of operating facilities; however, such dispersion can substantially reduce or even eliminate vulnerability to trade barriers.

A specific contribution of this chapter is the introduction of the effect of product–life cycle considerations into the process of operational strategy. With this extension Davidson adds a characterization of product and market maturity, and operating concentration or decentralization, to the list of factors that determine the effect of protectionist action on corporate values and performance.

Davidson also offers a simulation of gross margin performance under tariff imposition and within various types of operating structures. These simulations demonstrate the nature and extent of the impact of *various* protectionist measures, acting on different operating systems, on corporate performance. By examining these relationships at the corporate level, Davidson describes the corporate dynamics that underlie the simulations presented earlier in this volume by both Drobnick and Enzer (Chapter 2) and Aronson (Chapter 4). The aggregate effects of tariff imposition, as described in those earlier chapters, is the sum of the effects on individual corporations, as suggested here.

The simulations also relate to those provided in the following chapter by Hekman, who expands beyond the sensitivity of operating margins to consider the effects of protectionist legislation on corporate value.

Finally, without offering direct guidelines for design of operating strategy, the chapter's insights expand understanding of the nature of basic relationships important to strategic design of operations.

Host country trade policies and practices play a critical role in determining performance for multinational corporations (MNCs). Shipments of goods within multinational corporate systems account for an estimated 25–30 percent of all international trade. Those flows of products and services are highly vulnerable to restrictive trade policies. Host government initiatives that reduce market access, or increase the cost of access, will reduce profits for firms serving markets from foreign sources.

While MNCs appear to be primary victims of trade restrictions, the impact of such policies on their performance varies sharply. Firms serving foreign markets from self-sufficient facilities within each country could benefit from trade restrictions. Such firms might fear trade liberalization initiatives rather than restrictions. Clearly, the impact of trade policies on corporate performance is a function of the firm's operating strategy.

GENERIC OPERATING STRATEGIES

Any corporation's degree of vulnerability to restrictive trade policies and practices depends fundamentally on its operating configuration. Multinational corporations may choose to serve foreign markets in several distinctive operating modes. Export-oriented systems, those that serve host markets from a foreign source, are of course highly dependent on international trade conditions. Single-source export systems, those that serve would-be markets from a central manufacturing facility, can enjoy a variety of benefits, including scale economies, location advantages for factor costs, transportation and tax benefits, and government subsidies and grants. Firms utilizing centralized export facilities to serve foreign markets also face a number of risks. Such systems are vulnerable not only to trade restrictions, but to foreign exchange rate movements, among other factors. Bulova Corporation centralized its watch manufacturing activities in Switzerland in the 1960s, only to experience a dramatic increase in costs as the Swiss franc appreciated. Labor disruptions can also cripple single-source operations. Despite these concerns, Japanese, Korean, German, and other MNCs have successfully served world markets in this mode for decades.

In contrast, an MNC may choose to manufacture its products partially or fully within host markets. United States corporations typically establish a local manufacturing facility inside each significant foreign market. Such an approach significantly reduces vulnerability to trade restrictions. Alternatively, networks that manage coordinated transshipments between specialized facilities provide an operating approach with some immunity to trade restrictions.

Most MNCs exhibit an operating strategy that conforms generally to one of these approaches. While there exists a strong correlation between the nationality of a corporation and its operating strategy, different industries also exhibit markedly different patterns of operating activity. Underlying economic characteristics will determine the range of operating options available to firms in any industry. Prevailing operating patterns in an industry will be closely tied to its capital intensity and minimum-efficient scale levels. These variables will determine the maximum number of facilities within a corporate system. For example, modern automobile engine facilities require an investment of more than $300 million to reach minimum efficient production levels. In such instances, production within a number of host markets will not be feasible. In order to serve a wide range of markets, firms must conduct some form of trade activity.

PARADIGMS AND PRINCIPLES

While home country and industry strongly predetermine operating strategies, a firm's operating configuration also correlates highly with the maturity of its international activities. According to the product life cycle model of international trade and investment, foreign markets are initially served from an export base in the home country of the multinational firm (Vernon, 1966). According to the life cycle model, once sales in the foreign market achieve a minimum volume level, there will be a transfer of production technology to the host country, and a local source of the product will be developed. The minimum volume level represents the sales quantity at which local unit production costs fall below the cost of importing the product from a foreign source.

Two distinctive factors affect the timing of technology transfer and the initiation of production in the host country. The first is the impact of tariffs, which have the effect of reducing the trigger volume level. Any rise in tariffs would lead to an increase in the cost of serving the market through an export strategy and would stimulate more rapid transition to local sourcing. Restrictive trade policies would have a similar effect.

Under this paradigm, corporations will naturally increase their indigenous activities as market development and sales volume increase. Given a strong commitment to a host market, it would seem that the primary choice between export activity and local production is highly sensitive to trade policy variables. This phenomenon appears to be particularly important in explaining a recent surge in Japanese direct investment in the United States. Japanese direct investment in manufacturing facilities surged from about $6 billion in 1985 to about $13 billion in 1986. Many investments appeared to be directly linked to new tariffs and quotas in industries such as automobiles, television, steel, optic fiber cable, and semiconductors. Much of this surge in direct investment, in fact, occurred before the strengthening of the yen in late 1986.

Any policy or initiative that increased the cost of serving the market through an export strategy would tend to move operations toward indigenous sourcing. However, this economic logic may not translate directly into corporate decisions to establish or expand local operations.

Policies that penalize export-oriented operations might induce multinational firms to increase manufacturing activities inside a host country market. However, restrictive trade policies in the form of tariffs, quotas, and market reserve activities may also affect the attractiveness of the market itself. Restrictive policies may negatively influence the multinational's desire to maintain a presence in that market. The research on this subject shows mixed results. Dunning (1980) found a positive correlation between tariff levels and foreign direct investment activity. However, Davidson and McFetride (1985) found no correlation between tariff levels and corporate propensity to invest in a host country.

Restrictive trade policies and practices in and of themselves need not reduce the firm's perception of market attractiveness. In fact, significant import restrictions could be attractive to firms contemplating initiation or expansion of local operations. Such barriers would limit competition from imports and provide a barrier to market entry. However, uncertain trade policy conditions, or scheduled liberalization, would limit these benefits.

In relatively large, affluent, and otherwise attractive markets, significant and stable import restrictions could stimulate direct investment by MNCs. However, when restrictive trade policies are accompanied by restrictive investment and foreign exchange regulations, as is frequently the case, the attractiveness of local operations will be reduced. In such cases, the firm may postpone or avoid the decision to manufacture locally.

Even when economics indicate that local operations will provide a more efficient source of product, firms may opt not to shift to local sourcing. Restrictions on equity ownership or repatriation of profits, for example, would reduce the attractiveness of that option. These host country policy variables interact with trade policies in influencing corporate operating decisions.

Decisions to establish local operations can also be influenced by political risk and instability (Kobrin, 1976; Ghadar and Moran, 1984). Concern over marginal or full expropriation of corporate assets will argue against local manufacturing, despite favorable economics. Environmental uncertainty was found to reduce firms' propensity to commit to local operations in a recent study by Anderson and Gatignon (1986). While there is mixed evidence that political risk and environmental uncertainty in the host country can deter local operations, it has been widely observed that firms with little international operating experience are generally slower to initiate international operations (Vernon, 1983; Stopford and Wells, 1972; Davidson, 1980; Root, 1983). Corporate uncertainty stemming from ignorance of host country conditions and market characteristics, can lead firms to discount or avoid local operating options significantly (Davidson, 1980). Inexperienced firms exhibit a strong preference for export-oriented sourcing solutions. They are generally reluctant to commit to local operations. Firms with extensive foreign operating experience might be more responsive to the economics of local manufacturing and hence more responsive to trade policies and practices in their operating activities.

All of these factors interact with trade policies to influence corporate operating strategies. It is difficult to isolate the effects of trade policy variables on corporate operating decisions. It is readily possible, however, to examine how changes in trade policies and practices affect the performance of firms pursuing different operating strategies.

TRADE POLICIES AND CORPORATE PERFORMANCE

The effects of trade policy on corporate performance can be examined by studying how different generic operating systems respond to changes in the trade environment. Four generic operating systems can be identified: the pure export strategy, local final assembly, self-sufficient indigeneous production, and the networked system.

Japanese and Korean firms provide excellent examples of the export-oriented operating strategies. In many instances, world markets are served solely from facilities in the home country. Little or no activity is conducted in the host country. Many Japanese, Korean, and other firms have developed extensive markets around the world that are served almost exclusively through exports. This approach is of course most vulnerable to restrictive trade policies.

In the local assembly mode, some assembly work is performed in all host markets. The value-added content of local activity may be a small fraction of the total, but the firm possesses an operating presence of some magnitude in each significant host market. Honda Motors, an exception to the Japanese rule, represents a classic practitioner of this strategy. Honda operates more than 60 foreign assembly plants for its motorcycles. Its operating strategy emphasizes local assembly in all foreign markets. Such an approach can greatly increase access to foreign markets and reduce vulnerability to trade restrictions.

Indigenous operating strategies are found in many American MNCs. American multinational firms generally have highly developed foreign markets, and they exhibit correspondingly mature international operating networks. In most cases, these firms have already completed the process of initial market development through export activity. As markets have grown, they are served increasingly by local facilities. American firms generally exhibit operating strategies that emphasize self-sufficient indigenous production (Davidson, 1982).

The pure form of indigenous sourcing is presumably highly impervious to restrictive trade policies. However, the process of establishing local sourcing centers involves several phases that are highly sensitive to trade policies. In most cases, the initial phase of local production involves only a limited number of final assembly steps in the manufacture of the finished product (Stobaugh,

1976). Subassemblies and components will continue to be exported to the local market, and only the more labor-intensive assembly operations will be performed locally. Over time, there will be a tendency to increase the local content and expand the scope of local manufacturing activities. In the interim, components or subassemblies that are being transported to the local affiliate remain vulnerable to trade restrictions. In such cases, trade policy initiatives by a host country may damage embryonic manufacturing facilities in the early stages of localization of manufacturing content.

NETWORKED SYSTEMS

The product cycle model focuses on a series of decisions that are likely to be addressed in the development and evolution of an MNCs activities in individual foreign markets. The evolution of MNCs suggests that there is indeed a tendency to follow the pattern of expansion in individual markets as described above. However, there is another, distinct phase in the evolution of international operations that should be described.

In addition to the export, assembly, and local production modes, another systemic approach to international operations is probably more reflective of reality in the modern world of multinational corporations. This approach to international operations involves the development of a manufacturing network that exhibits a large number of facilities in foreign markets but does not require extensive self-sufficiency within each local market.

As an example, consider a corporation that serves a dozen markets, sells a dozen products in each market, and operates a manufacturing facility in each of the 12 countries. In addition, each of the 12 products requires a dozen components. Rather than producing 12 components and 12 products in each of 12 countries, the firm might choose to operate a facility in each country that specializes in the production of one final product and a set of components. If among the components used in all of these manufacturing facilities there are 48 unique items, a fully rationalized manufacturing network would involve the production of four components and one final product in each of a dozen facilities. Each facility would then serve the needs of all other markets for its final product and supply the other manufacturing facilities in the network with necessary components. As a result, this system will exhibit significant economies of scale and lower manufacturing costs.

This approach clearly requires substantial coordination and logistics management. Nonetheless, it may offer substantial economic benefits to the multinational corporation, while permitting local production in each country to satisfy host country desires for local employment and value added. IBM Corporation's European regional unit represents a classic example of a rationalized network. Facilities in Germany, France, Italy, the United Kingdom, and other countries provide the company's requirements for the entire region for individual components or products. Extensive shipments between affiliates characterize this system. Manufacturing rationalization along these lines has been a common phenomenon in Europe, as firms attempt to convert existing multiproduct plants to specialized facilities serving the entire European market. Several firms in the automotive industry have attempted to adopt this approach on a worldwide basis (Doz, 1986).

This rationalized approach to international operations represents a powerful compromise between the economic and the political imperatives of international business. It allows the firm to realize economies of scale and greater efficiency in specialized production facilities. It eliminates duplication of investment and allows more efficient utilization of capacity. The economic benefit of this approach can be substantial. The political benefits also seem to be positive.

This approach is responsive to host governments' needs for balance-of-payments performance, employment, local tax revenue, technology transfer, and other benefits. However, it can be seen that this latter approach is highly sensitive to trade policies. Any general increase in the cost of international trade, whether in the form of tariffs, quotas, restrictions, or simply administrative activities associated with trade, reduces the attractiveness of this approach relative to the option of self-sufficient indigenous manufacturing in each foreign market.

SIMULATION

The potential costs of trade restrictions can be seen in the simulation presented below. The simulation depicts the results associated with four distinctive operating strategies in different trade scenarios. The four operating strategies examined include (1) a pure export approach in which all foreign markets are assumed to be served from a domestic facility in the home country of the multinational firm; (2) an approach in which an assembly facility is present for each product sold in each host market, with extensive reliance on imported components; (3) a self-sufficient indigenous sourcing strategy in which all products and components are manufactured in the host country; and (4) a generic strategy, representing a rationalized network in which specialized facilities exist to serve world markets for individual components and products.

A number of factors, including transportation costs, wage rates, labor intensity, capital intensity, and other variables, would have an important impact on the performance of each of these strategies under different scenarios. In this simulation, the product contains medium value-added content, involves some skilled labor inputs, and is of medium capital intensity. Holding these variables constant allows us to examine the direct impact of different trade environments on the performance of these four operating strategies.

Several trade scenarios are depicted. Trade scenario A depicts essentially a free trade environment with modest administrative, direct, and political costs associated with international trade. All 10 of the national markets assumed in this simulation apply 5 percent tariffs to imports and permit open market access. In the second scenario, roughly a third of the world market contains

Table 11.1 A Simulation of Four Operating Approaches Under Different Trade Scenarios

Operating Strategy	Revenue	CGS	Tariff	Transport	Gross Margin
Scenario A: Free trade					
Export	$110M	$54.0M	$5.50M	$11.00M	$39.5M
Local assembly	110M	56.7M	2.75M	8.25M	42.3M
Indigenous production[a]	68M	63.2M	0	0	4.8M
Transshipment network[b]	110M	47.5M	6.80M	13.30M	42.6M
Scenario B: One third administered[c] two thirds free					
Export	$106.60M	$52.64M	$9.92	$10.66	$33.38
Local assembly	109.66M	55.71M	4.45	7.995	41.505
Indigenous production	67.86M	62.78M	0	0	5.08
Transshipment network	107.86M	46.65M	7.8	12.9	40.51
Scenario C: One third restricted, two thirds administered					
Export[d]	$68.40M	$35.36M	$13.68M	6.84M	$12.52M
Local assembly	109.24M	46.31M	23.84M	6.405M	32.68
Indigenous production[e]	89.34M	79.36M	0	0	9.98M
Transshipment network[f]	89.24M	38.85M	6.84M	10.52M	33.03
Scenario D: Restricted world trade					
Local assembly	$110M	$35.85M	$55.0M	$4.125M	$15.005M
Indigenous production[g]	98M	69.1M	0	0	29.9M
Transshipment network[h]	52M	26.5M	15.6M	13.05M	6.85M

[a] Sales only in markets with volume sufficient to warrant a local facility (markets 1, 2, 3, and 4).

[b] Facilities in markets 1, 2, and 4.

[c] One third equals markets 4, 6, 8, and 10, or 17 million units of goods at initial prices. Wholesale prices in these markets rise by 20% (and 100%) under scenarios B, C, and D.

[d] Sales in nonrestricted markets only.

[e] Sales in markets 1, 2, 3, 4, 5, and 6.

[f] Facilities in markets 1, 2, and 4 avoid final product tariffs, but tariffs on component and preassembled goods prevail. Sales in markets 1, 2, 3, 4, 5, 7, and 9.

[g] Sales in markets 1, 2, 3, 4, 5, 6, and 7.

[h] Sales in markets 1, 2, and 4 only.

ASSUMPTIONS:

(1) Wholesale price is $2/unit initially. Product sold from factory to independent distributors.

(2) There are 10 foreign market zones in this simulation, with initial unit volume for the product as follows:

Market   1 = 10 million units

Market   2 = 9 million units

extensive costs associated with international trade activity: market access costs rise from 5 percent to 20 percent in four of the 10 countries in the simulation. In the third scenario, the other six countries exhibit 20 percent access costs, and the original four countries are virtually closed to international trade with tariffs and trade compliance costs equal to 100 percent of the product's value. In the final scenario, the entire world market exhibits 100 percent tariff levels (Table 11.1).

The simulation shows that an open, free trade environment permits positive results from the export-oriented, local assembly, or transshipment network approaches to international operations. The choice of operating strategy does not critically influence performance in this scenario. Each of these three strategies performs well in a free trade scenario, and they have almost identical gross margin results. Indigenous production is not warranted in such an environment, however. A firm following this pure strategy would not participate in markets with sales volumes below break-even levels for a self-sufficient manufacturing policy. This extreme assumption results in lower sales levels for this generic strategy. In this simulation, results for each operating strategy are calculated based on the assumption that no other competitors are present. If the element of competition is introduced, the indigenous operating strategy clearly fails relative to the other options.

As the trade environment becomes increasingly restrictive in scenarios B, C, and D, the export-based operating system becomes increasingly unattractive. In a world of complete trade restrictions (scenario D), the export approach is no longer a viable option. In contrast, the indigenous sourcing strategy becomes attractive only in the most severe trade scenario. This approach benefits from higher unit prices associated with high tariff levels. Prices are assumed to rise at levels equal to tariff rates. Local assembly appears to have the greatest range of positive performance, although this approach is also adversely affected by the severe trade restrictions of scenario D. The transshipment approach performs

---

Market   3 = 8 million units

⋮

Market 10 = 1 million units

(2) Demand for the product follows the same function in all markets; $D = Db + 0.25Db(\$2.0\text{-}P)$ where Db = base demand specified in previous sentence, and P is the retail price of the product. Markets 1, 2, 3, and 4 are considered OECD markets; others are non-OECD markets.

(3) Transportation costs = $0.20/unit.

(4) Tariffs and trade compliance costs = 5% of wholesale revenues in free trade markets, 20% in administered markets, and 100% in restricted markets.

(5) Cost of goods =

$$A) \ \$10 \text{ million} + \$0.8Q$$

or

$$B) \ \$5 \text{ million} + \$0.6Q$$

where Q = volume produced in the sourcing facility, A = OECD countries (1, 2, 3, 4), and B = other countries with low labor costs. Of the variable cost, half is labor, and half is materials.

(6) Local assembly option involves displacing one-half of labor content. This generates a cost savings of $0.10 per unit in non-OECD countries but involves a $500,000 annual fixed cost per assembly location. This strategy reduces transportation and insurance costs by $0.05 per unit and reduces tariffs by 50% as well.

(7) Transshipment involves use of least cost location for component, preassembly, and assembly activities. Cost reduction of 25% assumed for each stage, but fixed costs increase so that CGS = $20M + 0.5Q. Transportation and insurance increase by 20%.

very well in a world of limited trade restrictions as simulated in scenarios A, B, and C but fares less well under severe restrictions. Given complete uncertainty about future trade conditions, the best operating strategy for multinational firms is the local assembly option. It has the highest expected performance level given equal probabilities for all four trade scenarios. It provides the widest range of positive performance. Also, it may permit the greatest degree of flexibility in terms of permitting transitions to other operating models.

This simulation examines the immediate impact of four distinctive trade scenarios on the performance of firms pursuing four generic operating strategies. Firms would presumably be able to alter their operating configurations to respond to new trade realities, given time, but each of these configurations exhibits some inflexibility. The central export approach can presumably shift to a local assembly mode fairly quickly, but such transitions are not without cost. Firms with existing assembly sites operate at a significant advantage over their export-based competitors when trade barriers arise. Honda Corporation, for example, operates a network of foreign assembly plants, while other Japanese vendors emphasize export activity. With significant capacity for automobile and motorcycle production in the United States, Honda has sprinted ahead of other Japanese firms since the recent imposition of tariffs and quotas in these industries. It is now the leading foreign vendor of automobiles in the United States, with plans to expand local production to 710,000 vehicles per year by 1990.

The indigenous production approach can revert to local assembly if trade liberalization occurs, but the resulting facility configuration will not be optimal. In fact, the threat of reductions in tariff levels can be highly unsettling to firms committed to indigenous production. The removal of internal tariffs in the European Economic Community necessitated a shift from multiple full-line facilities to central or specialized sites for many corporations.* Reductions in tariffs in Canada have been linked to reduced United States direct investment and divestment of existing facilities (Davidson and McFetridge, 1985b).

The critical issue for multinational corporations, presumably, is to predict the trade scenario and develop the appropriate operating configuration. It is clear that there are preferred strategies for MNCs given any global trade environment. One of the items on the corporate strategy agenda is therefore analysis and forecasting of the international trade environment, which can lead to appropriate action on the international operations front. Proper forecasting of the trade environment becomes critical to long-term operating strategy and investment. Shifts from one configuration to another involve significant costs and should be avoided.

A CONTINGENCY APPROACH

It is not the task of this chapter to forecast future trade environments. It attempts to examine the impact of different trade environment scenarios on

---

* See, for example, DAAG Europe (A) or Chandler Home Products case studies, Harvard Case Clearing House, Nos. 9–374–037 and 9–377–232, respectively.

different corporate operating strategies. However, it is appropriate to suggest that a global view of trade policies is simplistic in terms of assessing how corporate strategies and public policies interact. For example, in many countries with highly restrictive trade regimes, such as Brazil, there are tariffs, quotas, and other restrictions in place that effectively prohibit international firms from serving the Brazilian market from foreign sources. However, the administration of trade policy in Brazil is quite sophisticated. Individual firms are able to negotiate access to Brazilian markets on the basis of company-specific trade balances. A firm that exports $200 million a year from Brazil might be granted market access for $400 million worth of imports into the Brazilian market. In essence, it is critical that the multinational firm examine not only global trade environment scenarios, but also the specific trade policies and trade administration practices of individual host countries.

It is appropriate to examine how individual operating strategies might be applied in countries with different trade environments. In viewing trade policy from the prespective of an individual country, it is important to consider the prevailing structure and process of trade policy administration, key policy variables, and the trade performance of the host country. It is also important to consider the foreign exchange position of the host country. In considering these variables, it is possible to identify several generic environments faced by multinational corporations intent on conducting business in a specific host market.

One extreme case would involve a host country with highly restricted market access, highly restrictive foreign exchange controls, and highly restrictive direct investment regulations. In such a case, multinational corporations would find it difficult, if not impossible, to serve the local market from an export base. It would be very difficult to exchange and repatriate local currency derived from commercial activity in the host market. It would also be difficult, because of equity participation restrictions, to establish and control a local affiliate in the host country. Given severe restrictions on market access, foreign exchange conversion, and equity investment, many multinational corporation might choose to avoid participation in markets with such policies. In fact, several Latin American countries (notably those in the Andean Pact), India, and other nations exhibit conditions in each of these three areas that severely restrict MNCs' activities (Balasubramanyam, 1973; Furnish, 1976). Foreign investment levels in those countries have lagged notably behind levels in neighboring countries (Davidson and McFetridge, 1985b).

At the other end of the extreme would be a market that granted ready access to imported products, free conversion of foreign exchange, and open direct investment activity. The United States, the Scandinavian countries, Hong Kong, and certain other markets best typify this end of the spectrum. In between, countries exhibit different levels of restrictions in each of the three policy areas. For example, Canada exhibits relatively free market access and free foreign exchange conversion but does regulate foreign direct investment to some extent. In evaluating a specific host country's trade, foreign exchange, and direct investment policies, the MNC must then choose a specific operating orientation for that host country.

In reality, the four operating modes described above are never found in pure form within any individual corporation. For the most part, the corporation must customize its operating strategy to individual markets. It would thus be possible to witness a corporation that chose to serve a certain set of markets from a central export base, chose to organize another set of markets within a transshipment network, and chose to serve a third set of markets with local assembly or self-sufficient indigenous manufacturing facilities. These clusters of countries would be determined by the nature of the prevailing trade regime and other characteristics of the individual host country. Thus, Venezuela, because of its relatively open trade regime, might be served from a United States-based, or Japanese-based, or German-based manufacturing facility. Colombia, as a member of the LAFTA trade regime, might be served from a Brazilian affiliate that specialized in one line of products. A sister Colombian facility might produce other product and components for sale in Colombia and the rest of the LAFTA market. India, on the other hand, would be served by a self-sufficient local manufacturing facility, as would other restricted markets that are not part of trade communities.

This contingency approach to operating strategy permits the firm to be flexible in terms of its operating strategy for serving individual markets. Given a diversity of trade, foreign exchange, and direct investment policies in the world today, such an approach is seemingly inevitable.

PARTICIPATION POLICIES

It is important to view the question of operating strategies from another perspective as well. The choice between export, indigenous, and network approaches to international operations is intimately linked to the question of participation policies. Firms must choose not only whether and how to serve a market, but through what form of business organization. In examining operating options, the firm may choose to establish local manufacturing through a licensing agreement, a joint venture, other forms of collaborative production, or a wholly owned subsidiary. The choice of format is presumably less sensitive to trade conditions than to other market and firm characteristics (Davidson and McFetridge, 1984). However, in markets with restrictive trade, investment, and foreign exchange regulations, firms can be expected to exhibit preference for lower levels of direct participation in the market. Market size and political stability (Anderson and Gatignon, 1986) can also be expected to influence participation decisions.

When participation options are added to the contingency approach discussed above, the complexity of international operations increases sharply. In addition, it is important to suggest that certain participation patterns can restrict a firm's flexibility in the face of shifting trade conditions. It may be difficult to include a licensee or joint venture in a globally rationalized manufacturing network, for example. Problems associated with transfer pricing, cost allocation, coordination, and decision and incentive structures

(Contractor, 1984; Killing, 1982) accompany efforts to integrate such units into the network. Firms that have used licensing and joint venture agreements as their primary vehicle for initiating local production within foreign markets may find it difficult to develop and administer a rationalized network. That could be a disadvantage under a variety of trade conditions.

CONCLUSION

While it is critical to focus on trade regimes within individual countries, it is also appropriate to question the general trend and direction in these key public policy areas. To the extent that a homogeneous trade environment appears across all countries, it becomes possible for the corporation to adopt a more homogeneous operating strategy. In the immediate postwar period, with an increasingly open trade environment and the development of regional economic communities, it was possible to adopt an approach which focused on specialized facilities within regional economic communities. Inter- and intraregional trade flourished. These facilities could openly serve markets inside the region and trade with facilities in other regional communities. While rising trade restrictions particularly threaten interregional trade, trade within regional trading blocs may remain relatively open (see Drobnick and Enzer, Chapter 2). To the extent that trade restrictions reduce access to regional trade communities, such as the Eastern bloc, the EEC, LAFTA, and ASEAN, and do not reduce internal acess to member markets, it remains possible to retain many of the benefits of large-scale, specialized facilities designed to serve relatively large markets. To the extent that the trade environment becomes highly nationalized and restrictive at the level of individual nations, it appears that firms pursuing indigenous manufacturing strategies will gain in terms of competitive position within world markets.

The world does not appear to be homogeneous in terms of trade conditions, but it does appear that market access is becoming increasingly difficult in the majority of nations. Given this shift toward greater trade protectionism at the level of the individual nation, firms with the ability and the flexibility to establish local manufacturing affiliates in a large number of host countries would appear to have a competitive edge. Questions remain, however, about the degree to which host countries will permit the MNCs to utilize imported components and their ability to develop operating networks that rely on extensive transshipment from specialized facilities.

Many of the problem associated with trade restrictions can be finessed if host countries adopt company-specific trade balance targets. Transshipment activities would be permitted under such trade regimes. Under such a scenario, firms with countertrade capabilities will also possess a significant advantage in accessing foreign markets. This capability can provide a useful substitute for a local manufacturing presence. General Electric Corporation's trading arm implemented over $3 billion in countertrade agreements between 1982 and 1987, supporting GE exports of more than $5 billion. Countertrade agreements are formal contracts between the multinational corporation and a host government. Under such contracts, GE's international countertrade unit commits to export from the host market a certain percentage of the value of GE shipments into that host country. These agreements facilitate export-oriented operating strategies. Few other United States firms possess such countertrade capabilities, but Japanese firms, which are most vulnerable to trade restrictions, can utilize the unparalleled services of their affiliated trading companies. Creative corporate strategies involving countertrade are an increasingly important fact of life in many host countries.

The primary issue for the average corporation remains concern about fundamental tensions between economic and political imperatives. Tensions between home and host governments will increase as trade frictions heat up. In a world of aggressive public trade policies, the multinational corporation can only feel increased pressure for trade and other contributions to its host markets. The ability of corporations to respond creatively and flexibly to these pressures will determine the ultimate cost, in efficiency and growth losses, associated with rising trade restrictions.

REFERENCES

Anderson, E.; and Gatignon, H.: "Modes of Foreign Entry," *Journal of International Business Studies* (Fall 1986), pp. 1–26.

Balasubramanyam, V.N.: *International Transfer of Technology to India* (New York: Praeger, 1973).

Contractor, F.J.: "Choosing Between Direct Investment and Licensing," *Journal of International Business Studies* (Winter 1984), pp. 167–188.

Davidson, W.H.: *Experience Effects in International Investment and Technology Transfer* (Ann Arbor, MI: UMI Research Press, 1980).

Davidson, W.H.: *Global Strategic Management* (New York: John Wiley, 1982, Chapter 6).

Davidson, W.H.; and McFetridge, D.G.: "International Technology Transaction and the Theory of the Firm," *Journal of Industrial Economics*, 32 (March 1984), pp. 253–264.

Davidson, W.H.; and McFetridge, D.G.: "New Directions in Global Strategies: Portfolio Adjustment or Production Rationalization," *Columbia Journal of World Business* (Summer 1985a).

Davidson, W.H.; and McFetridge, D.G.: "Country Characteristics and the Choice of Technology Transfer Mode," *Journal of International Business Studies* (Fall 1985b).

Doz, Yves: "Managing Manufacturing Rationalization Within Multinational Corporations," *Columbia Journal of World Business* (Fall 1978).

Doz, Yves: "The International Automotive Industry," in M.S. Hochmuth, and W.H. Davidson, eds, *Revitalizing American Industry* (Cambridge, MA: Ballinger, 1986).

Dunning, John: "Toward and Eclectic Theory of International Production: Some Empirical Tests," *Journal of Business Studies* (Spring/Summer 1980), pp. 9–31.

Furnish, D.E.: "The Andean Markets Common Regime for Foreign Investment," in

K. Sauvant, and F.G. Lauipour, eds, *Controlling Multinational Enterprises* (Boulder, CO: Westview Press, 1976).

Ghadar, F.G.; and Moran, T. eds: *International Risk Management* (Washington, D.C.: Landegger Program in International Business Diplomacy, Georgetown University, 1984).

Killing, J.P.: "How to Make a Global Joint Venture Work," *Harvard Business Review* (May–June 1982), pp. 120–127.

Kobrin, S.J.: "Environmental Determinants of Foreign Direct Manufacturing Investments," *Journal of International Business Studies* (Fall/Winter 1976), pp. 29–42.

Root, F.J.: *Foreign Market Entry Strategies* (New York: AMACON, 1983).

Stobaugh, R.B.: *Nine Investments Abroad and Their Impact at Home* (Boston: Division of Research, Harvard Business School, 1976).

Stopford, J.M.; and Wells, L.T. Jr.: *Managing the Multinational Enterprise* (New York: Basic Books, 1972).

Vernon, R.: "International Trade and Investment in Product Life Cycle," *Quarterly Journal of Economics* (May 1966), pp. 190–207.

Vernon, T.: "Organizational and Institutional Responses to International Risk," in R.J. Herring, ed.: *Managing International Risk* (Cambridge, U.K.: Cambridge University Press, 1983).

Vernon, R.: *Storm Over the Multinationals* (Cambridge, MA: Harvard University Press, 1977).

12

Trade Barriers and Currency Risk

CHRISTINE R. HEKMAN

The subject of this chapter is, in some ways, very focused, and the work certainly prescribes a specific technical approach for a single functional area—financial management. However, it also provides a framework that summarizes and integrates the insights drawn from other functional perspectives introduced and explored earlier in this book. This section is dedicated to describing the many ways in which changes in trade policy affect corporate performance. This concluding chapter of Part II provides a framework that recognizes the contributions of each functional area to aggregate corporate sensitivity to trade policy shifts.

Professor Hekman analyzes the relationship between trade policy and the degree to which a particular company's returns are more or less sensitive to changes in foreign currency values. In deriving the description of the factors that determine this relationship, she addresses the contributions of marketing, production, financial portfolio strategy, and industrial organization. Thus, the model provided here as a framework for the narrower discussion of trade policy and risk management summarizes the relationships between the important elements in each of the underlying functional areas.

The integration of the complex web of corporate, organizational, and industrial factors that contribute to a company's response to policy shifts is accomplished through the specification of a single corporate objective or benchmark. That objective is the value of the company—or corporate returns. The conceptual basis for the relationship between changes in trade policy and changes in value and returns is presented here as a model, which recognizes the underlying, determining factors.

Focusing on a single performance outcome provides the framework within which to aggregate and relate the many mechanisms through which policy change affects value. The mechanisms include those internal corporate responses introduced in the preceding chapters. By drawing these response mechanisms under a single valuation umbrella, this chapter integrates the insights and experiences of each of the discrete, functional perspectives.

The chapter also recognizes and correlates the effects of change that are external to the company but that significantly influence its internal responses and its value. These influences act primarily through the industrial structure. Thus, a major integrating contribution of this chapter is the formalization of the role of industrial structure and dynamics. These dynamics are shown both to affect the constraints on the corporation's ability to respond to policy shifts and, in turn, to be affected by the responses of particular corporations.

By drawing together the external constraints and the internal corporate response, the chapter connects the chapters of this section to the aggregate perspective described in Part I. This connection derives from recognition that the effect of policy shifts on values, returns, and margins is ultimately determined by the effect of those shifts on industrial prices and corporate competitiveness. With this link, then, we return from study and characterization of a particular company's sensitivity to policy shifts to an understanding of the effects on the entire system.

Finally, this chapter attempts to explain why one company's risk profile is affected more strongly than another's by changes in trade policy. It also provides a framework for predicting such changes and for managing the individual functional areas so as to protect corporate flexibility and value from the effects of unexpected policy changes. In particular, it offers a framework for management of currency risk through the corporate financing and risk management function.

It is interesting to note that the approach offered here implies that the financial function is subsidiary to and dependent upon the other management functions. The approach recommends that managers of the financial function focus attention on residual vulnerability. This is the risk that remains after taking into account the capacities of other managers to alter pricing, sourcing, production, and scale economies; investment structure; and organizational structure to accommodate unexpected changes in policy. To the extent that flexibility in any or all of these functional areas allows recovery from policy shifts, protective financing or hedging is unnecessary. However, inability to recover results where cost considerations or sensitivity to economies of scale in any or all of these areas leads functional management to favor low cost rather than flexibility in investment and operations leaves the financial function with residual risk.

The framework offered at the conclusion of this chapter summarizes these cost/flexibility tradeoffs in a single financial profile. This profile is then taken to the capital markets as the basis for financing and risk management.

A model of the relationship between currency exposure and the system of setting industry prices is described in this chapter, and the extent to which foreign participants influence industry prices is explored. The conclusion of this exploration is that trade barriers in general, and quotas in particular, restrict the influence of foreign producers. This restriction reduces the sensitivity of the industry price to changes in foreign exchange rates and increases the share of the industry's value that is effectively denominated in the domestic currency. The result is reduced risk for investors in domestic businesses and increased value.

As quotas are lifted, the values of foreign currencies will influence the industry price more strongly so that the foreign currency exposure of domestic producers will increase. The implication is that the reduction of barriers to trade will reduce the value of current and incremental investment in the domestic industry.

Thus, this chapter addresses the following question: How dramatically will the imposition or elimination of trade barriers affect the currency exposure of a business? The question is addressed by considering a model from which the relationship between trade barriers and foreign exchange exposure is derived.

The relationship between the currency of industry pricing and the foreign exchange exposure of the domestic industry participants is captured in the corporate "foreign currency profile" that summarizes the company's foreign exchange exposure. Finally, that discussion is summarized in a study of the effect of quota imposition on the foreign currency profile.

FOREIGN EXCHANGE EXPOSURE

Measurement and remeasurement of foreign exchange exposure is an increasingly important component of the corporate financial and risk management function. As the perceived risk of the investment or business activity changes, so does the prescription for risk management. In the main, this implies a requirement for rebalancing the corporate capital structure along dimensions of currency and maturity mix. Rebalancing may be accomplished by using one or more of the many recently developed financial instruments such as currency swaps and foreign currency options. Such rebalancing in response to changes in exposure also explains much of the expanding demand for these instruments.

Assessment of foreign exchange exposure has also received increased attention, as risk management has become a recognized tool of competitive strategy. In fact, the ability to measure and manage risk has been shown to relate strongly to the ability to protect competitive position through appropriate investment analysis and commitment.

The central determinant of exposure for all companies is the industry pricing structure. In turn, industry pricing is influenced substantially by the presence or absence of foreign competition. Changes in the foreign economic environment in general, and foreign exchange rates in particular, affect domestic pricing as foreign competitors respond to the incentives provided by their investors. They may attempt to protect their investors' returns by raising prices when translated returns fall because of exchange rate changes. Conversely, they may respond to the opportunity to expand market share by reducing prices when a decline in the value of their currency increases the returns from foreign markets.

In the presence of strong foreign competition, industry prices are affected by foreign exchange rates. Likewise, the reduction or elimination, through tariffs or quotas, of foreign competition will reduce the potential influence of foreign exchange rates on industry prices. In sum, trade barriers are important determinants of foreign exchange exposure, because they define and constrain the influence of foreign competition on industrial structure and pricing.

FOREIGN EXCHANGE EXPOSURE AND THE CHARACTERISTICS
OF INDUSTRY PARTICIPANTS

The foreign exchange exposure of an investment is the sensitivity of the value of that investment to unexpected changes in foreign exchange rates. Any description of this sensitivity must look below the surface to the basic element upon which value depends. The model described here summarizes the developments described in two earlier papers and provides a comprehensive description of exposure (see Hekman, 1983 and Hekman, 1985, for the expanded models). These papers explore the effects of exchange rate changes on value, especially on the value of the future operating cash flows as described in the following equation:

$$\text{VCF} = \sum_{t=1} \frac{A_t X_0^{(1-\varepsilon)}}{(1+r)} \tag{1}$$

where VCF = the current value of operating flows,
A_t = a fixed parameter determined by industry production and demand characteristics in each period,
X = the current spot foreign exchange,
r = the cost of capital.

This sensitivity is captured in the exponent which relates the foreign exchange rate, X_0, to the value of the operating cash flows, VCF. This coefficient is the difference between unity and ε, where ε represents the relationship between operating revenue and the exchange rart.

$$R_t = B_t X_0^\varepsilon \tag{2}$$

where R_t = total revenue at time t,
B_t = a parameter constant at time t,
ε = the aggregate elasticity of revenue with respect to changes in the foreign exchange rate.

These equations describe the values of firms based in small countries and assess the effects of changes in exchange rates on these values. The effects are generalized through the effects of the exchange rate change on the cost of the firm's inputs. The cost of a traded and freely supplied input is directly affected by exchange rate changes; the cost of a nontraded input, which is in limited supply, responds to changes in the quantity of production. Thus, changes in exchange rates induce changes in costs, quantity supplied, price, and revenue.

With this framework, both supply and demand factors determine the degree of sensitivity of the system to changes in foreign exchange rates. On the supply side, the primary determinants of exposure are the supply of the constrained input, the extent to which its supply responds to changes in its cost, and the shares of the various inputs in the production process.

$$Q_t^s S p_t^{-\alpha} p^\beta \tag{3}$$

where Q_t^s = quantity supplied,

    S = fixed production and technology parametes,

    p_t = the price at time t of the traded input,

    α = the elasticity of supply with respect to the cost of traded inputs,

    β = the price elasticity of supply.

In this formulation, parameters of technology and production are captured in the constant parameter S. The effects of constrained inputs and the cost share of inputs are reflected in the exponent on the traded input's price. The relationship between industry price and the quantity produced is determined by the exponent, β.

Influential characteristics of industry demand include the price of potential substitutes and the strength of the market response to differences between the industry price and the prices of the substitutes.

$$Q_t^d = DP_f^{\eta_c}P^{-\eta} \tag{4}$$

where Q_t^d = quantity demanded,

    P_f = the price of competing foreign goods,

    η_c = the cross price elasticity of demand between domestic product and foreign product,

    D_t = fixed demand parameters which include the effects of income on demand,

    η = price elasticity of demand for domestic industry production.

Here the quantity demanded is a function of the price set by the foreign competitors and by the sensitivity of consumer response to the difference between prices set by domestic producers and prices set by foreign producers.

The price set by foreign competitors reflects both input costs and the currency preferences of investors. Thus, the foreign price is influenced by the rate of exchange of the relevant currencies.

$$P_f = P_h(X_0)^\sigma \tag{5}$$

where P_h = the price at which foreign producers supply their home market,

    σ = the elasticity of the price set by foreign producers with respect to the foreign exchange rate.

Foreign producer costs are captured in the price charged for the product in their home markets, P_h. The price charged abroad should cover these costs and offer a positive return to investors after translation at the foreign exchange rate. This translation requirement introduces a currency component while allowing that the price set by a foreign producer in his home market may be related to but different from the price set in foreign markets.

Thus, industry demand as seen by the domestic participants in the primary market includes traditional determinants plus a factor that recognizes the prices charged by foreign competition. These prices in turn reflect the costs and technologies available to foreign competitors as well as the exchange rate at which foreign competitors will translate earnings back to their home country investors.

Further, the formulation recognizes that the foreign competitors may price to offset some, but not all, of the effects of changes in foreign exchange rates on local investment returns.

$$Q_D = D[P_b(X_0)\sigma]^{\eta_c} P^{-\eta} \qquad (6)$$

The joint effects of these statements of supply-and-demand relationships is a description of the industry price and the production and revenues of the domestic producers.

$$P = [(D/S) p_t^{\alpha} p_b^{\eta_c} [1/(\beta + \eta)] X_0 \sigma \eta_c [1/(\beta + \eta)]] \qquad (7)$$

Price is a function of the fixed parameters of supply and demand, foreign and domestic production costs, and the exchange rate. To further isolate the relationship between exchange rates and domestic producers' revenues, assume that the production costs are fixed for both domestic and foreign producers and that parameters such as factor shares and input supply elasticities are also constant. In this case, the variable element of revenue for domestic producers is the foreign exchange rate. This rate affects domestic production revenue through its effect on foreign competitors and on the price they charge.

The effect of exchange rate changes on the price of competitive foreign production may be either mitigated or amplified. The extent of magnification is represented by σ, the elasticity (with respect to the exchange rate) of the price of foreign product.

Further, the subsequent effect on domestic producers' revenue depends on the price of domestic production and the degree to which consumers accept this price given the price offered by the foreign firms.

To summarize several levels of model development, note from Eqs 1 and 2 that the sensitivity to changes in exchange rates of the value of domestic operations is the exponent on the foreign exchange term in Eq. 8:

$$R = (S^{\eta} D^{\beta})[1/(\beta + \eta)] C_t X_0 \sigma \eta_c [\beta/(\beta + \eta)] \qquad (8)$$

where C_t = a function of fixed parameters which describe the costs of traded inputs for the domestic producers, foreign producers' costs, and their effects on industry price.

Note further that, having assumed constancy of many important parameters and variables, the exponent captures the interplay of foreign and domestic producers in a given market.

The foreign producers' response to the foreign exchange rate is an important determinant of the effect of trade barriers on domestic producers' exposure. This response is determined by the interaction between the sensitivity of foreign producers' prices to foreign exchange rate changes, σ, and the sensitivity of the consuming market to the resulting difference between prices of domestic and foreign goods, η_c. (Fixed parameters assume that the prices charged by domestic producers will respond to changes in foreign producers' prices in a way that maximizes domestic profits and values.)

The central assertion is that changes in quotas alter the relevant coefficient in a very predictable fashion. As a result, the basic character of the industrial pricing mechanism is altered. In particular, when quota limits for the producers are lifted, consumers' freedom of choice and, thereby, the cross-price elasticity of demand increases also. In other words, reducing the trade impediment increases domenstrated consumer sensitivity to changes in the prices of foreign products and to differences between those prices and the prices of domestic products.

Further, this consumer sensitivity may be magnified by the sensitivity of the foreign producers to the foreign exchange rate at which profits are translated into their own currency and evaluated as return by their investors. The parameter η_c captures this sensitivity of the foreign price to changes in the foreign exchange rate. Thus, if quota levels decline, domestic exposure will be unchanged, provided foreign investors accept the added risk without compensated increase in return.

In summary, quotas restrict the competitive influence of foreign producers on the industry price. This leaves the domestic producers with a greater share of pricing power than they would possess in the absence of the quota.

QUOTAS, PRICING POWER, AND FOREIGN CURRENCY PROFILES

Each investment group, foreign and domestic, attempts to maximize the stability of investment returns with reference to the costs of a consumption basket or to the return on an investment portfolio. To the extent that the producers in each group are a competitive force, that currency becomes a reference for industry pricing. The success of each group in influencing industry pricing determines the currency denomination of future cash flows accruing to industry production.

Quotas constrain the participation of foreign producers in the price-setting system. They also limit the extent to which those producers can exercise their power and defend the interest of their investors through their influence on the industry price. Under quotas, industry prices and the values of the participating producer firms will be more heavily affected by changes in the costs of domestic consumption and product than would be true in an environment that was free of restriction. Further, the smaller the quota relative to free trade import quantities, the greater the influence of domestic costs.

INDUSTRY PRICING AND CORPORATE FOREIGN CURRENCY PROFILES

Effective exposure is the proportionate sensitivity of corporate value to changes in foreign exchange rates. Effective sensitivity to each currency depends on the total response of the cash flows, either actual or expected, to changes in foreign exchange rates. In the aggregate, exposure or sensitivity to foreign exchange rate changes can be summarized in a corporate foreign currency profile. This profile summarizes, by currency, the effective foreign exchange exposure of the corporation.

The primary determinant of exposure and the corporate foreign currency profile is the currency of denomination of industry pricing. As an example, assume that a 10 percent revaluation of the Japanese yen forces Japanese firms in a particular industry to raise prices in United States markets by 5 percent. This represents a proportionate response of 50 percent of the change in the yen's value.

Assume further that the domestic United States segment of the industry follows the Japanese lead and also raises prices by 5 percent. If both the currency revaluation and the price increase are expected to persist, United States firms in the industry can look forward to a 5 percent increase in profits. As a consequence, the value of the United States firms can be expected to increase by 5 percent.

This response is equivalent in effect to a full 10 percent response on half of the exposed value. For this reason, the foreign currency profiles of each of the United States companies include a yen-based component equal to half of that company's total value. This component is equivalent, in terms of the effect on overall sensitivity to the value of the yen, to an investment in yen-denominated fixed-income securities of half of the company's total value.

Clearly, the key to assessing the magnitudes of the components of the foreign currency profile is recognition of the increase in prices, which is made possible by the response of the foreign competitors to changes in the yen/dollar exchange rate. This price increase reflects the foreign competition's willingness to sacrifice return in defense of market share by passing only half of the revaluation through to the United States market. It also reflects the commensurate response of the United States firms that match the price increase rather than use the opportunity to expand market share.

It is also important to note the conclusion that a significant share of the values of the United States firms depend on the value of the yen even though these firms may not invest in Japan, export to Japan, or import from Japan. This substantial exposure derives from the presence of Japanese competitors in the United States market. The magnitude of the exposure reflects the market dominance of the Japanese firms.

FOREIGN EXCHANGE EXPOSURE AND FOREIGN CURRENCY PROFILES

A foreign currency profile is a characterization of corporate assets that focuses on the underlying currency denomination. This profile disaggregates the overall sensitivity of value into the sensitivities of each component to changes in particular exchange rates.

As an example of a foreign currency profile, consider Table 12.1, which describes the foreign currency profile of a hypothetical United States investment company. The company's assets are as follows: an investment in British gilts, partial ownership of a German firm, and partial ownership of the United States firm in the industry described above. The dollar values of the three investments are equal at $33 million each. The foreign currency profile of

Table 12.1   Corporate Foreign Currency Profile

Assets	Balance Sheet ($ million)	Net Worth		Currency Profile	
British gilts	$33.3	Equity	$100.0	£	$33.3
Investment in Germany	33.3			DM	33.3
Investment in the United States	33.3			Y	16.5
Total assets	$100.0	Net worth	$100.0	$	16.5

the investment company reflects the effective exposure to the risk of changes in the dollar/pound sterling rate, the deutschmark/dollar exchange rate, and the yen/dollar exchange rate.

Exposure to changes in the dollar value of the pound sterling reflect the fixed denomination in pound sterling of the investment in gilts. Declines in the dollar value of sterling will be directly reflected in declines in the dollar value of the investment. Thus, the foreign currency profile includes a $33 million component denominated effectively in pounds sterling.

Investment in the German company is also assumed to be fully exposed. This investment is purely domestic—that is, dollar returns on the investment directly reflect any changes in the deutschmark/dollar rate. In other words, deutschmark returns are totally insensitive to changes in the foreign exchange rate. Such an assumption might be valid for a firm that neither exported nor imported, and that confronted no foreign competition. The German investment is responsible for the deutschmark exposure component of the foreign currency profile equivalent to $33 million.

The remaining asset, the investment in the United States company, generates both the dollar and the yen exposure components. The yen component of $16.5 million reflects the presence in the market of Japanese competition and the consequent response of industry prices to changes in the yen/dollar rate. The 50 percent response to changes in the exchange rate is effectively equivalent to a 100 percent response on half of the invested value. Thus, we can state the fully exposed equivalent value as $16.5 million, half of the total value of $33 million.

The residual value is considered unexposed, or denominated in dollars. In this case the unexposed value is $16.5 million. Overall, the corporate foreign currency profile is a blend of the values of the pound sterling, deutschmark, yen, and dollar. The magnitudes are summarized in Table 12.1.

The introduction of quotas in this example eliminates the incentive for Japanese competitors to increase market share by cutting prices in response to a strengthening yen. The effect on the foreign currency profile would be an elimination of yen from the profile. In this case the domestic business would be truly domestic in the sense that industry pricing would be completely insensitive to exchange rate changes.

CONCLUSION

Introduction or expansion of quotas reduces the incentives for foreign producers to influence industry pricing. As a result, the industry pricing preferences of foreign investors are repressed.

Conversely, when quota limits are raised, the abilities of foreign producers to promote the preferences of their investors are increased. As foreign firms attempt to stabilize prices with respect to foreign consumption baskets, the sensitivity of domestic industry prices to changes in foreign exchange rates is increased.

Further, the greater the difference between foreign and domestic consumption baskets and wealth portfolios, the greater the increase in currency risk for investment in domestic productive capacity.

In corporate finance terms, the increase in currency risk associated with foreign influence in pricing translates to a greater effective share of foreign currency in the currency profile. Such shifts recommend expanded use of foreign currency debt, foreign currency options, swaps, and other financial hedging instruments.

Shifts in the currency profile also have implications for investment value, the topic of initial interest. As changes in industry pricing increase the foreign component of the currency profile, the risk of investment in the industry increases. Thus, the values of both current and prospective investment in the industry fall. This is especially true in cases where reasonably priced hedging instruments are not available.

REFERENCES

Adler, M.; and Dumas, B.: "The Microeconomics of the Firm in an Open Economy." *American Economic Review* (Feb. 1977), 180–89.

Dornbusch, R.: "Money, Exchange Rates, and Employment." *Open Economy Macroeconomics* (New York: Basic Books, 1980).

Heckerman, D.: "The Exchange Risk of Foreign Operations." *Journal of Business* (Jan. 1972).

Hekman, C.R.: "A Financial model of Foreign Exchange Exposure," *Journal of International Business Studies* (Summer 1985), 83–99.

Hekman, C.R.: "The Real Effects of Foreign Exchange Rate Changes on a Competitive, Profit-Maximizing Firm." Unpublished mimeo, 1983.

Hodder, J.E.: "Exposure to Exchange Rate Movements." *Journal of International Economics* (Nov. 1982). 375–86.

Lessard, D.R.: "Evaluating Foreign Projects: An Adjusted Present Value Approach." In D.R. Lessard, ed., International Financial Management, pp. 577–92. (Boston: Warren, Gorham and Lamont, 1979).

Levi, Maurice: "Economic Exposure." *International Finance*, Chap. 13, pp. 323–57. (New York: McGraw-Hill Book Company, 1983).

Lindgren, B.W.: *Statistical Theory* (London: The MacMillan Company, second edition, 1968).

Shapiro, A.C.: "Exchange Rate Changes, Inflation, and the Value of the Multinational Corporation." *Journal of Finance* (May 1975), 485–502.

III

CORPORATE RESPONSES
TO TRADE POLICIES:
THREE CASE HISTORIES

The only way to evaluate the real effects of trade policies on the corporation is by observing actual behavior in the market. This is done in this section. Although each case is somewhat unique, together they provide us with a validation of the general argument presented and discussed in the two previous parts of the book. This general argument can be summarized as follows.

United States trade policy is inherently risky for the corporate sector. The level of protection on the average is stable, but the incidence of protection and the instruments used to implement the policy change from one time to another and from one industry to another. Corporate management responds to the risks and opportunities of trade policy by seeking protection when it suits its purpose, as in the case of American manufacturers in the semiconductor industry, the United States steel industry, and other protected industries over the years. Often, management has to respond to indirect effects of trade policies, like changes in the exchange rates. This factor is demonstrated in the case of Japanese corporations that export to the United States in this period of dollar depreciation. Responses range from cost cutting to operational changes and relocation of production to reduced profits. In other cases, like the one concerning the semiconductor industry, the response took the form of gray market transactions and other circumventive tactics. The purpose of these actions is to maintain value. The connection between the value of firms and trade policy is manifested in the stock market, which is a reflection of corporate values. As the value changes with shift changes in current and expected trade policy, and with the way in which management responds to trade policies, so do the prices in the stock market.

In Chapter 13 we move from the level of the single corporation to the level of the industry with Pugel's discussion of the semiconductor industry. This industry has been the subject of much action in international trade, culminating in the Arrangement Concerning Trade in Semiconductor Products of July 1986. This Arrangement was negotiated and signed in response to a decline in the demand for semiconductors in the world's markets, coupled with an increase in the Japanese proportion of the industry. Contrary to its intent, the Arrangement creates an incentive for circumvention, has an effect on the way in which business is conducted, and may even harm the United States industry it purports to help.

Johny Johansson's chapter examines the way in which corporations respond to changes in exchange rates, one of the major indirect outcomes of the trade situation. Trade policies, and associated exchange rate changes, have created a risky situation for the major Japanese exporters to the United States, and their responses are based on long-term strategic considerations, which seem to contradict the simplistic, short-term economic model which predicts a decrease in Japanese exports to the United States as the dollar depreciates against the yen.

Canto and Dietrich bring the same empirical argument to the level of the American economy as a whole. They do so by examining the behavior of share prices of United States firms that were the subject of protection. As in the semiconductor case, protection is associated with the business cycle. Whenever the United States experiences a recession, the probability of protectionistic policy increases. If the down cycle is restricted to a given industry, protectionistic action is even more likely.

The effects of current and expected trade policy, as well as the strategic and tactical responses of management, is traceable at all levels of economic activity. Trade policy figures importantly in the policy of single firms or industries, and in the business policy of the corporate sector as a whole. The three case histories presented and discussed in this part of the book are just one set of examples of what has become an economywide phenomenon.

13

Japanese and American Response to Trade Friction: The Semiconductor Industry

THOMAS A. PUGEL

Trade policy is a balance of many economic, political, moralistic, and organizational factors. It is generated and formulated in the political sector, but the only way to measure its real impact is to observe its effect on the business community. More specifically, because trade policy may impact individual industries in different manners, a useful way to examine the real effects of trade policy in a particular period is to look into the effects of trade policy on a particular industry. This is done in the following chapter.

The semiconductor industry has been the focus of much discussion pertaining to international trade. The general feeling in the United States is that this industry is of strategic importance to the United States and is threatened by Japanese competition based on "unfair" trade practices. This is also a case, like some others described in the Canto and Dietrich study, where trade policy, in both the United States and Japan, was brought to bear in an effort to correct the situation via a bilateral agreement. The Arrangement Concerning Trade in Semiconductor Products affects individual manufacturers in the United States and Japan, as well as the entire industry.

The trade arrangement was a response to two different factors affecting the semiconductor industry: the general condition of the world economy and the electronics industry, and the international structure of the semiconductor industry. The first factor determines, to a great extent, industry efforts to initiate protective measures; the second factor determines the form of protection. In other words, the initiation of protectionist measures by United States industry is directly related to the level of demand for its products in the global market. A decline in worldwide demand for semiconductors brings about an increased demand for protection. The nature of the protective measures, if and when they are put into effect, is determined to a great extent by the international composition of the industry—in this case by the well-being of the Japanese producers. In the future, as the Koreans, and maybe others, join the industry in a substantial way, the process will become multilateral rather than bilateral, as it has been in the period discussed in this chapter. Then, different considerations will enter into the picture.

The semiconductor industry is among the fastest growing and most technologically dynamic of all manufacturing industries. Semiconductors are key inputs into a variety of electronics products and other products whose electrical functions are defined or controlled by semiconductors.

United States firms have been dominant in the industry since its inception, but the competitiveness of Japanese firms has been rising. Trade friction between the United States and Japan has developed because of what United States firms and the United States government view as unfair practices and policies used by Japanese firms and the Japanese government to enhance Japanese competitiveness.

In 1985 these United States complaints became formal trade actions: three dumping cases and an investigation under Section 301 of possible unfair trade practices by the Japanese government. In July 1986 the United States and Japanese governments agreed to an Arrangement Concerning Trade in Semiconductor Products to resolve these complaints.

This chapter discusses the responses of Japanese and United States firms to the emergence of semiconductor trade friction, focusing on responses to the 1986 Arrangement. The first two sections describe important trends in the industry and the trade friction and Arrangement. The third section discusses responses by Japanese firms to their reduced ability to compete on the basis of price for export sales. The fourth section explores the impact of the Arrangement on the product strategies of United States firms. The fifth section analyzes responses to improve market penetration in Japan, and the sixth section discusses the impact of the Arrangement on international cooperative agreements. The final section provides conclusions regarding the responses of United States and Japanese firms to trade friction and the 1986 Arrangement.

TRENDS IN THE SEMICONDUCTOR INDUSTRY

The global value of production of semiconductors totaled almost $34 billion in 1986, excluding production by the Soviet bloc. The value of semiconductor production has grown by about 16 percent annually, on average, over the past quarter century, even as the price per unit of production has steadily declined. Industry production and sales also exhibit pronounced boom-and-bust cycles.

Until the 1980s, United States firms were predominant in the industry in terms of innovation and global sales. However, the competitiveness of Japanese firms has been rising since at least the mid-1970s, and Japanese firms are clearly challenging the United States predominance.[1] Table 13.1 shows production by firms based in the United States, Japan, Western Europe, and the rest of the world, for 1980, 1983, and 1986.[2] For each area, production is broken down into that of discrete devices such as transistors and diodes, the more mature and slower-growing segment of the industry, and that of integrated circuits (ICs), which include a number of active elements on a single chip. In addition, for the United States, two types of producers can be identified: merchant firms, those that produce semiconductors largely for sale

Table 13.1   Semiconductor Production, 1980, 1983, and 1986, in Millions of Dollars

Region and Product	Production[a]		
	1980	1983	1986
United States[b]	11,085	13,620	16,915
IC	9,055	11,475	14,675
Merchant	6,360	7,850	9,800
Captive	2,695	3,625	4,875
Discrete[c]	2,030	2,145	2,240
Japan	3,645	6,210	12,755
IC	2,290	4,420	9,555
Discrete	1,355	1,790	3,200
Western Europe	1,600	1,795	3,240
IC	710	1,040	1,790
Discrete	890	935	1,450
Rest of world[c]	315	430	975
IC	130	230	650
Discrete	185	200	325
Total	16,645	22,235	33,885
IC	12,185	17,1652	6,670
Discrete	4,460	5,070	7,215

[a] According to the home base of the producing firm, as categorized by the Integrated Circuit Engineering Corporation. Several United States firms owned by European firms are considered United States based.
[b] Includes Canada.
[c] Includes both merchant and captive production.
[d] Excludes the Soviet Union and Eastern Europe.
SOURCES: Adapted from Integrated Circuit Engineering Corporation (1982, 1985, 1987).

into the open market, and captive firms, those that produce mostly or solely for in-house consumption. All producers of any significance based outside the United States are considered merchant firms, even though they may consume part of their production in-house.

Table 13.1 clearly shows the relative decline of the United States-based firms and the rise of the Japanese. The United States share of world semiconductor production was about two thirds in 1980. This share fell to about three fifths in 1983 and to about one half in 1986. During this same period the Japanese share of world semiconductor production rose from a little more than one fifth to almost two fifths. For ICs only, the United States share of world production fell from about three fourths in 1980 to about two thirds in 1983 and to a little more than one half in 1986, while the share of Japanese firms rose from a little less than one fifth to over one third during the same period. If captive production of ICs by United States-based firms such as IBM and AT&T is excluded, the value of IC production by United States-based merchant firms was almost three times that of Japanese firms in 1980, but the two were almost equal in 1986. Japan is also increasingly important as a market for semiconductor sales: in 1986 the size of the Japanese market surpassed that of the United States for the first time.

Japanese firms have made particularly strong gains in the merchant market for one general type of IC—MOS memory ICs—which include dynamic random-access memory (DRAM) ICs, static random-access memory (SRAM) ICs, and erasable, programmable read-only memory (EPROM) ICs as its major products. In 1980 United States firms accounted for 73 percent of global sales of MOS memory ICs, but this share fell to 33 percent in 1986. The share of Japanese firms rose from 26 percent to 58 percent during this same period.[3] Within this general product area, DRAMs have received particular attention. Japanese firms achieved a share of about 40 percent of the world merchant market for 16K DRAMs in the late 1970s; a share of about 60 percent for the next generation, the 64K DRAMs, in the early 1980s; and a share of about 80–90 percent for 256K DRAMs in the mid-1980s. The share of Japanese firms in the emerging market for 1M DRAMs is expected to be about 80–90 percent.

The rising competitiveness of Japanese firms can also be seen in bilateral data. The United States had a semiconductor trade surplus with Japan through 1979. In 1980 a small deficit of $11 million emerged, and this deficit grew to $834 million in 1984, a boom year. The deficit has since shrunk to $350 million in 1986 as the industry experienced a serious recession.[4] The United States share of Japanese semiconductor consumption has been rather steady since at least the mid-1970s, averaging a little more than 10 percent. The United States share of Japanese IC consumption has also been rather steady, averaging a little over 15 percent during this same period. In contrast, the Japanese share of United States IC consumption has risen from about 1 percent in 1976 to almsot 10 percent (if captive consumption of captive production is included in the denominator) or about 15 percent (if captive production–consumption is excluded) in 1986.[5]

These trends in production, trade, and market shares are imbedded within broader trends that are influencing competition in the industry. The most important general trend is the continuously rising complexity of ICs. The number of active elements on the most advanced chips has approximately doubled each year since the invention of the IC. Rising complexity has a number of important implications for the industry, implications that have had an impact on trade friction in the industry.

First, the rising complexity of ICs has increased the cost and difficulty of designing new ICs. Rising costs of research and development have increased concerns over the ability to achieve returns on these investments. Second, rising complexity has increased the cost of production facilities, because increasingly precise equipment must be used, and increasingly pure or clean environments must be established for production. These first two implications together create rising capital requirements to enter or remain in the industry.

Third, rising complexity has increased the challenge of mastering advanced techniques to produce the most complex ICs. In production, learning economies are achieved by making small, trial-and-error adjustments to the production process, in order to improve the yields of usable chips and thus lower unit costs. Increasingly, these learning economies are apparently best achieved using mass production of standard chips of relatively straightforward design, especially MOS memory ICs.

Fourth, rising complexity implies that the functions of electronic systems and systems products are increasingly determined by one or a small set of advanced ICs. Thus, coordination between systems design and chip design is increasingly important, because the chip design increasingly determines the functioning and differentiation of the systems product. Such coordination can be enhanced in a number of ways. One is through vertical integration. Another is through improvement in interactions between the semiconductor producer and the customer buying the semiconductors and producing the systems product. This could simply involve more attention to customer interactions and technical services offered by the semiconductor firm, but it increasingly involves various forms of contractual ties, including technology development contracts, joint development efforts, and minority equity ownership positions.

Another aspect of complexity in the semiconductor industry deserves mention—complexity of business strategy and the diversity of strategies that appear to be viable in the industry. Strategies can and do vary along such dimensions as the breadth of products produced; the relative emphasis on low-cost production of standard products, on production of proprietary products, or on production of custom or semicustom products; the orientation of research and development (or technology strategy); and the extent of vertical integration with systems products. Japanese firms are often characterized as following a strategy of low-cost mass production of standard commodity products, although differences in strategies are also evident if Japanese firms are examined closely.[6] United States firms are characterized as following a diverse set of strategies but often emphasizing innovations in design.[7]

SEMICONDUCTOR TRADE FRICTION AND THE TRADE ARRANGEMENT

As the share of Japanese firms in global and United States semiconductor sales has risen, United States semiconductor firms and the United States government have periodically voiced complaints about the practices and policies of Japanese semiconductor firms and the Japanese government. However, no formal actions had been instituted prior to 1985. Indeed, 1984 was a boom year for the semiconductor industry, and firms spent most of their energies attempting to meet demand. However, the boom ended in late 1984, and a serious industry recession began, one from which the industry recovered only in 1987.

The extent of the recession became evident in early 1985, as sales, prices, and profits declined severely. United States complaints about Japanese practices and policies resumed, and in June 1985 such complaints culminated in formal trade actions against Japan.[8] In June the first of three suits alleging dumping of

Japanese semiconductor exports was filed. These three dumping cases covered 64K DRAMs, 256K and 1M DRAMs, and EPROMs. Also in June 1985, the Semiconductor Industry Association (SIA), the trade association of United States semiconductor producers, filed a petition requesting that the United States government investigate allegedly unfair trade practices by the Japanese government, under Section 301 of the 1974 Trade Act, as amended in 1984. The SIA charged the Japanese government with encouraging practices in Japan to deny United States firms access to the Japanese semiconductor market, and encouraging or condoning conditions that led to chronic dumping of Japanese semiconductors in the United States market.

Dumping is defined under United States law as selling imports into the United States market at a price that is less than fair market value, where fair market value is either the price in the home (or third-country) market or fully allocated unit cost plus a profit margin. All three dumping cases were investigated under the cost definition of fair market value. Dumping violates United States law if it exists and if it causes injury to United States industry. All preliminary findings in these three cases concluded that dumping and injury were occurring, and in April to May 1986, final determinations in the 46K DRAM case resulted in the imposition of antidumping duties of 12–35 percent on imports from various Japanese producers.

In a Section 301 case, United States trade law requires government-to-government negotiations simultaneous with the investigation of the existence and importance of the alleged unfair trade practices. Most of the United States government action with respect to the Section 301 semiconductor case focused on these negotiations. Little progress was made until early in 1986, when it became clear that the decisions in the dumping cases would go against the Japanese firms. In May 1986 a preliminary agreement was reached between the United States and Japanese governments to resolve both the Section 301 case and the two remaining dumping cases. Serious differences then developed over the details of the agreement. Under pressure of deadlines for the completion of all three investigations, the two governments concluded the Arrangement Concerning Trade in Semiconductor Products in late July 1986.[9]

The Arrangement provides for governmental actions to prevent dumping of semiconductors by Japanese producers and to improve foreign access to the Japanese semiconductor market. The Section 301 investigation and the two unresolved dumping cases were suspended, although the United States government reserved the right to reopen these cases, and possibly to take other punitive actions, if the Japanese government fails to adhere to the Arrangement. The Arrangement is effective for 5 years—to July 31, 1991.

Several mechanisms were created by the Arrangement to prevent dumping. For products covered by the suspended dumping suits, Japanese producers on a quarterly basis provide cost data to the United States Department of Commerce, which calculates fair market values for each firm for each product, informs each firm of its values, and monitors the prices of exports to the United States. For a number of other semiconductor products, the Japanese producers quarterly provide cost data to the Japan Ministry of International Trade and

Industry (MITI), which uses the United States formula to calculate fair market values for each firm for each product, informs each firm of its values, and monitors the prices of exports of these products to the United States. On all of these products MITI is also required to monitor the prices of exports to third countries to prevent dumping in these markets.

To improve access to the Japanese market, the Japanese government agreed to encourage the purchase of more foreign semiconductors by Japanese buyers and to set up a government organization to promote such sales. Apparently, an understanding also exists that the United States share of the Japanese market should approximately double to 20 percent by 1991.

SEMICONDUCTOR SALES BY JAPANESE FIRMS

Under the terms of the 1986 Arrangement, the United States and Japanese governments undertake to prevent export sales by Japanese firms at prices less than fair market value, as defined by the United States antidumping law. Such monitoring is to apply to any export to any country, not only on exports to the United States. The Arrangement thus potentially constrains the ability of Japanese firms to compete for sales outside of Japan, by requiring any sales to carry prices that cover the full unit cost of production and yield an 8 percent profit margin. Furthermore, the fair market values are calculated for each company and for each product, and they are revised only quarterly. Thus, firms judged to be high-cost producers will have an especially difficult time in competing for sales outside of Japan. For instance, the initial determination by the United States Department of Commerce assigned the lowest fair market values for 256K DRAMs to NEC and Toshiba. These companies were able to maintain or expand their exports to the United States for this product, while other Japanese producers saw their legitimate exports decline to low levels.

A number of responses by Japanese firms to this aspect of the Arrangement are possible. First, Japanese firms could accept the decline in export volume but derive benefits from the higher prices and profit margins on this smaller volume. Second, the firms could seek ways to circumvent the Arrangement and maintain price competition in order to minimize the loss of export volume. Foreign buyers want to purchase at the lowest possible price, so they are likely to support such efforts at circumvention. However, the United States government is likely to complain that such circumvention is a violation of the Arrangement. Third, the firms could shift production out of Japan, so that their sales to the United States and third-country markets would not be covered by the pricing rules of the Arrangement.

Circumvention

The initial Japanese response to the pricing rules of the Arrangement was apparently to ignore them, at least for exports to countries other than the United States. United States firms and the United States government quickly became aware of this failure to enforce the Arrangement, however, and complained to the Japanese government. In November 1986, MITI responded to these complaints by issuing guidance on pricing to Japanese firms and by tightening up on the issuance of export licenses. At the same time, Japanese firms and the Japanese government complained that the Arrangement allowed United States and other (e.g., Korean) firms to undercut Japanese firms' prices for sales outside of Japan.

Perhaps the major development in response to the efforts to enforce this part of the Arrangement was the emergence of a substantial gray market in Japanese ICs. The initial incentive for the gray market comes from the fact that the Arrangement does not set prices for Japanese ICs within Japan. Pricing within Japan remains competitive and below the fair market values for many products. Indeed, to the extent that the Arrangement reduces legitimate exports from Japan, some supply is shifted to Japanese sales, further widening the price difference.

Various methods were developed to utilize the gray market. Intermediaries may purchase ICs in Japan and apply for an export license that includes a phony invoice for sales at fair market value, or such export sales may occur at what appears to be fair market value, but a rebate is then granted to the foreign purchaser. Exports may also occur without an export license, since tens of thousands of chips fit into a suitcase. Many of these gray market ICs are bound for consumers in third countries, but a substantial number are imported into the United States. One method to import into the United States is again in suitcases. Penalties for such "smuggling," if detected, are apparently minor, perhaps because there is no duty on semiconductor imports. Another is to assemble the ICs onto phony circuit boards and export these boards to the United States, where they are disassembled. Such boards are not covered by the Arrangement. The existence of this gray market is evident in the availability of Japanese 256K DRAMs for prices of $1.60 to $1.80 in Taiwan in early 1987, when the fair market value was about $2.50.[10]

The extent to which the Japanese firms themselves actively used or promoted the gray market is unclear, but it is clear that they benefited from the ability to continue to compete on the basis of price for export sales. Only one case of a direct sale by a Japanese firm at less than fair market value has been reported, a sale by Oki to Hong Kong at a price that might be more than a third below Oki's fair market value for the product. An interesting side note is that in February 1987 NEC lost a court suit in the United States seeking to block sales of gray market ICs by an unauthorized United States importer–distributor.

The initial response of MITI to United States complaints about the existence of this gray market was to deny its existence. However, by early 1987 even MITI recognized its existence—it was reported that a MITI survey concluded that 20–30 percent of Japanese exports to third countries were being made at less than fair market values, with a substantial portion of these ultimately destined for the United States.[11] In the face of continued complaints from the United States, MITI attempted to further restrict the issuance of export licenses and also took steps to reduce the incentive for gray market exports. In February

1987 MITI issued administrative guidance to Japanese producers to reduce output of certain semiconductors, most importantly 256K DRAMs and EPROMs, by an average of 10 percent from the fourth quarter of 1986 to the first quarter of 1987. The guidance was in the form of a revision of the "semiconductor production forecast." The actual reduction in production seems to have been about 23 percent. In March 1987, MITI offered further guidance in the form of a forecast that overall semiconductor production should decline by 11 percent from the first to the second quarter, with 256K DRAMs to decline by 32 percent. In June, MITI's guidance suggested increases in third-quarter production of 10 percent for 256K DRAMs and EPROMs. Nonetheless, production of 256K DRAMs would still be 24 percent below its peak in the fourth quarter of 1986.

The stated goal of this guidance has been to firm up prices in Japan and reduce the incentive for gray market exports, thereby more closely meeting the goals of the Arrangement. Evidence from Taiwan suggests that the policy had some effect rather quickly—gray market chips were not so plentiful or so cheap in March as they had been previously. However, MITI may also have had other purposes in adopting the approach of administrative guidance for production cuts. Japanese firms were taking heavy losses in their semiconductor divisions, and they accumulated very large inventories of unsold chips, especially of 256K DRAMs. Thus, MITI may have used the Arrangement as a pretext for organizing an informal "recession cartel" to benefit the Japanese producers. In any case production of 256K DRAMs would have declined, because Japanese firms were shifting to production of 1M DRAMs, the next generation of this product.

Sanctions

As noted already, by early 1987 the United States government concluded that the Arrangement was not having its intended effects to prevent dumping, especially for exports to third countries. A study by the United States Department of Commerce concluded that Japanese exports of DRAMs and EPROMs to third countries occurred at an average of about 40 percent below fair market values during February. In March both houses of Congress unanimously passed resolutions favoring sanctions against Japan for failing to abide by the Arrangement. Later in March, President Reagan announced the possibility of temporary sanctions against Japan, in the form of higher tariffs on some United States imports from Japan. The products affected were to be chosen from a list of 19 possible categories. The criteria for selecting the products affected were (1) to minimize the harm to United States consumers by choosing products in which the Japanese had a small share of the United States market for the product, and (2) to choose products exported especially by the six largest Japanese semiconductor producers. By the first criterion semiconductors themselves were not a possible target.

In April President Reagan announced punitive tariffs of 100 percent on 16-bit laptop and desktop computers; 18-, 19-, and 20-inch color television sets; and certain power handtools, effectively stopping their import from Japan. The total value of imports affected was $300 million, equal to the estimated losses to United States semiconductor firms from Japanese failure to enforce the Arrangement. Of this $300 million, $135 million was the estimated loss from continued Japanese dumping, and $165 million was the estimated loss from the lack of improvement in access to the Japanese market.

In the next months, the extent of dumping of Japanese exports of semiconductors declined substantially. In June, citing reductions in the dumping of DRAMs, President Reagan ended the tariff sanctions on 20-inch color TVs, representing $51 million of affected imports. In early November, the United States government concluded that all Japanese dumping was essentially ended. President Reagan lifted the tariff sanctions on certain low-performance desktop computers, the other color TVs, and most of the power handtools, representing about $84 million more of affected imports. Tariff sanctions on about $165 million of Japanese exports, mostly laptop and other desktop computers, remained in effect because of lack of improvement in the United States share of the Japanese semiconductor market (see the last section of this chapter for additional discussion of this issue).

Thus, the circumvention of the antidumping provisions of the Arrangement induced the United States government to apply tariff sanctions on certain Japanese exports to the United States. As the dumping was ended, the sanctions were removed. However, it is not clear that the sanctions resulted in substantially more effective enforcement by MITI of these provisions. Rather, the general recovery of global demand for semiconductors during 1987, by firming prices through rising demand, was probably the most important force in the ending of Japanese dumping.

Shifting the Location of Production

A second major area of response by Japanese firms to the effects of the Arrangement on their ability to make sales outside of Japan has been to shift production out of Japan. In contrast to the first response, the development of a gray market, which involved evasion of the terms of the Arrangement, this second response may largely involve avoidance and thus not violate the terms of the Arrangement.

One shift is in the location of assembly of chips fabricated in Japan. Exports of unassembled chips are subject to fair market values, but these are lower than those for fully assembled ICs. Furthermore, pricing of the unassembled chips exported to assembly affiliates is rather arbitrary, as this is merely a transfer price on intrafirm trade. Once the assembled ICs are sold by the assembly affiliate, it is more difficult for the Japanese or United States government to monitor the price or determine whether the ultimate sale is at fair market value, especially for sales to countries other than the United States. NEC reportedly expanded its assembly of 256K DRAMs in Malaysia, Singapore, and the United Kingdom, with a substantial part of the increase then exported to the United States. Hitachi and Toshiba are also reported to have expanded assembly of

256K DRAMs in Malaysia, and Matsushita to have expanded its assembly of ICs in Singapore, for export to the United States and Europe.

Full production within the United States by Japanese firms is not covered by the pricing rules of the Arrangement, and United States assembly of chips fabricated in Japan places the company in a different category of fair market values, as discussed earlier. Prior to the rise of semiconductor trade friction in 1985, a number of Japanese firms had established or were constructing production facilities in the United States. A recent study of this foreign direct investment characterized the approach taken by the Japanese firms as rather cautious and conservative.[12] Thus, as of 1985 only two Japanese firms had full-

Table 13.2 Foreign Direct Investment by Japanese Semiconductor Firms in United States Production Facilities

| Japanese Firm | FDI as of 1985 | | Developments Since 1985 |
	Year Established	Information	
NEC	1978	Acquisition of Electronic Arrays for $9 million. Facilities previously used for production of memory ICs, now used only for assembly of ICs	
	1984	Large, highly automated plant for full production of memory ICs, gate arrays, and microprocessors	Expansion planned
Hitachi	1978	Assembly of memory ICs	Establishment of full production of ICs by 1987
Toshiba	1980	Acquisition of Maruman IC. Full production of gate arrays and assembly of memory ICs and microprocessors	Expansion of full production planned
Fujitsu	1980 1984	Assembly of memory ICs Construction of a plant for full production announced, then postponed in 1985	Proposed acquisition of 80% of Fairchild in 1986, then withdrew offer in 1987. Subsequently, revived plan for construction of plant for full production, with IC production expected to begin in late 1988
Mitsubishi	1985	Assembly of DRAMs	Expanding assembly facility. Considering expansion to full production
Oki	1985	Assembly of DRAMs and gate arrays	Planning full production by 1989
Matsushita	—	—	Planning full production by 1989

SOURCES: Adapted from Integrated Circuit Engineering Corporation (1987) and Yano Research Institute (1984).

production (fabrication and assembly) facilities in the United States, and only one of these, NEC, was of substantial size. Four others had or were completing assembly facilities. Table 13.2 shows the facilities of these companies and the year of establishment.

Table 13.2 also shows developments since the trade friction became severe. A number of incentives for United States production by Japanese firms can be identified. Full production in the United States would permit pricing without regard to the fair market values set by the Arrangement. This would be of particular benefit to firms whose values have been set at levels higher than those of their competitors. The strengthening of the yen also favors shifting production into the United States. However, a number of disincentives also exist. Japanese firms are concerned about their ability to manage United States workers and achieve yields and quality levels comparable to those in Japan. In addition, the effectiveness of the Arrangement (or any successor policy) appears uncertain. Furthermore, the expansion of capacity with a de novo investment would exacerbate the problem of low-capacity utilization rates in the industry.

As shown in Table 13.2, the approach taken by Japanese firms to foreign direct investment in the United States continues for the most part to be cautious. NEC is reported to have doubled production of 256K DRAMs in the United States in 1986 and plans to expand its DRAM production capacity. Hitachi is expected to have full-production capacity ready in 1987, although planning for this predates the severe trade friction. Toshiba has announced plans to expand its United States production facilities. Mitsubishi is expanding its assembly of DRAMs and considering the establishment of full production. Oki and Matsushita have announced plans to establish full production by 1989.

By far the most interesting development in this area, and one that was decidedly not cautious, involves Fujitsu. Of the four largest Japanese semiconductor producers, Fujitsu had the smallest presence in United States production by 1985. In 1984 Fujitsu announced plans to build a full-production facility in Oregon, but the industry recession starting in late 1984 led Fujitsu to postpone construction of this facility. When the first set of fair market values was issued by the United States Department of Commerce for 256K DRAMs in 1986, the value for Fujitsu was more than triple that of the lowest values for some of the other firms, and Fujitsu recognized that it had a serious problem.

Based on negotiations initiated by Fairchild, Fujitsu announced an offer to acquire 80 percent of Fairchild, a company usually considered a United States semiconductor producer, although it had been acquired by Schlumberger, the French oil exploration company, in 1979. Fairchild has been plagued by losses and technological problems, especially in the production of MOS ICs, since before the 1979 acquisition. Fujitsu apparently offered to pay between $200 million and $250 million for this 80 percent ownership share. The Fairchild management was to receive responsibility for Fujitsu production and sales of semiconductors in the United States and Europe. Fujitsu would receive access to Fairchild's production facilities and its extensive United States sales and distribution network, a network of a sort that no other Japanese firm has yet developed. Fujitsu also would receive access to Fairchild technology, especially in the areas of bipolar logic ICs and microprocessors, although it is debatable how much Fujitsu would actually benefit from this, given that its own technology, including bipolar logic, is generally very good.

The announcement of this proposed acquisition set off substantial discussion in the United States. Some simply accused Japanese firms of weakening United States semiconductor firms and then planning to buy them at distress prices, even though Fairchild's problems were of long standing. Some others seemed most concerned that the merged Fujitsu–Fairchild would be a formidable competitor, combining Fujitsu's technology and products with Fairchild's distribution capabilities. Much of the discussion, however, focused on the implications for national security, given that Fairchild was a supplier of advanced ICs for defense electronics systems. The dangers of having such a supplier owned by a Japanese firm were pointed out, although others noted that Fairchild was already owned by a foreign firm and that the ICs supplied by Fairchild were not that important in any case. Nonetheless, the discussion continued, and it became clear that the Secretaries of Defense and Commerce both opposed and sale. Although no obvious law exists to oppose the acquisition, conditions such as the revoking of defense contracts could be used to discourage it. Others in the United States government favored allowing the sale, and the eventual outcome in terms of the United States government position never became clear. At the same time, an investigation of the antitrust implications of the acquisition was proceeding, but no major problems were expected.

As a result of the public discussion and the opposition voiced by various government officials, Fujitsu decided in March 1987 to withdraw its offer. This experience is likely to discourage other Japanese semiconductor firms from seeking acquisitions in the United States.

In August 1987 Fujitsu revived its plan to build a full production facility in Oregon. Production is expected to commence in late 1988 at the earliest, but in the meantime Fujitsu is without a major production presence in the United States. In October 1987 National Semiconductor purchased Fairchild for $122 million, thus becoming the third largest United States merchant producer.

PRODUCT STRATEGIES OF UNITED STATES FIRMS

A major aspect of the investigation of dumping is the demonstration of injury to United States industry. Much of the discussion of the injury done by Japanese dumping of semiconductors has focused on memory ICs. United States firms alleged that Japanese firms were driving them out of these commodity products, with injury resulting through several channels. United States firms lost returns on their investments in developing and producing these chips, but more importantly, United States firms lost economies of scope derived from producing these chips. High-volume memory ICs are considered "technology process drivers"—production of these chips can be used to quickly master advances and refinements in production process technology that can then be applied to other, often lower volume ICs.

A major issue concerning the effects and effectiveness of the Arrangement is, then, the extent to which United States firms have reentered into production of these commodity memory chips, or at least not abandoned production of them. A discussion of this issue also requires consideration of broader trends in the product strategies adopted by United States firms, and it leads into a discussion of the proposed consortium of United States firms to advance and diffuse production process technology.

Memory ICs

In 1985 and 1986 four major United States firms—Intel, Motorola, National Semiconductor, and AMD—stopped production of 256K DRAMs, in the face of falling demand and plummeting prices. A major focus of two of the dumping suits and the 1986 Arrangement has been to end Japanese dumping of DRAMs and permit continued United States production of these ICs. Yet through mid-1987, no United States firm announced reentry into such production following the implementation of the Arrangement. The four United States firms that were producing DRAMs in mid-1986 were still the only United States firms doing so. One of these, TI, produces DRAMs in both the United States and Japan, and its exports from Japan are actually covered by the Arrangement. TI has explicitly stated that it plans to remain in the production of DRAMs because of the scope economies of producing this type of product. Another United States producer of DRAMs, Micron Technology, also continues to produce DRAMs, although it is in a precarious financial condition. Micron Technology specializes almost completely in the production of DRAMs, so it gains almost no scope economies from this production. The other two United States producers of DRAMs, IBM and AT&T, produce solely for in-house use. AT&T has expressed interest in open-market sales, but it has not been able to expand production fast enough to generate a surplus beyond its own requirements, and in any case its marketing capabilities for such sales appear to be weak.

Thus, with respect to the production of DRAMs, the responses by United States firms suggest that the Arrangement has had little effect on or benefit to the United States economy. Three of the four United States producers of DRAMs—TI, IBM, and AT&T—presumably would have continued production of DRAMs, with or without the Arrangement. The other United States producer, Micron Technology, may have remained in production because of the Arrangement, but it derives none of the scope economies that figured so prominently in the discussion of injury.

The clearest response by a United States firm in this area has been the agreement between Motorola and Toshiba, under which Motorola purchases unassembled DRAM chips produced by Toshiba in Japan, ships them for assembly in Malaysia, and then markets the assembled DRAMs under the Motorola name. Some United States firms have charged that this is largely a method for Toshiba to circumvent the pricing rules of the Arrangement.

Two other types of memory ICs, EPROMs and SRAMs, also can be used as process drivers. EPROMs were the focus of one dumping suit, and both of these types of memory ICs are covered by the antidumping provisions of the Arrangement. Only one "United States" firm, Signetics, has announced entry or reentry into these product areas, through a program to develop and produce a 256K CMOS EPROM. However, Signetics is actually owned by Philips, the Dutch electronics company. Other United States firms have remained in the production of these products. Intel and Motorola use both EPROMs and SRAMs as process drivers, AMD uses EPROMs, and Fairchild has used SRAMs. Given the importance of having a technology driver, it seems likely that these firms would have remained in production of these memory ICs without the Arrangement, so the Arrangement may have had little impact on United States production of these products as well. National Semiconductor has apparently been using the production of gate arrays and logic ICs as process drivers rather than reenter into production of memory ICs.

There may be several reasons why United States firms have not entered or reentered into the production of memory ICs. First, the cost of doing so is rather high. Designing the most advanced memory chips and determining the appropriate production processes costs tens of millions of dollars, and the cost of a single production facility for mass fabrication of these ICs is approaching $200 million. Given the uncertainties of the effects of the Arrangement and the poor financial condition of many United States merchant semiconductor firms, none of them has been willing to undertake the necessary investment.

Second, such entry into commodity memory ICs runs counter to general product trends in the industry. The cost of designing custom or semicustom chips, called application-specific ICs (ASICs), has been declining because of advances in computer design automation. ASICs accounted for 9 percent of the worldwide merchant IC market in 1983, and this share had grown to 14 percent by 1986. Many forecasts suggest that the share will grow to over 20 percent by 1990.[13] Most United States firms, including major firms, smaller producers, and new entrants, are focusing attention on this part of the market. Process technology is of importance in implementing a strategy of emphasizing ASICs, and process drivers can be used to master advanced production process techniques. However, other process technology may be at least as important— the ability to produce limited runs of specific products with the flexibility to shift production quickly and smoothly between product types. Process drivers do not contribute to the mastery of this flexibility.

Close customer relations are another major requirement of effective implementation of this product strategy. Such relations are of much less importance in marketing commodity memory IC. United States firms are responding to the challenge of customer relations in a variety of innovative ways. TI is seeking long-term contracts and guaranteeing just-in-time delivery. National Semiconductor and Xerox have entered into a long-term relationship to share proprietary information about the development of Xerox's systems products and the corresponding development of proprietery ICs to enhance the differentiation of Xerox's products. Intel and IBM, which has been purchasing 15–20 percent of Intel's semiconductor output (and until 1987 owned 20 percent of Intel), have entered into an extensive agreement to exchange technologies and production rights. Intel gains access to IBM's ASIC designs in both gate arrays and standard cells, to IBM's system for computer design of these types of ASICs, and to some of IBM's technology for the manufacture of these ASICs. IBM gains access to Intel's microprocessor and related design technology, with the right to use and modify this technology to create proprietary IBM chips that may be more resistant to cloning, as well as to Intel's ASIC designs.

Thus, an important trend in the industry is toward greater differentiation of IC products. The antidumping provisions of the 1986 Arrangement, with their emphasis on commodity and standardized products, can be viewed as a diversion. However, the Arrangement, by reducing the ability of Japanese firms to compete for the commodity business, may spur Japanese firms to shift their own emphasis toward more differentiated products more quickly. Such an effect would then ultimately increase, rather than muffle, the degree of competition from Japanese firms felt by United States semiconductor firms.

Consortium

Although United States firms have not individually entered or reentered into the production of advanced memory ICs that can be used as process drivers, they continue to express concerns that their production technology is falling behind that of the Japanese firms. In 1986 informal discussion began of a cooperative effort among United States firms to enhance their production process capabilities.

In February 1987 the Defense Science Board, a group of scientists and business people acting as advisors to the Pentagon, issued a report supporting large-scale government funding of such a cooperative effort. The report notes that United States firms lag behind Japanese firms in a number of areas of semiconductor technology and that the United States lead in other areas is generally shrinking. The Board views this as unacceptable to the national security, and recommends a number of actions by the United States government. The report supports the establishment of a cooperative to focus on research into semiconductor manufacturing technology. The United States government should support such an effort through funding by the Department of Defense of about half of its cost, up to $200 million per year for 5 years, and through an antitrust exemption for its activities. The report also recommends a parallel program on chip design involving a number of universities, with funding by the Department of Defense of about $500 million over 5 years. The overall goal of these programs would be to regain the lead in many areas of semiconductor technology, especially in the cost and quality achieved by United States production.

In March 1987 the SIA approved the formation of the Semiconductor Manufacturing Technology Institute, known as Sematech. Sematech is aimed to develop state-of-the-art production techniques for member companies for use in their own production operations.[14] Discussion within the SIA focused largely on the breadth of the proposed consortium. Some firms, most notably Intel, favored a venture to mass-produce at least one product, in order to develop the full experience benefits with the advanced production techniques. Other companies, including IBM and TI, favored a venture that would focus on research and development, with only low-volume production of prototype products. They argued that such an approach would involve lower cost and could be geared up faster, and that such an approach was much less likely to face problems with the antitrust laws. In addition, IBM feared that it might be forced to purchase much of the output from a high-volume operation, regardless of its cost or quality, while TI feared that high-volume production of DRAMs, the most likely product to be produced by the consortium, would compete with its own DRAM production. The SIA finally decided to approve a nonprofit consortium focusing on research, development, and low-volume production.

Planning the details of the operation of Sematech continued through 1987. It is expected to have an annula budget of about $250 million per year for 6 years. The SIA hopes that government funding, mostly from the Department of Defense, will cover about half of the budget. By mid-1987, 16 United States firms had committed about 80 percent of the money to cover the industry half of the budget. Members of the consortium include merchant firms such as TI, Motorola, National Semiconductor, Intel, and AMD and captive producers such as IBM, DEC, and Hewlett-Packard.

The involvement of IBM in the consortium is viewed by many as a key to its success. IBM may contribute the product design, perhaps a 4M or 16M DRAM, on which the consortium focuses its production efforts. IBM may also contribute some of its production expertise. Such involvement by IBM, which has been very protective of its semiconductor technology in the past, suggests that IBM has concerns about the trends in United States semiconductor capabilities. IBM is the world's largest buyer of semiconductors on the open market as well as the world's largest producer (solely for in-house consumption). IBM is apparently concerned that the decline of United States merchant firms would force IBM to purchase more ICs from Japanese firms that also compete with IBM in many systems products.[15] IBM is also concerned that United States firms producing semiconductor manufacturing equipment and pure materials are also declining, again forcing it to turn to Japanese firms for such equipment and materials. IBM thus appears to believe that the transfer of some of its technology to outside firms is a reasonable price to pay for the strengthening of these supplier industries in the United States.

It is possible to view the creation of this consortium as a response to the 1986 Arrangement, in that the consortium is a response to the failure of the Arrangement to induce United States firms to enter or reenter into the manufacture of memory ICs independently. Nonetheless, a number of questions exist about the likely ability of the consortium to achieve its objectives. First, government funding is not assured, and such funding is likely to be politically controversial. Second, government funding, if it is granted, will be channeled largely through the Department of Defense. Conflict could develop over the direction of research undertaken, with the Department of Defense emphasizing defense objectives and the firms emphasizing commercial objectives. Third, the member firms will also need to contribute research personnel to the consortium. Each will have some incentive to "free-ride," by withholding their best personnel. Fourth, and perhaps most important, it may prove to be difficult to transfer any manufacturing technology developed by the consortium back to the member firms. Semiconductor manufacturing is exacting and idiosyncratic. Firms often run into serious problems transferring technology even intrafirm from one plant to another.

SALES OF UNITED STATES SEMICONDUCTORS IN JAPAN

The second major aspect of the 1986 Arrangement is the encouragement by the Japanese government of Japanese purchases of foreign semiconductors. Although it is not part of the written agreement, a goal of a United States share of the Japanese semiconductor market of 20 percent by 1991 appears to exist.

Responses by both Japanese firms and United States firms are relevant to an analysis of this aspect of the Arrangement. In Japan, the major semiconductor producers are also among the major semiconductor buyers and consumers. They are large producers of electronic systems products, but their actual level of internal integration is generally moderate. Thus, the same Japanese firms that are affected by the antidumping provisions of the Arrangement are also affected by its market access provisions.

Japanese firms have stated that they purchase rather modest amounts of semiconductors from United States firms because of problems of relying on United States firms as suppliers. United States products are viewed to be of lower quality and reliability, and United States firms are viewed as less responsive to customer needs and as offering less technical and sales service. United States firms dispute the validity of these criticisms. United States firms instead charge that a form of collusion has developed to exclude outsiders, although they offer no clear evidence of such collusion.

To the extent that it is negative perceptions of United States semiconductor firms (or even distrust of foreigners in general) that limit sales of United States semiconductors in Japan, much of the response to overcome these problems must come from United States firms willing to invest in order to develop sales in Japan. One problem for United States firms attempting to sell semiconductors in Japan is their lack of production facilities in Japan. Japanese buyers cite this lack as a contributor to concerns over delivery delays and the lack of responsiveness to buyer requests. As shown in Table 13.3, only two United States firms, TI and Motorola, had full-production facilities in Japan by 1985, while two other firms had assembly facilities for ICs. Since the trade friction became severe, no other United States firm has announced plans to develop its own production facilities in Japan, although a number of joint ventures have

Table 13.3 Foreign Direct Investment by United States Semiconductor Firms in Japanese Production Facilities

United States Firm	FDI as of 1985		Developments Since 1985
	Year Established	Information	
Texas Instruments	1968	Three plants fabricate MOS and bipolar ICs	Expansion planned
Motorola	1980	Acquired 50% of Aizu Toko to establish a joint venture to produce MOS ICs. Raised share to 100% in 1982	Construction of a second plant
Analog Devices	1980	Assembly and testing of bipolar ICs	—
Fairchild	1984	Assembly and testing bipolar ICs	Construction of a full production plant for MOS ICs completed by 1987. This new plant was not sold to National Semiconductor in its acquisition of Fairchild. Instead, it is offered for sale to a separate buyer.

See also Table 13.4 for major joint ventures and similar cooperative agreements established since 1985.

SOURCES: Adapted from Integrated Circuit Engineering Corporation (1987), Organization for Economic Cooperation and Development (1985), and Yano Research Institute (1984).

been announced, as discussed in the next section. As shown in Table 13.3, three of the four United States firms already in Japan are expanding their facilities. In comparison with foreign direct investment by United States semiconductor firms in Europe, where these firms continue to compete successfully for sales, direct investment in Japan is remarkably small.

Another form of investment that is needed in Japan is marketing to reverse the perception of low United States quality, if, as United States firms claim, quality differences are not actually that large. AMD is establishing a quality assurance center in Japan and also plans to add an IC design center. Motorola and Signetics have announced "zero defect warranty" programs for some of their customers, but it is not clear to what extent these apply to Japanese buyers.

Another strategy that might be used to boost sales in Japan is the maintenance of proprietary product technology. For instance, in the past Intel and Motorola have been relatively liberal in licensing their microprocessor designs to Japanese and other firms. While they receive returns from licensing, they do not gain the sales revenues earned by these second sources. It appears that Intel and Motorola will not be so liberal in licensing their designs for 32-bit microprocessors, the most advanced currently available. Recent laws enacted to protect IC circuit designs and court rulings in the United States extending copyright protection to microcode instructions etched onto the microprocessor chips should enhance their ability to protect their proprietary designs. At least in the short run, this strategy should lead to additional sales of United States ICs in Japan. A danger of the strategy in the longer term is that it is also providing an additional incentive for several Japanese firms to attempt to develop their own designs for these microprocessors.

By early 1987, United States firms and the United States government were complaining that the United States share of the Japanese semiconductor market had not risen. The Japanese government responded that it was too soon to see much increase. In addition, semiconductor prices in Japan were depressed by the antidumping provisions of the Arrangement, making sales by United States firms more difficult. In March 1987 MITI set up an organization to encourage Japanese purchases of foreign semiconductors—the International Semiconductor Cooperation Center in Tokyo. Ten Japanese semiconductor producer–buyers and one French firm, Thomson, joined, but no United States firm did so immediately. United States firms indicated that they could not justify the cost of joining, since the Center largely duplicated their own marketing efforts, although many left open the possibility of joining in the future. Later in 1987 two United States firms, TI and LSI Logic, became members.

Also in March, MITI issued administrative guidance to the 10 largest Japanesen semiconductor producing firms to increase their purchases of foreign semiconductors. These firms did increase their purchases of United States ICs somewhat, but this increase appeared to be a short-term expedient rather than a long-term commitment. Under further United States prodding, MITI began encouraging other Japanese firms to buy United States ICs. This guidance might lead to more long-term commitments, but the effects through late 1987 have been modest.

By late 1987, the United States share of Japanese semiconductor consumption had increased about 1 percent from its rather low level of mid-1986. United States firms and the United States government were unhappy with this slow progress. The portion of the tariff sanctions covering the lack of market access were continued in November 1987, when the portion covering dumping was lifted. In the absence of more determined efforts by United States firms to convince the middle-level decision makers in these Japanese firms of the quality and reliability of United States semiconductors and firms, however, it is not clear that guidance from MITI can have a substantial, or a lasting, effect.

INTERNATIONAL COOPERATIVE AGREEMENTS

A trend evident in recent years in the semiconductor industry is the growing number of international cooperative agreements. Such agreements increasingly go beyond licensing and cross-licensing of the rights to produce proprietary product designs, to active collaboration to develop and produce semiconductors jointly. These agreements take a number of forms beyond licensing, including technology exchanges with further joint development efforts, agreements to combine complementary technologies (e.g., design technology with production capabilities), joint ventures for technology development, and joint ventures for production.

A number of reasons have been advanced for the increasing prevalence of these major cooperative agreements. The cost of development of semiconductor technology has been rising steadily as the complexity of ICs increases. The cost of establishing a state-of-the-art production facility has also been rising rather rapidly. Cooperative agreements provide a mechanism to spread the financing and risk of these investments. They also provide a method of combining complementary assets between firms, in a setting where internal development of some of these assets is increasingly costly. Such combinations may involve different technological strengths, technology with financing capability, or technology with marketing capability.

Table 13.4   Major Cooperative Agreements Between United States and Japanese Firms Since 1985

United States Firm	Japanese Firm	Agreement
Motorola	Toshiba	Motorola gains access to Toshiba design and production technologies for memory ICs, especially DRAMs. Toshiba gains access to Motorola design technology for 8-bit, 16-bit, and 32-bit microprocessors. The two firms also plan to build a joint production facility in Japan to produce memory ICs and microprocessors
National Semiconductor	NMB	Long-term agreement to design, produce, and market advanced ICs in Japan. SRAMs are the initial focus. National provides design and marketing expertise. NMB provides production facilities
AMD	Sony	Agreement for joint development of ICs for industrial and consumer applications. AMD strength is in the industrial area. Sony strength is in the consumer area
LSI Logic	Kawasaki Steel	Formation of a joint venture, Nihon Semiconductor Inc., to produce ASICs in Japan
Standard Microsystems	Sumitomo Metal	Joint venture to produce ASICs in Japan
Fairchild[a]	Fujitsu	Following withdrawal of Fujitsu's offer to acquire 80% of Fairchild, the two firms agreed to pursue a series of technology exchange and development programs. Joint production in both the United States and Japan planned

[a] Fairchild was subsequently acquired by National Semiconductor.

SOURCES: Adapted from Integrated Circuit Engineering Corporation (1987) and accounts in various newspapers and magazines.

Table 13.4 shows major cooperative agreements between United States and Japanese firms announced since about the end of 1985. It is not clear the exact extent to which semiconductor trade friction and the 1986 Arrangement have had an influence on such agreements, but some influence is likely. The clearest influence is apparent in the agreement between Fairchild and Fujitsu, although this has been superseded by the purchase of Fairchild by National Semiconductor in October 1987. Fujitsu presumably entertained the initial idea of acquiring Fairchild largely because of the problems created for Fujitsu by the Arrangement. After Fujitsu withdrew its acquisition offer, Fujitsu and Fairchild agreed to engage in a number of techology exchange, joint development, and joint production efforts. Thus, through these cooperative arrangements, Fujitsu would have accomplished a number of the objectives it had sought to accomplish through the acquisition. Interestingly, United States government officials did not complain about any threats to national security caused by these cooperative agreements.

The timing and scope of the agreements between Motorola and Toshiba may also have been influenced by the Arrangement. Toshiba's willingness to share its DRAM technology could have been influenced by the pricing rules covering Toshiba's DRAM exports from Japan. As noted previously, Toshiba is also selling unassembled DRAM chips to Motorola, an arrangement that may allow Toshiba to partially circumvent these rules. The announcements of the plans to build joint production facilities in Japan by both Motorola–Toshiba and Fairchild–Fujitsu may also be influenced by the friction, in the sense that the Japanese firms may intend to use them to diffuse some of the United States criticism that Japanese firms are aiming to drive United States firms out of the business and that the Japanese market is collusively closed to outsiders.

Several other of these major cooperative agreements were agreements essentially unaffected by the friction and the Arrangement, in that they would have occurred in any case. AMD and Sony are sharing complementary technology strengths in order for each to become a broader-line producer. NMB is a pure producer (a "foundry") in Japan seeking alliances with other firms that can supply design and marketing capabilities. Both Kawasaki Steel and Sumitomo Metal are seeking to diversify out of declining industries. While they can supply financing, they are pursuing partners to provide technology in their effort to enter the high-growth semiconductor industry.

CONCLUSIONS

The 1986 Arrangement Concerning Trade in Semiconductor Products was intended to address several aspects of what United States firms and the United States government view as unfair practices and policies used by Japanese semiconductor firms and the Japanese government. The two major areas of complaint have been chronic dumping by Japanese firms and lack of access to the Japanese market. The United States government has made it clear that promises from the Japanese government and Japanese firms to reform their practices and policies are not enough—the United States government will judge the Arrangement by the results obtained. Many of these results depend on the responses of business to the Arrangement.

Through 1987, the Arrangement appears to have had rather little effect in some areas and somewhat surprising results in others. With respect to the prevention of dumping, the major result was the development of a large gray market in ICs exported from Japan in circumvention of the Arrangement. Thus, the Arrangement had a lesser effect on transaction prices for export sales of Japanese ICs than might have been expected. In response to United States pressure, MITI moved to reduce the incentive for these gray market exports by attempting to reduce Japanese output of ICs and thus raise the price in Japan. In effect, the pricing rules of the Arrangement began to apply within Japan, although the Arrangement formally covers only exports from Japan. The cartelization of the industry, a typical result of such negotiated sectoral agreements to address trade friction, is being extended.

The Arrangement has had rather small impacts in other areas of business decision making, perhaps because the effectiveness of the Arrangement was debatable even as it was enacted, and because the emergence of the gray market reinforced concerns over its effectiveness. Japanese firms made rather modest efforts to shift production out of Japan, and United States firms have not altered their product strategies to any noticeable extent. Most importantly, the Arrangement has not led to substantial entry or reentry of United States firms into production of MOS memory ICs. Instead, United States firms are now planning a cooperative effort to advance their production technology, and they are seeking substantial government funding of this consortium.

The Arrangement also has not yet had much impact on the United States share of the Japanese semiconductor market. The Japanese government has apparently been encouraging expanded purchases of foreign semiconductors, and it states that it is too early to judge the effectiveness of this aspect of the Arrangement. However, the increase in share depends mainly on the willingness of United States firms to invest in marketing, quality guarantees, customer servicing, and probably production in Japan. United States firms apparently remain rather pessimistic about their prospects for sales in Japan, and such additional investments have been modest. A few have expanded marketing efforts and are addressing Japanese perceptions that United States products are generally of low quality and that United States firms offer rather poor customer service. No new firms have announced plans for wholly owned production facilities in Japan, although several new joint ventures for production in Japan have been announced. The firms that already have production facilities in Japan are expanding. Nonetheless, the overall level of additional investment is modest.

Thus, the Arrangement, which has the appearance of a major change in trade policy, had a rather modest impact in its first year. The major effects were the development of a gray market for Japanese exports, the incipient cartelization of Japanese producers, and the tariff sanctions imposed by the United States government on certain United States imports from Japan, in retaliation for the failure of the Arrangement to have substantial effects. By late 1987, the Japanese dumping ended, and a portion of the tariff sanctions were lifted. The general recovery of global market demand for semiconductors, however, and not the Arrangement, was probably most important in eliminating dumping.

The portion of the tariff sanctions related to access to the Japanese market remained in effect in late 1987. In this area, the Arrangement is vague, probably overly ambitious, and not well designed to elicit the kinds of business responses that would lead to the results desired. Under the Arrangement, United States firms have an incentive to rely on MITI encouragement to expand their sales in Japan. They can view such encouragement as something of a substitute for their own commitment of resources to selling in Japan. Government encouragement is not likely to produce the kind of long-term selling relationships that the United States firms desire. Disputes over the ineffectiveness of the market access aspect of the Arrangement are likely to continue.

NOTES

1. For a discussion of somewhat contrasting views of the basis for the rising competitiveness of Japanese firms, see Pugel et al. (1984) and Borrus et al. (1986).
2. The Integrated Circuit Engineering Corporation categorizes three firms as United States based, although they are (or were) owned by European parents (Signetics by Philips, Fairchild by Schlumberger, and Interdesign by Ferranti), and one firm as European based, although its corporate headquarters is in the United States (ITT). Recategorization of these firms according to the base of their parent headquarters would alter the shares implied by Table 13.1, lowering the United States share and raising the European share by several percentage points. Fairchild was acquired by United States based National Semiconductor in October 1987.
3. Integrated Circuit Engineering Corporation (1987).
4. Based on trade data compiled by the Japan Ministry of Finance, which appears to be the most accurate source.
5. For further discussion of these market share estimates, see Pugel (1987).
6. See Kimura (1986) for further discussion of the strategies of Japanese semiconductor producers.
7. See Wilson et al. (1980) for a discussion of the strategies of United States semiconductor producers.
8. Discussion of the legal validity and economic implications of these actions is beyond the scope of this paper. See Pugel (1987) for a discussion of these actions and an analysis of their legal and economic aspects.
9. See Pugel (1987) for further discussion of this Arrangement and its economic implications. The Arrangement is often also referred to as the Agreement on Semiconductor Trade.
10. Kristof, Nicholas D.: "Gray Market for Chips Shrinking but Still Big," *New York Times*, March 26, 1987.
11. Chira, Susan: "Japan Asks for Less Chip Output," *New York Times*, Feb 19, 1987.
12. Moses and Pugel (1986).
13. Integrated Circuit Engineering Corporation (1987).

14. In some ways the objective of Sematech parallels that of the Japanese VLSI project of the late 1970s.
15. See Pugel (1987) for a discussion of the transactional infirmities inherent in such purchasing.

REFERENCES

Borrus, Michael; Tyson, Laura D'Andrea; and Zysman, John: "Creating Advantage: How Government Policies Shape International Trade in the Semiconductor Industry," in Paul R. Krugman, ed., *Strategic Trade Policy and the New International Economics* (Cambridge, MA: MIT Press, 1986).

————, *Status 1982* (Scottsdale, AZ: Integrated Circuit Engineering Corporation, 1982).

————, *Status 1985* (Scottsdale, AZ: Integrated Circuit Engineering Corporation, 1985).

Integrated Circuit Engineering Corporation, *Status 1987* (Scottsdale, AZ: Integrated Circuit Engineering Corporation, 1987).

Kimura, Yui: *Competitive Strategies and Strategic Groups in the Japanese Semiconductor Industry*, Ph.D. Dissertation, New York University, Graduate School of Business Administration (1986).

Moses, Frederick A.; and Pugel, Thomas A.: "Foreign Direct Investment in the United States: The Electronics Industries," in H. Peter Gray, ed., *Uncle Sam as Host* (Greenwich, CT: JAI Press, 1986).

Organization for Economic Cooperation and Development, *The Semiconductor Industry: Trade Related Issues* (Paris: OECD, 1985).

Pugel, Thomas A.: "Limits of Trade Policy Toward High Technology Industries: The Case of Semiconductors," in Ryuzo Sato, and Paul Wachtel, eds, *Trade Friction and Economic Policy: Problems and Prospects for Japan and the United States.* (New York: Cambridge University Press, 1987).

————: "United States–Japan Trade Friction in the Semiconductor Industry," *Harvard International Review*, 9(3) (1987), pp. 26–29.

————; Kimura, Yui; and Hawkins, Robert G.: "Semiconductors and Computers: Emerging Competitive Battlegrounds in the Asia–Pacific Region," in Richard W. Moxon, Thomas W. Roehl, and J.F. Truitt, eds, *International Business Strategies in the Asia–Pacific Region* (Greenwich, CT: JAI Press, 1984).

Wilson, Robert W.; Ashton, Peter K.; and Egan, Thomas P.: *Innovation Competition, and Government Policy in the Semiconductor Industry* (Lexington, MA: Heath, Lexington Books, 1980).

Yano Research Institute: *Japanese Semiconductor and IC Industry* (Tokyo: Yano Research Institute, 1984).

14

Stronger Yen and the United States–Japanese Trade Balance: Marketing Policies of Japanese Firms in the United States Market

JOHNY JOHANSSON

As textbooks in international trade would have it, changes in the exchange rates are one of the primary mechanisms that adjust the trade balance. When country A is running a trade deficit with country B, the currency of country A will often depreciate in terms of the currency of country B. This occurs owing to an excess demand in country A for goods from country B. As the currency of A depreciates, the prices of imported goods in that country rise, and the prices of A's goods in country B fall. Therefore, the residents of country A will buy fewer goods from country B (and the residents of country B will buy more goods from country A), and thus the trade account will adjust itself.

In the period 1985–88, the United States dollar depreciated against the Japanese yen to the tune of about 50 percent. This should have acted to "correct" the trade deficit between the United States and Japan. It has not done so. Japanese firms continue to export to the United States and to maintain stable prices in United States dollars in the face of rapidly declining yen prices and yen revenues for them.

This apparent inconsistency provides an excellent opportunity to gauge the real complexity of corporate responses to changes in trade policies. As we have indicated earlier, there is a difference between the short-term and long-term effects of changes in the exchange rates on corporate values. In deciding on pricing policies in the face appreciating yen, the management of large Japanese corporations with substantial exports to the United States had to consider their competitive position with regard to other exporters as well as with regard to domestic United States firms. The reduced revenues in the present had to be balanced against future losses as a result of a reduced market share. In some ways, this is a similar issue to the one that is the focal point of Part II of this book—the tradeoff between cost effectiveness and flexibility. In this case, the management of the Japanese major exporters to the United States had to balance immediate profits, which would have been helped by an increase in dollar prices, to maintain more stable yen prices and revenues, with a higher degree of flexibility by maintaining their market share. The cost of keeping the flexibility is a reduction in revenues and a profits squeeze.

This decision is affected by the expectation of management with regard to the duration and size of the changes in the exchange rates, which are partially affected by current and perceived future changes in trade policy. In this particular case, the Japanese firms decided that future flexibility is worth more, in terms of the value of their firms, than current cost effectiveness. Flexibility can be seen also as a way to "buy time" while the operational, marketing, and other functional aspects of management are adjusted to reflect the new situation.

In the past couple of years, actual and anticipated tariff barriers have induced Japanese exporters to turn increasingly to FDI in manufacturing. From September 1985 on, they have also been faced with an indirect attack from an appreciating yen. In the 17 month period since the concerted drive against the United States dollar began, it has declined by more than 40 percent against the yen and by about 15–20 percent against the German mark and other European currencies. While some argue that the dollar is still overvalued vis-à-vis the Japanese currency, the current level of about 150 yen to the dollar has been pronounced (February 1987) roughly acceptable to the governments of the major countries.

Part of the rationale for the push against the yen was to reduce the Japanese–United States trade imbalance, in fact to reduce these huge revenues and profits scored by the Japanese. As we all know, their success in the United States markets in the first half of the 1980s, when the dollar was strong, led to unprecedented profits for the Japanese (partly "windfall" profits in the case of the auto companies, because of the voluntary quota restrictions).

How were the Japanese exporters supposed to react to this new and radically different yen rate? The standard economic theory prediction, elaborated further below, is that the appreciated yen will force them to raise prices in the markets abroad and thus lose sales to lower-priced competitors. A marketing theory argument, also elaborated below, would suggest that the higher prices will be accompanied by a concentration on more value-added products and on specialty niches of the markets, an attempt to protect profits at the expense of total revenues. The outcome under both scenarios would be a loss of market share in terms of volume.

The theory of the multinational corporation, on the other hand, would predict that the erosion of market share could be stopped by investment in manufacturing abroad. As a solution in the long run, it has some obvious appeal, but one would expect it to go counter to the Japanese corporation's need to maintain employment at home.

The present study assesses the actual damage done to Japanese companies' profitability and examines the remedial measures instituted, particularly in preserving market shares abroad and jobs at home. The empirical data presented derive from published annual reports, newspaper articles in Japan, and interviews with some of the Japanese companies and government agencies (including MITI).

In what follows, the three theoretical arguments will first be developed in more detail. Then a section discussing the repertory of actions available to the typical Japanese exporting company will be presented. The empirical data collected will then be introduced and analyzed with the aim of assessing how accurately the theories predict behavior. The uncovered deviations are then analyzed further, and a, richer framework, which would predict the Japanese firms' behavior better, is proposed.

THE ECONOMIC ARGUMENT

There is no real need to get very profound when explaining why an appreciated yen would lead to lower sales for the Japanese in the United States. To the extent the exporting is done from Japan, export prices will be quoted in yen. This would usually be the case whether sales go through a sales subsidiary abroad (the typical Japanese case in the United States) or through an independent agent/distributor network. As the yen appreciates, the quoted prices will necessarily rise in the market country currency. The "passthrough" of the rising yen is immediate.

In reality, of course, there are delays in the dynamics of this mechanism. The *inventory* of already-imported units serves as a buffer. The sales subsidiary has a choice of raising prices immediately on items in inventory to gain a windfall profit or to avoid raising prices until the new shipments come on the market.

The degree to which the buy-and-sell *contracts* specify prices, in what currency, and for how long will also serve to slow down the impact. Furthermore, if the yen appreciation (and the dollar decline) was anticipated, there are of course avenues for the company to hedge against overexposure. The effect, again, is to slow the price changes in the market.

Economic theory would suggest that the only alternative to raising prices (whether sooner or later) is to accept *lower profit* margins. This would happen if the Japanese yen prices quoted are reduced. The company ships the same quantity to the United States as before, but at a lower price. Unavoidably, the profit margins on the products will be lower.

There is also another source for the profit squeeze. In the United States, prices might be held down and the same volume might be sold as before. In such a case the revenues (and profits) shown by the sales subsidiary in dollars might be the same, but when translated into yen they are lower.

Thus, both the headquarters and the subsidiary will show lower earnings. It would seem safe to predict that the yen increase would be passed through to the customer it at all possible, and at least in the longer run. Although non-Japanese competitors are sure to gain sales, there are limits to which the American consumer can be "subsidized" by lower earnings in Japan.

THE MARKETING ARGUMENT

From marketing theory, one can develop a more articulate prediction of what will happen to the Japanese marketing mixes in addition to price changes (under the asumption that some price increases are unavoidable).

In marketing strategy terms, a price increase directly affects a product's positioning. In terms of a product space dimension (typically an axis like "Economy"), the position has now shifted relative to the other products of the market. This means it might have to shift its appeal to target another segment in the market, generally a more upscale segment where the higher price is no distraction (or perhaps an attraction).

For many in the market, the product will no longer be on the efficient frontier, as there are other products providing the same benefits at lower per-dollar cost. For yet others, the dollar price puts the product out of reach, beyond the budget constraint.

Unless a way can be found to soften the impact of the higher price (via constructive installment credit arrangements or the like), and assuming that the competitors are not also raising prices, a new marketing mix has to be formulated around each product's new position and target segment. It would be very difficult for a marketer to accept the implicit assumption in the economic argument that price will simply be increased.

Quite generally, the new mixes can be predicted to center around more upscale products, with added features and increased versality, backed by advertising and other promotional means to educate customers anout the new possibilities.

Where the new segments are located in the market space depends on the present positioning. If the products were previously at the lower end of the market, they will now aim for the middle. If the middle core of the market had been targeted before, the new target will be upscale. And so on.

How the new products will be developed depends also on a number of things. Some low-end products might be dropped from the market altogether. Others will be upgraded by the addition of new features. New lower-end products with simplified designs might be introduced to cover lower-end segments.

The product activity required for an effective marketing job could be very expensive. The cost–benefit analysis determining whether the company deems it justified depends on the *importance of the market* (in terms of sales, profits, now and in the long run) and the *resources required* to stay competitive (if new products and features are already available in the home market, for example, the investment requirements are lessened considerably). In the present case, it would take little imagination to see that (1) the United States market *is* very important for most of the Japanese exporters, and (2) many have new products already introduced in the home market or under way in prototype stages. One would predict that there would be a number of introductions of new products in the United States market following the rise of the yen.

From a marketing viewpoint, the advertising and other promotional instruments would need to be beefed up. The new products would have to be introduced with proper support and the customers (re-)educated. Were the products to stay largely unchanged, the higher prices would have to be explained and justified. Reducing promotional spending would only be justified in the case where prices were kept at their old levels, and costs needed to be slashed to maintain profits. As a short-run tactic this might work, but if competition was strong enough, such a strategy would be a road to extinction.

The predicted marketing reactions by the Japanese can be summarized as "differentiation" (or, in a few cases like Subaru's autos, where the product line is limited, "focus") strategies in Porter's (1981) framework, encompassing as they do reformulations of existing products and product line extentions. But the company can also consider "diversification" into new markets. One could in fact predict that as a result of the yen rise, there would be an increase in the attention paid to markets where the yen rise has not been so steep. One would expect the Japanese to intensify their penetration effort in major European markets, like Germany, whose currencies have also risen against the dollar.

In sum, from what marketing teaches us, the consequence of the rising yen would be an emphasis on differentiation in the United States market, with increases in advertising to support a smaller but upgraded fleet of Japanese products, many with new features, and with new entries at the upper end of the market. This marketing strategy thrust, which came to characterize the Japanese in the auto market during the run of the voluntary quotas, is thus foisted upon them again by external forces.

THE MULTINATIONAL ARGUMENT

The theory of multinational production can also be used to develop some predictions of what will happen when a currency appreciates. Assuming the change is expected to be more or less permanent, and given a sufficiently long-term perspective, the theory suggests that the response would consist of an increase in FDI manufacturing.

If the market country is sufficiently important, as is the United States, and market positions need to be protected, the multinational prediction would be that the Japanese will invest in manufacturing in the United States (or a third country with a currency better aligned with the dollar, such as Canada or Taiwan). The appreciation of the currency has to be seen as permanent, since these investments require time to be implemented and to generate a positive cash flow. Since indications at least in the latter half of 1986 have been that the new rate is here to stay, one would predict an increased activity in FDI among the Japanese, at least over some longer span of time.

However, there are related developments that could occur in the short run. Most of the Japanese exporters have some offshore manufacturing and assembly plants in place already. To the extent that these are located in countries with currencies aligned to the dollar, one could predict that these facilities will exhibit increased capacity utilization and expansion.

The expansion could take several forms. One would expect standardized parts and subassemblies to be shifted there as soon as possible; where labor and machinery are of sufficient quality for more skilled jobs, they would be allocated new responsibilities. Where the product built or assembled is of the simpler kind, additional features making it suitable for the lower end of the American market will be considered so as to enable direct shipment to the United States.

The multinational theory would also suggest that jobs will be shifted out of

Japan into other countries for subsidiary manufacturing and then imported to Japan for reexportation. In general, the high value of the yen could be predicted to help make the reluctant exporting giants of Japan to finally become true multinationals.

THE JAPANESE FIRM'S REPERTORY

A more pragmatic and atheoretical way of predicting what the Japanese reaction might be is simply to enumerate the feasoble actions open to them. This style of analysis is reminiscent of the Harvard Business case approach and amounts to a statement of the Japanese firms' repertory of counteractions. The advantage of the pragmatic stance is its obvious relevance. Where a theory's underlying assumptions might be unrealistic in the particular case—and thus invalidate the theory's predictions—the repertory listing will always be in the realistic domain (even if at times it is unimagivative precisely because of its atheoretical perspective).

REFINING THE PREDICTIONS

The *economic* argument is that price increases will be passed on via a stable price quoted in yen. This would seem an entirely feasible outcome. On the other hand, there are cases where the consequently eliminated profits for the Japanese sales subsidiary in the United States have led to investigations by the IRS. The reason is that the lack of profits leads to no tax revenues and thus a suspicion of transfer pricing to shift profits in Japan. On the other hand, *not* raising prices in dollars might lead to charges that the product is being sold under cost—that is, dumping.

When these practical considerations are taken into account, the economic prediction will have to be refined to say that it is likely that *some* adjustments of prices will take place, but probably not by the full amount of the currency fluctuation.

Are the predicted *marketing* changes feasible? The advertising and related promotional shifts would seem quite within the reach of the typical Japanese exporter. The financial requirements for the suggested product changes might be prohibitive for some (smaller) firms. There is also the possibility that organizational obstacles would impede the required changes. New products are never sure bets, and there might be differences within management about the need to take such great risks or the permanence of the new currency alignment. Sticking with tried and true products might well seem a preferable option.

These considerations make it likely that marketing predictions need to be shifted away from new products previously suggested. Instead, a more conservative stance could be expected, where a major counterbalance to the anticipated increases in price consists of improvements in existing products supported by advertising announcing the value of the new features.

This more conservative stance on new products would also lead to a stronger emphasis on the opportunities in new markets where the yen rise is less pronounced. Thus, the earlier predicted thrust toward some of the European markets could be expected to intensify as the profitability of the American market declined.

The expansion to offshore manufacturing facilities suggested by the *multinational* theory needs to be refined by the introduction of several modifying factors. They include the desire to provide employment for existing employees, lack of familiarity with manufacturing management abroad, doubts as to whether Japanese management techniques can be transferred intact, and uncertainty about overseas labor skills. Add to this the longer-term perspective involved, and it is likely that manufacturing expansion abroad is seen more as an unavoidable long-term nightmare than are an appropriate solution to current exchange rate problems.

The more limited multinationalism involved in assigning existing offshore plants more products and tasks, on the other hand, seems entirely feasible. The stages in the production processes usually assigned to overseas units involve less demanding processes and work, and the lack of skills might prohibit further offshore activities. But in all likelihood there has already been gradual training in many of these plants, and the labor skills in Japanese subsidiaries in countries like Indonesia, Thailand, and the United States must be increasing gradually.

Furthermore, since robotization in recent years has come to mean that some of the simpler tasks have been repatriated back to Japan, one could hypothesize that the high yen might even slow down this drive toward FMS and a reshipment of jobs abroad. But this would seem to go against the "constant improvement" manufacturing philosophy that the Japanese companies are so proud of, and one would hesitate before making such a prediction.

Other Possibilities

Other activities are also feasible for the Japanese companies attempting to fend off the high yen's impact. One obvious question is to what extent the government can provide some assistance. One does not have to think in terms of outright subsidies or currency intervention—the Japanese exporters are in most cases much too large today to warrant those—but some "administrative guidance" might be useful. Could MITI alleviate the currency problems?

The question is not so farfetched as it might appear at first glance. If one remembers that in many cases the Japanese manufacturers abroad tend to dominate certain niches of a market—for some time they constituted the entire market for products such as VCRs and compact disk players—the idea that MITI could engender some collective action is attractive. Why could the Japanese producers not get together and collectively raise prices by a given target percentage?

When it comes to competition, most Japanese firms abroad are mainly worried about their Japanese compatriots. If a company were sure its Japanese competitors would follow suit, raising prices would be considerably more palatable. In fact, for markets where the Japanese are dominant, one would expect more of a price increase than in others, where non-Japanese competition is fiercer. Knowing the Japanese experience with competition from the NICs (and lack of it from many Western companies), one could even predict that the only real obstacle to such collusive action would be the emergence of competitors from Taiwan and, in particular, Korea.

The Japanese companies also have a tendency to absorb low profits in the short run if the long-term prospects look acceptable. Thus one could expect that management and workers would show a recognition of the need to "tighten the belts," the bonuses would become smaller, and part-timers would be asked to stay home—all so that the prices abroad could be kept stable.

Despite the Japanese reluctance to run their subsidiaries as stand-alone profit centers, one would still expect them to start considering a more decentralized structure. For as the yen rose at different rates in different countries, it would become natural to allow the local sales subsidiary to make the decision as to what the final price ought to be. Such a delegation of power would also allow headquarters to minimize their price schedule restructuring in Tokyo.

THE EMPIRICAL EVIDENCE

The First Year

The predictions generated above could have been made at the time the attack against the yen/dollar rate was getting under way in September 1985. During the next year or so, the actual responses and outcomes were being reported intermittently by the press. It was becoming clear that the predicted rise in prices of Japanese products was very slow in coming. There was no strong advertising emphasizing that "this is your last chance before prices go up," and there seemed to be no rush in the United States to buy Japanese products before prices rose.

In the absence of immediate and significant price increases, there was no strong evidence that the Japanese were shifting their product lines upward. True, the upper ends were stretched in accordance with an already discernible trend. Sometimes this stretching met without much evident success, as in the case of the Acura automobile. In other cases, the stretch had more impact but did not generate as much profit as could be expected because of intense competition between many Japanese makers, as in the case of large-screen television sets.

But the lower end of the markets was not easily surrendered to other competitors. Newcomers from Japan (like Isuzu in autos) and new models from existing manufactures took care of that. Neither was the middle core yielded. In the traditional Japanese strongholds—autos, cameras, consumer electronics— the only major low-end competition still came from the Koreans and the other NICs, just as before, perhaps with the addition of some oddity like the Yugo. Moreover, the price disadvantage of the Japanese did not seem to increase as much as one would have guessed a year earlier. The Japanese companies were holding the line on price, and this meant their marketing effort could be pursued in much the same manner as before.

The increase in FDI that did seem to take place during the year was generally attributed more to the fear of tariff barriers than to currency problems as such. Not many new projects were announced where the dominant motivating force was not connected with actual or potential trade barriers.

Not surprisingly, there was very little change in the increases in the United States–Japan trade imbalance. The Japanese continued to rack up gains in exports, and the proponents of currency realignment as a cure for the American trade deficit were at pains defining how long is long (as in "the long run").

If the picture in the United States was amazingly "more of the same," the news emanating from Japan was decidedly different. Now we heard about squeezed profits and actual losses in leading companies like Hitachi and Nissan, about worker and management layoffs in structurally declining steel companies like Kawasaki, and about a generally depressed economy with low consumer spending and corporate retrenching. It was an economy where exporters has taken a blow and where imported products has yet to come down much in price. About the only ones doing well were the importing middlemen, who reaped the benefits of buying low and selling high.

The Company Interviews

The field interviews for the present study took place in Japan in December 1986. The aim was to find out what had actually happened in the companies. Why had they decided not to increase prices in the United States, but instead to virtually subsidize the United States consumer out of company profits and to the detriment of their own laid-off workers.

The interviews were arranged with help from Jetro and my colleague Professor Ikujiro Nonaka at Hitotsubashi University, who also accompanied me to several of the interviews. The companies visited included Canon in optical products, NEC and JVC in electronics, Nissan in autos, and Asahi Diamonds, a midsize industrial firm. In the companies, the people interviewed were generally of *bucho* ranking and connected with international planning and/or sales.

In addition, I met with representatives of MITI, Japan Economic Foundation, and Jetro. Also, some informal talks were held with a division manager of a Swedish subsidiary in Japan (Gadelius) and academicians at Hitotsubashi.

This is, of course, a very limited sample of the representative opinion in Japan. Nevertheless, as with all qualitative research, quality is more important than quantity. The fact is that the picture of what was happening become quite clear after only a couple of interviews, and with the pattern repeating itself, I could rapidly get convergence on the main threads of the story.

Was the Yen Appreciation Anticipated?

All of the people interviewed had foreseen that some kind of yen/dollar realignment had to come sooner or later. These did not seem to be Monday morning quarterbacking comments, either. In the bigger companies, there had been a standing policy for the previous couple of years to operate with a yen dollar exchange rate of 200, far below the rate of 240–250 then reigning. The smaller Asahi company had gone so far as to source as much as possible of their raw materials and supplies in the West (all diamonds were imported, for example), and with only 9 percent export ratio they were in fact gaining from the strong yen.

The companies had not been expecting such a drastic or rapid revaluation as the one actually occurring. The 150–160 yen dollar rate was seen as "very difficult" for them. According to newspaper reports, Mazda was an exception. A year earlier, Mazda's prediction had been for a rate of about 160, and the corporate strategy (including United States transfer prices) had been premised on this lower rate since then. But the expectations of most companies had been closer to the 200 level, and there had been no contingency planning for the lower level. But, clearly in the spirit of the already prepared cost efficiencies, their first and most striking reaction was that now the company had to make money at the new rate.

Cutting Costs

Thus, the most common immediate reaction to the currency crisis was one of the cost cutting. In the interviews, this was the first and biggest answer for all the companies interviewed. They had no easy "let's pass it on to the customer" solution, not even as a simple toss-away at the start of the conversations. One got the sense that such sentences do not exist among the Japanese.

As so often occurs in Japanese firms, the large companies had all instituted formal campaigns to slash costs. They came in various names and guises ("Campaign 160" at Nissan, for example), and all centered around the theme of being able to make money at the new yen rate. Not all were convinced the high rate would stay, and some suggested it might stabilize at 170 or even 180, but all saw it as absolutely necessary to try to "make it" at the new rate without tinkering with prices.

The campaigns were generally structured around a 2- to 3-year period. Canon "would be able to make it as 185 now," according to one of their interviewees, but the typical response was that it would take another couple of years to be able to get down to 150–160. In 2 years, NEC expected to be able to make it at 160. Were they sure they were going to make it? "We must and we will," was the typically laconic Japanese answer.

Part of the reason for the determined optimism was of course that Japanese companies have done this sort of thing before. After the first oil crisis, many corporations cut costs and rationalized their entire operations in order to save energy and to be able to operate profitably at relatively low levels of capacity utilization. As Japanese workers' wages grew uncompetitive with those of neighboring NICs, the companies turned increasingly to investments in robotics to modernize their factories and to generate cost savings. By linking the size of the bonuses to performance, a legitimate profit squeeze can be directly translated into lower pay without strongly demoralizing the work force.

Such practices make a large portion of wages a variable cost even in the short run. In the extreme case, people are given only their base pay, and at the managerial levels—down to *bucho* or even *kacho*—a severe downturn might mean that the base pay is also reduced. A standard practice is to send people from Tokyo headquarters to a sales job with a subsidiary in the provinces. In one company, newly hired people with MBAs from prestigious United States schools had been "demoted" with a "2-year stint" in the field. Typically the family of such an employee had opted to stay in Tokyo, with money sent to them often directly from the company and the hapless father able to see his family only on weekends at best.

There was also the fact that much of the cost cutting amounted to putting the squeeze on subcontractors and independent parts suppliers. Although it is a touchy issue and one not covered directly in the interviews, according to my academic colleagues, most of the Japanese companies have asked their suppliers to share in the cost-cutting burden by drastically reducing their prices. According to the press, some companies in the steel and shipbuilding industries have also trimmed their costs by simply terminating some of their suppliers. People have been laid off.

One factor that helped support the cost-cutting policy was the expectation, expressed in two of the companies, that the deflationary impact in Japan from the strong yen (and the corresponding inflationary pressure in the United States from the weakening dollar) would work to bring about a new "normal" realignment at the higher yen value. Thus, the profit squeeze would be transitory, and with the new cost efficiencies and later "normal" price increases, the Japanese companies would come back to their previous positions even better off than before.

A Multinational Thrust

There was also considerable evidence that a trend toward sourcing abroad was involved in the cost cutting. Combined with the termination of supplier contracts and the trimming of the work forces was a reallocation of parts and supplies to existing subsidiaries in foreign countries. These mainly involved subsidiaries in countries close to Japan, but the possibility of sourcing from subs in the United States and Europe was clearly under consideration in all the companies, including the possibility of supplying the United States market from a third country (a practice that in semiconductors would have been a way to circumvent the Japan–United States agreement and that the United States Department of Commerce was policing vigorously). The transportation charges from the suppliers were obviously a factor in these decisions, the Southeast Asian countries having a strong cost advantage.

There had also been evaluations of the feasibility of manufacturing the final product abroad. For example, Canon had tentatively decided to move more of its camera production to Taiwan. Its plant there already makes the low-end Canon unit, and it would take on more of the product line items in the future.

In the high-tech end of production, however, Japan was still seen as the manufacturer of choice.

There was also more sourcing abroad from independent suppliers. As mentioned, the Asahi company had in fact developed global sourcing early enough to gain from the sinking dollar. Some hesitation about this mode of sourcing was expressed among the larger companies, understandably since they have long been accustomed to very close relationships to their suppliers. There was no evidence that the usual Japanese insistence on prompt deliveries, zero-defect quality control, and low inventory levels was about to be relinquished. One could sense some uneasiness on this score with overseas suppliers, and this clearly limited the extent to which offshore sourcing was seen as a transferring technology to neighboring countries; in several instances the determination to plug any leakage was palpable. The scare of a "hollowing out" of the manufacturing sector was real.

In the longer term, the multinational expansion was seen as proceeding as already planned although perhaps intensified by the currency realignment. There was a strong sentiment that Japan could not turn back this tide, mainly because of trade barriers, actual or potential, rather than currency problems. But it was clear in December 1986, as the yen realignment seemed more and more permanent, that the new manufacturing sites would have to take on a much greater share of production than initially anticipated. Thus, scale economies were becoming a concern, and it was suggested in two of the interviews that specialization of models between subsidiaries was necessary, perhaps with overseas plants exporting back to Japan. The outcome could possibly be a more limited choice of models abroad, with the offshore plants concentrated on one or two models.

The Role of Government

There was strong agreement among all that MITI would have been unable to generate any collective action even if an attempt had been made. The big companies were not about to listen to the government, and MITI had shifted its attention to smaller and medium-size businesses, partly in order to protect them from being overly pressured by their big customers. MITI has in fact publicly encouraged the large companies to cut costs by importing more, even though this goes against their support of smaller companies. (Again, more recent evidence suggests that this exhortation is giving place to an appeal to work hard for the good of everybody and attempts to stimulate domestic demand.)

Another kind of government role was seen as potentially important, however. The expectations were generally that the fiscal year ending in March 1987 would show considerably losses for many companies. Deficits for a large number of exporters would be a strong basis for a collective appeal to government to assist ailing companies during an intermediate term of adjustment. It was clear that the companies saw a political avenue to influence the government, but only after the currency damage had been sufficiently severe.

One strength of this cautious fallback position was that the parent companies' annual results (contrary to much writing) are very important for the stockmarket and for the confidence of the Japanese people in the future—and thus for their discretionary spending behavior. Since losses abroad could be made up by increased consumption at home, such consumer pessimism would neutralize one beneficial effect of the yen appreciation, leaving the companies losing both abroad and at home.

Why Were Price Increases Avoided?

The typical argument against raising prices was quite naturally the competitive situation in the United States, but also the notion that the United States consumer would not be able to pay a higher price (quite apart from this willingness to pay). The companies were worried about their Japanese compatriots, the NICs, and their Western competitors, in that order. The lack of fear of the American companies was clear. One foundation was apparently the fact that United States companies have not reduced prices in Japan but instead tried to profit on the (for them) favorable yen rate. The sense was that if the Japanese would raise prices in the United States markets, the Americans would also do it. (Recently published data suggest that in fact there has been some price decreases of American products in Japan—Stern, 1987).

New product introductions from the NICs were seen as a potentially dangerous factor, especially those from Korea, where a lot of Japanese technology has been leaked through licensing and FDI. The threat from the NICs seemed also to be a factor in the decision not to approach MITI for some consensus solution. "If the Japanese manufacturers agreed to raise prices, it would leave the United States market wide open for the Koreans," in the words of one of the interviewees at NEC.

With the large exporters free of government "guidance" abroad, none of them could any longer expect the Japanese competitors to follow suit if a price increase was implemented. This uncertainty seemed all the more serious, since the customary marketing strategy of most Japanese companies is to keep close to other Japanese companies. Thus, substitutability among the Japanese products in the United States market was seen as high, with products positioned close to each other and with the "Made in Japan" label common to all.

But there have actually been *some* adjustments of the prices of Japanese products in the United States. Although the figures vary considerably by industry, most of the autos, electronics, and optical products have had price increases in the range of 10–20 percent in deflated figures since the currency realignment started. The figures are higher in industries like copiers, cameras, motorcycles, and autos, where the Japanese have, if not dominant market shares, at least strong brand franchises, and lower in VCRs and integrted circuits, where they have less secure positions (partly because of the NICs). Most of the shifts did not, of course, cover even half of the actual increase of about 40 percent.

According to the interviews, these price increases would have been even greater if the full transfer price adjustments from headquarters had been allowed to pass through to the market. There have been considerable price increases for products going from Japan to the sales subsidiaries in the United States. The exact data are of course proprietary, but in two of the companies the American subsidiary had passed through only about half of the total price rise. There seemed to a common understanding that headquarters and subsidiaries should share the burden.

It was apparently the American subsidiary that had decided not to pass through the increased prices. One should recognize that these units are all managed at the top by Japanese expatriates with profit responsibility, so the delegation of the authority for the final decision is perhaps not so surprising. The closer to the market, the more informed the call. It is noteworthy, however, that in no instance did the interviewees talk about any conflicts or second-guessing in the relationship between Tokyo and the United States. There was a lot of communicating going on, and consensus seemed to have been reached.

What About Marketing Changes?

Initial Reaction
With the early reluctance to raise prices, much of the impetus for making immediate changes to the marketing mix had evaporated. The product line policies were pursued pretty much as before, with the addition to the upper-end products coming right on schedule and those of the lower and middle ends continuing strong. Initially, advertising was not increased or changed much.

New Markets?
There was little or no evidence that the European (or any other) markets had been given more attention at the expense of the United States. The United States is the No. 1 foreign market for a great majority of the large Japanese exporters, partly because the European market is so relatively fragmented and less open than the American. A case in point is Canon, whose 75 percent export ratio is made up of 40 points from the United States and 10 points from Europe. In all, the respondents tended to see the United States as a special market, and to make tradeoffs of the marketing effort there and focus more upon Europe seemed suicidal—the Japanese competitors would move right in.

Product Line Stretching?
As the increases in prices were beginning to be seen as necessary and permanent, there was a lot of talk about "adding value" to the product. The Japanese have long been fond of saying that "any importer to the Japanese market must realize that he has to provide some special and strong reason for the Japanese customer to buy his product. To be a me-too follower is just not enough." The idea is that the average, run-of-the-mill product is as easily supplied by the Japanese themselves. This emphasis on a competitive

advantage was clearly behind the sentiment that a price increase must always be justified by some product change—by a new feature or added versatility.

This was not idle talk, either. Canon had boosted its R&D spending considerably, to an amazingly high 11 percent of sales. NEC had also "substantially" increased its R&D expenditures. Clearly the product line "upgrading" proposition was supported. As the early disbelief was giving way to a conviction that maybe the high yen rate was here to stay, the companies were all in agreement that a cornerstone of their future survival strategy must be a high value-added offering in the market, with a correspondigly higher profit margin.

But the upgrading was not followed willingly by a sacrifice of their existing strong middle-of-the-market positions. The products aimed at the lower end would be sourced largely from abroad, with some more advanced subcomponent work in Japan and assembly perhaps in the market country. It was clear that the Japanese did not want to repeat the American mistake that opened the door the Japanese by relinquishing the lower end of the market. Nevertheless, the number of models available at the lower end might be less than otherwise because of the overseas sourcing and the required scale economies.

Pricing Policy

The companies were monitoring the market reactions to their price increases closely, and one got the sense that in the short run they were attempting to identify the extent to which they could trade on their good brand name and loyal following. If a negative reaction emerged, they were prepared to backtrack a step—such as offering the rebates and cash back now seen for cars. This sort of "incrementalism" comes naturally to the Japanese, who are used to staying close to the customers and modifying any strategy according to feedback from the market place.

Gone forever—and mourned—were the good old days when the Japanese products could be sold easily with a superior price/quality ratio. In such a setting companies can hold the line on price, a comfortable position enjoyed by the Japanese back home. As most seemed to realize, with the new currency alignment, the Japanese would have to do the same jockeying for price points and cents off that has long characterized the way in which their American competitors have operated. Only by upgrading would there be a chance to again hold the line on price.

Advertising

Changes in advertising and other promotional techniques are of course quite different to monitor because of the variety and complexity of the messages. But after the early lack of reaction, the interviews suggested that the the Japanese will have to fight two quite different battles in their advertising campaigns.

The upgrading of their product line involves a more sophisticated audience less drawn by the life-style appeals so common for the Japanese products today. Instead, more status-oriented and selective appeals will become necessary. Furthermore, the sales message has to be more subtle and appeal to upscale consumers. The way this will be done is perhaps already fairly clear. There has been some evidence that more soft-sell, Japanese-style advertising is becoming more common in the United States. Obviously not independent of changing audience tastes in general, the shift is also very compatible with the upgrading of the product line. The approach will apparently be the soft and exquisite image-oriented style of Japanese advertising at home.

But if the Japanese are not about to give up the core of the market, their unique selling points in that market have to contain more of the price information than has been their wont. No longer will we see Japanese products advertised by the most American-looking people on TV, but hard-sell, cash-back, attributes-and-price kind of meat-and-potatoes advertising. It is price competition that drives this advertising, and it seems unavoidable that the Japanese will have to do it or relinquish the low-to-middle core of their markets in the United States.

SUMMARY AND CONCLUSIONS

How well did our predictions hold up? The economic argument did not come through very well, the price increases emerging only slowly and reflective of only about 20–30 percent of the adjustment after more than a year of a high yen rate.

The marketing prediction of more diversification into other markets was not held up—the United States market is too important to give up. The product line stretching at the upper end *did* receive support—but the Japanese are also staying with the lower-end products. The advertising is changing—not because it is supporting a smaller set of products, but because it supports a wider product line.

The multinational argument fared quite well, with some immediate shifting of sourcing abroad, consequent increased imports, and more foreign parts in Japanese-made products. The long-term predictions failed to materialize strongly, the currency shift being only a very weak driver of offshore manufacturing expansion.

The underlying reason for the predictive failures of the frameworks is the same in all three cases: they ignore the Japanese companies' clear tendency to treat most costs as variable even in the short run. It is perhaps arguable that when it comes to a less important market than the United States, the view of manufacturing costs as "givens" might be valid in the short run. But if the American market is at stake, no sacrifice is too big.

Other writers have pointed out that an unusually large portion of the costs in the Japanese corporation are variable or at least not fixed for a long time period (e.g., Abegglen and Stalk, 1985). What this study bears witness to is the *strategic* use of this flexibility to circumvent extenal pressures aimed at forcing a change in marketing strategy. One is reminded of the old cliché that in business all problems are disguised opportunities.

Incorporating the cost flexibility into the theories employed for the predictions seems a fruitful task for another study. Nevertheless, one can sketch out briefly the reformulations necessary.

The economists will naturally argue that all it takes is a clear specification of what costs are actually variable and which are fixed during the planning stage of the companies. But this fails to recognize the depth of the cost cutting involved. Firms will actually redefine their production processes in many cases. They will, in the economists' jargon, shift to another production function. It is not even clear that the production possibility frontiers stay put. With these underpinnings possibly movable, the economists will be in deep waters predicting company reactions.

Marketers will argue in their defense that even if pricing is within their domain, they have no responsibility for manufacturing costs. These have to be taken as givens, as in the typical Harvard Business School case. For the Japanese corporation, this is an assumption that makes the rest of the marketing strategy a house built on sand. The Japanese company is apparently able to make manufacturing costs a function of what the market price needs to be. Thus, the Japanese marketers can decide on a competitive price, and the rest of the organization will try to make a profit at that price. No more cost-plus formulas for pricing, no more marketing decisions to maximize profits. On the other hand, the standard Japanese preoccupation with sales and market share becomes quite natural.

The reason the predictions of the multinational theories fared well is precisely that the production location is viewed there very much in terms of cost advantages. Thus the success with the sourcing predictions. But again, as in the case of economic theory, the multinational predictions are based on the idea that in the short run there is a given cost structure that guides production location decisions.

It is perhaps small wonder that United States multinationals tend to go offshore and to divest unprofitable ventures at a much higher rate than the Japanese. Viewing costs not as givens but as figures that can be reduced by hard work makes the Japanese much more willing to stay with a business than the United States managers eager to get on with their stars. One should not be surprised if the only onew who find it worthwhile to manufacture in the United States in the future are the Japanese.

REFERENCES

Abegglen, J.C.; and Stalk, G. Jr.: *Kaisha: The Japanese Corporation* (New York: Basic Books, 1985).

Porter, M.E.: *Competitive Strategy* (New York: Free Press, 1981).

Stern, J.P.: "The High Yen: Mixed Blessing," *Japan Electronics Update*, 1(9) (1987), pp. 1–8.

15

Effect of Restrictive Trade Policies on Earnings and Employment Levels in Protected Industries

VICTOR A. CANTO

J. KIMBAL DIETRICH

As conventional wisdom would have it, restrictive trade policy is bad for the welfare of the country, but it is beneficial to those industries that are protected. The data and analysis presented by Canto and Dietrich in this chapter contradict this allegation. Indeed, wherever restrictive trade policies were implemented, the effects on the level of employment and profits in the protected industry were negatively affected or not affected at all.

This chapter begins with a description of the dynamic process by which protectionism is enacted. It provides a concrete example, at the single-industry level, of the general process by which United States trade policy is determined, a process described and analyzed in Chapter 3 by Odell and Willett. The dynamics of protectionism are initiated, according to the findings presented by Canto and Dietrich, by falling employment and decreasing returns in some industries. The relative decline experienced by the industry triggers political pressure for protectionism. If successful, this pressure is translated into some form of restrictive trade policy, such as an "orderly marketing agreement," a "voluntary restraint," or a similar action. However, the protectionist measures do not help employment, or contribute to profits as expected. Employment and profits of protected industries increased only in those cases where the protection was circumvented by the foreign competitors.

Therefore, it is argued that protectionism, as expressed by restrictive trade policies, does not improve the welfare of those who initiated the process. Labor does not enjoy higher rates of employment in the declining industries, and management and shareholders do not receive higher profits. Moreover, in most cases, the restrictive trade policy does not reverse the trend in trade patterns. Those industries that enjoy protection continue to delcine. The determining factor, according to Canto and Dietrich, is to what extent the market succeeds in circumventing the restrictions. Indeed, the data presented and analyzed in this chapter cast doubt on the conventional analysis of protectionism as a way to help some interest groups that are suffering from foreign competition. True, restrictive trade policies afford some protection to the protected industries, but they also provide even greater opportunities for those who find a way to circumvent these policies. Thus, the "voluntary restraint" on the importation of Japanese cars to the United States may have afforded some relief to labor and shareholders of the United States automobile industry, but it created bigger profit opportunities for the Japanese automobile industry, via a change in marketing and pricing policies (moving to bigger, more expensive cars), and for the Korean automobile industry (by vacating a niche in the United State market).

There is a growing body of literature investigating the way in which political forces shape United States trade policies (Marvel and Ray, 1983; Ray and Marvel, 1984; Ray, 1981a, b). The purpose of this chapter is to document further the importance of special interest groups on the determinants of industry's special trade policies. We take our analysis a step further and investigate whether the imposition of industry specific protectionist policies does in fact improve the profitability and/or employment levels.

The results we report in the first section of this chapter are interesting, for they suggest that the industry profitability and employment levels are important determinants of industry-specific trade policies. This result is in accord with recent empirical findings by Marvel and Ray (1983, 1984), who report a strong and negative relationship between industry growth and tariff reduction. Earlier literature in this area (Stern, 1964) suggests that tariff protection is most pronounced in industries susceptible to import penetration. In contrast, our empirical findings are similar to Ray's (1981a, b) in finding that import penetration does not have a significant effect on the determinants of industry-specific trade restrictions.

Analysis of the effects of industry-specific trade restrictions on selected industries reported in the second section also yields interesting results. In the case of the leather shoe, color TV, and automobile industries, the industries' stock return and employment performance appear to be negatively affected. However, in most cases the employment results were not statistically significant. These results suggests that a minimum requirement for an effective trade policy (i.e., an increase in profitability and/or employment) was not evident. In contrast, the results for the automobile and shoe industries suggest that the protectionist policy resulted in lower stock returns. An explanation for the failure of the protectionist policies to help the leather shoe, color TV, and automobile industries is presented in the third section. The explanation for this result is that American consumers and foreign suppliers found ways of circumventing the trade restrictions. To the extent that domestic firms made their investment and production decisions without anticipating the partial or total circumvention of the trade restriction, their investment are unlikely to yield the expected returns, and hence profits would actually be lower than they otherwise would have been. The final section of the chapter pesents concluding remarks.

DETERMINING THE RESTRICTIONS ON TRADE
IN INDIVIDUAL COMMODTIES

Trade restrictions may give rise to ecnomic rents to workers and capital owners in protected industries. These benefits will occur largely at the expense of other sectors of the economy and/or foreign competitors. In turn, the potential rents generated by the trade restriction will give rise to rent-seeking behavior. To the extent that different special interest groups that benefit from the protectionist action can organize effectively, the political process may result in protectionist policies.[1]

Brock et al. (1985) provide a theoretical justification that links the rise in protectionist policies in an industry to the industry employment and profit levels as well as the market share of imports. The model focuses on a hierarchical game that incorporates three distinct special-interest groups: workers, capital, and political parties. Their model explores the behavior of lobbies and political parties in the setting of international commercial and industrial policy. In their framework, policies are set by political parties that are power brokers among special-interest groups. Protectionist and antiprotectionist lobbies channel resources to their favoured parties to maximize their probability of elections Brock et al.'s analysis suggests that special -interest groups use political pressure to force the government to intervene when competition from abroad threatens the earnings of labor and capital in their industry.

In a somewhat different context, similar conclusions are reached by Peltzman (1976), who argues that regulators serve the special-interest groups. However, they are constrained by the political risks associated with imposing costs on some of their constituents in order to help the special-interest groups.

These theoretical contributions provide the basis for much of the analysis of the empirical determinants of industry-specific trade policies presented in this chapter.

Sample Selection

Interventions in trade for individual industries are called "microevents" in this chapter. To perform the empirical analysis, trade restrictions imposed since 1960 were classified according to the standard industrial classification (SIC) industry most affected by the trade restrictions (as shown in Table 15.1). For each industry affected by a micro trade event, 10 years of historical data up to and inclusive of the event year, on employment, imports, and returns on capital was obtianed. The sources for the employment in industries and import measures were SIC classifications of employment in industries and imports.[2] SIC industry indices were calculated using the Center of the Study of Security Prices (CRSP) file of returns. After netting out industries for which inadequate data were available, 11 industries were included in the sample: they are listed on Table 15.2.[3] In addition to the sample of industries directly affected by trade policy, a sample of seven industries not affected by trade policy was selected at random, SICs for those are also given in Table 15.2.[4]

Table 15.1   Summary of the Industry-Specific Trade Restrictions: 1960–1982

Industry	SIC[a]	Year	Action Taken
Textiles	22	1961	Voluntary quotas established limiting the importation of cotton textiles
		1968	Voluntary quota on exports to the United States of woolen and synthetic fiber
		1974	Multifiber Arrangement restricted textile imports
Sheet glass and carpets	227	1962	Raised tariffs on sheet glass and carpets
Meat	201	1964	Meat Import Act of 1964 designed to protect domestic cattle industry; quotas come into effect when imports exceed adjusted base by 10$ (trigger level); President was given authority to suspend quotas
		1969	Informal restraints on major meat-supplying countries; special bilateral restrictions with Honduras
		1970	Voluntary restraints on meat imports negotiated with additional countries
		1971	Restraint program on meat continued, allowing for 1971 imports to be higher than the suspended trigger level but below negotiated restraint levels
		1972	Voluntary restraints negotiated on meat
		1975	Voluntary restraints negotiated on meat
		1977	Voluntary restraints on meat imports negotiated
Financial institutions	60	mid-1960s	The Interest Equalization Tax, designed to restrict the availability to foreigners of banking services in the United States.
		mid-1960s	Foreign Direct Investment Program, designed to restrict United States financing of foreign direct investments by United States firms
Steel	331	1969	Voluntary Restraint Agreement imposed on imports of steel
		1972	Voluntary Restraint Agreement on steel extended from 1971 to 1974
		1978	Trigger Price Mechanism on steel implemented
		1982	Steel quotas negotiated with European countries
Specialty steel	332	1971	Tariffs on stainless-steel flatware raised
		1976	Quotas placed on specialty steel

Table 15.1 (Contd.)

Industry	SIC[a]	Year	Action Taken
Fruit	017	1982	Negotiated voluntary quotas on Mexican fruit and vegetables (1971) allowed to lapse
Soybean	0116	1974	United States soybean export embargo
Nonrubber footwear	314		Orderly Marketing Agreement negotiated with Korea and Taiwan to restrict imports on nonrubber footwear to 1976 levels
Color TVs	365	1977	Orderly Marketing Agreement with Japan to restrict imports of color TV
		1980	Orderly Marketing agreement with Korea and Taiwan to restrict imports of color TV
Industrial fasteners	3452	1979	Restraints on imports of industrial fasteners, after once failing at the ITC, were imposed; the Commission was required to consider it again following Ways and Means Committee request
Lightweight chassis	3713	1980	25% tariff imposed on lightweight chassis trucks
Automobiles	3711	1980	"Voluntary" export restraint negotiated with Japan to restrict automobile imports

[a]Standard Industrial Code.

Table 15.2   Industry Classifications Used in Empirical Analysis

With Trade Action		With No Trade Action	
SIC Code	Industry	SIC Code	Industry
01	Agricultural products	207	Fats and oils
017	Fruits and nuts	265	Paper containers
222	Textiles (synthetic)	394	Toys
223	Textiles (wool)	2111	Tobacco (cigarettes)
331	Steel	2732	Printing (books)
2211	Textiles (cotton)	3172	Leather goods
2279	Carpets		
3149	Footwear (nonrubber)		
3211	Flat glass		
3651	Radio, TV sets		
3711	Autos		

The data for statistical analysis of micro effects were constructed from the sample of industries affected by trade policy as follows. First, the growth rates of employment and imports in the SIC industry were computed for the 2 years prior to the intervention of trade policy. The growth rates were then expressed as the difference of the SIC industry employment growth from United States aggregate growth in employment and growth in SIC imports relative to total United States import growth. One observation therefore consists of the qualitative designation of trade intervention (typically a quota), the growth rate in employment and growth of imports expressed as differences from national averages, and the associated SIC industry stock returns.

In addition to these observations, the historical data from the affected industries in nonintervention years 4 and 7 years earlier and the nonintervention sample were used to produce observations where no trade policy intervention occurred. With the historical series on affected industries, growth rates in employment and imports, again expressed as differences for United States averages, were computed for the years 4 and 5 and the years 7 and 8 prior to the trade policy intervention to be comparable to intervention years described in the previous paragraph. With the firms from the matching sample, growth rates and returns were computed as with affected industries, where the time periods were staggered for the industries randomly and in some instances, owing to data availability, 5-year growth periods were used. The final sample for the microevent analysis used all observations for which complete data were available and consisted of 60 observations.

Empirical Results

The dependent variable in the trade intervention analysis is the qualitative variable indicating intervention or nonintervention in trade. Logit analysis was chosen to predict a policy of trade intervention given the measures of injury to industries affected by trade. Logit analysis has minimal requirements concerning the statistical properties of error terms in the regression. These requirements are met in the case of the political uncertainties associated with the intervention in trade that are the source of the stochastic error terms. Logit analysis estimates a

Table 15.3 Determinants of Industry-Specific Trade Restrictions: Results of the Logit Estimations[a]

Independent Variable	Coefficient	Standard Error	Significance Level
Intercept	−1.269	0.355	0.0004
Relative growth in employment (SIC)	−9.616	5.36	0.073
Relative stock returns	−2.97	1.42	0.074
Relative growth in imports	−1.83	1.67	0.197
Model chi-square	4.58		0.126

[a]Industry-specific trade-reducing policy intervention (dependent variable = 0.1).

logistic probability curve as a function of the explanatory variables. Maximum likelihood estimates of parameters are derived using the statistical analysis system (SAS) logit routines. Results are provided in Table 15.3.

The employment and stock return relative to the economy's average prove to be the most significant explanatory variables in explaining trade intervention by industry. Slow growth or decline in employment in affected industries relative to aggregate United States experience produces an increase in the probability of a trade-reducing policy intervention which is significant at the 90 percent level.

The empirical results reported in Table 15.3 are interesting when compared to the results previously discussed in the literature. Most of the literature uses ordinary least-squares with a cross-section analysis to estimate these effects. This makes the comparability of our results somewhat of a problem. In a recent paper, Ray (1981) reports both ordinary least-squares and Probit cross-sectional analysis of the United States trade restriction for the year 1970. Ray's results indicate that for specific industries (i.e., microresults), the percent change in imports does not play a significant role. This is similar to the result reported in this chapter.[5]

In an analysis of the Kennedy tax round, Marvel and Ray (1983) report a strong negative correlation between domestic industry growth and tariff rate exchanges. In general, one will expect employment growth and profitability to be correlated with industry growth.[6] Thus, our result that employment growth relative to the natural economy and the industry stock return net of the market average are significant determinants of trade restrictions is consistent with Marvel and Ray's finding. However, the extent that interest of workers and owners of capital does not coincide with industry employment growth and stock returns will be a better proxy of the protectionist pressure than the industry output growth. Furthermore, since we net the economy's average from each of our variables, an argument can be made that our variables are a better proxy for the special-interest groups' protectionist pressures.[7]

STOCK MARKET AND EMPLOYMENT EFFECTS OF TRADE INTERVENTION

Advocates of protectionsit trade policies argue that trade restrictions devised to protect particular industries, if effective, will restrict foreign imports and result in a higher level of employment and profits than would otherwise be obtained in the absence of the restrictions. However, to the extent that the restriction generates a price differential between the domestic and foreign markets, economic agents will have an incentive to circumvent the restriction. Thus, if easily circumvented, it is possible that the industry-specific restriction will not afford the desired degree of protection and could, under certain conditions, end up hurting the "protected" industry. The analysis presented in this section investigates the effect of trade restrictions on selected industries.

The "event time methodology," pioneered by Fama et al. (1969), is now used to estimate the impact of the industry-specific trade policy on the industries' stock returns and employment. For the purpose of this study we selected four industries as defined by the SIC codes; (1) leather shoe, (2) color TV, (3) automobile, and (4) steel. The events methodology requires an equilibrium model of the expected change in equity values (i.e., the rate of return). Alternative models have been used to estimate the expected rate of return of aggregate equity indexes. One commonly used model, which will be adopted in this chapter, is the market model.

The Market Model

In the market model, the expected return for a group of stocks is related to a general stock index, and departures from the expected return are unsystematic sources of returns. The relationship between the returns on a portfolio of stocks in an industry and the market is measured by the regression coefficient (beta) estimated by using a sample of the returns over a prespecified time prior to the event period. The market-adjusted return is computed during the event period using the value of the general stock index and the market sensitivity factor (beta).[8] Deviations from the expected return over the event period are attributed to the trade action. Therefore, these forecast errors (i.e., deviations from the market-adjusted return) and used as a proxy for the event-related abnormal return.

The length of the event period is usually chosen arbitrarily. For purposes of this study, the event period spans 12 months preceding the announcement of the trade action (EM − 12) and the 6 months following the announcement of the trade action (EM + 6). For an industry-specific event that encompassed more than one trade action, such as the steel industry, event periods are aligned by pivoting the data around the announcement time. The average excess return (AER) is calculated as follows:

$$AER_t = \frac{1}{J_t} \sum_{j=t}^{J=k} ER_{jt}$$

where J_t is the number of trade actions selected, t denotes time relative to the event period, and ER_{jt} denotes the excess return for the particular event in the month relative to the event time. The statistical significance of the abnormal performance is determined by constructing a statistic for the cumulative excess return (CER) where

$$CER_{t_1, t_2} = \sum_{t=t_1}^{t_2} AER_t$$

Significance of the CER is determined by the "t-test" statistics calculated from the ratio of the cumulative excess return to its estimated standard deviation (see Ruback, 1982). The standard deviation is estimated from the time series of the industry index adjusted as discussed later.

The major problem with the estimation of the t-statistics is the time series dependency of the data used to estimate the variance. Most event studies have ignored this issue. However, if the prediction errors exhibit first-order autocorrelation, the variance of the CER will be undervalued (Brown and Warner, 1985). In cases where there is first-order autocorrelation, the following formula will be used to estimate the variance:

$$Var(CER_{t_1,t_2}) = t\, Var(AER_t) + 2\frac{t-1}{t} COV(AER_t, AER_{t+1})$$

A second major problem arising from the estimation of the variance in event studies is the evidence that the variance of the stock return increases around the event announcement (Beaver, 1981). This will result in an underestimation of the true t-test value. We shall use the event period—a high-variance period—to estimate the variance of the CER. This will cause our results to be on the conservative side. Another problem may arise if an incorrect universal event period is imposed for all the events selected. It has been argued that an arbitrary choice of event period may lead to suboptimal results (Brown et al., 1983). Despite the possibility of bias in parameter estimations due to a misspecified event period, most event time studies have used an arbitrary universal event period for estimating event-related effects.[9]

Empirical Results

The analyses of the impact of the effects of industry-specific trade restrictions on the industry stock return indexes are reported in Table 15.4 for several definitions of the event period. The majority of the cumulative excess returns for the various stock indexes is consistently negative, and for the automobile and shoe industries the results are statistically significant at the usual confidence levels (i.e., 95 percent), although the tests for overlapping periods are not independent. However, it is worthwhile to note that a large fraction of the decline in the stock return index occurs before the event date. One possible explanation for this result is that the decline in stock return results in the imposition of trade restriction. If this is the case, the cumulative excess returns and the significance of the results are being overstated. However, with the exception of the automobile industry, if one calculates the cumulative gain for the 6 months following the event, it is apparent that the gain is not much different from its standard error. In turn, this suggests that the minimum requirement for an effective protection (i.e., an increase in pofitability and/or employment) is nonexistent.

If a given trade restriction is easily circumvented, the trade restriction will be ineffective in protecting the domestic industry. This could explain why an industry stock index will not improve in response to the trade restriction. Furthermore, if domestic firms make investment and production decisions based on the misguided belief that the restrictions will be completely effective, their investments are unlikely to yield the expected returns, and hence profits will unambiguously decline. In cases where restrictions are aimed at particular industries, such as the recent auto import quotas, the profit umbrella hoisted by restrictions on the low-cost competitors opens the way for new competitors to enter the market. This would further impair the protected industry's future

Table 15.4   Effect of Micro Trade Policies on Stock Returns Cumulative Average Prediction Error (CAPE) Estimation Period (1960–1982)*

Cumulation period in the event interval	Industry Indices			
	Steel SIC331	Automobile SIC371	T.V. SIC365	Footwear SIC
	CAPE	CAPE	CAPE	CAPE
EM-12 to EM0	−3.02	−18.70**	−8.44	−35.30**
	(−0.48)	(−2.15)	(−1.49)	(−2.78)
EM-12 to EM6	−10.41	−32.26**	−7.42	−30.26**
	(−1.36)	(−3.06)	(−1.08)	(−1.98)
EM-12 to EM-1	−4.54	−18.00**	−7.71	−34.30**
	(−0.75)	(−2.15)	(−1.42)	(−2.81)
Average error (APE)	−0.85	−1.68	−0.38	−1.33
Auto-correlation lag1	−0.15	−0.16	−0.10	0.03
lag2	0.05	−0.05	−0.17	−0.03
Variance (APE)	3.06	5.84	2.46	12.24

*Expected Return in the Event Interval is Estimated using the Market Beta Model $(R_i = \text{Beta} * R_m + \text{Const})$.
  t-values are in parentheses.
**Significant at a confidence level of 95.0%.

    EM-12 = 12th month preceding the event month.
    EM0 = the event month.
    EM6 = 6th month following the event month.
    EM-1 = 1st month preceding the event period.

      Var (APE) = Variance of prediction errors in the event interval
      Auto Corr = Auto-correlation of prediction errors (lag = 1 month)

profitability. We explore these effects of trade restrictions in the next section.

The cumulative excess return for the shoe industry stock index is consistently negative (Table 15.4, column 1). This result suggests that the imposition of restrictions on leather shoe imports is associated with depressed returns to capital in the domestic shoe industry. Taken at face value, the estimates show an average decline of 1.2 percent per month in the stock index during the interval period.

The effects of trade restrictions on the stock indexes of the automobile industry are similar to those obtained for the leather shoe industry. Taken at face value, the results suggest that, on average, trade restriction are associated with a decline of approximately 1.2 percent per month for the shoe and automobile industry indexes and a decline of 0.5 percent or less per month for the steel and and color TV industry indexes; however, the latter are not statistically significant.

An approach parallel to the one used to examine the effect of trade policies on equity values is applied in the analysis of the impact of trade policies on

Table 15.5   Expected Employment Growth Models: Hours Worked Dependent Variable Growth in Industry

Dependent Variables	Industry			
	Steel SIC331	Automobile SIC371	T.V. SIC365	Footwear SIC314
Intercept	−0.004 (1.74)	−0.001 (0.169)	−0.003 (0.931)	−0.005 (0.02)
Aggregate Employment	—	4.652 (5.365)	2.334 (5.142)	1.878 (2.73)
Aggregate Employment (−1)	1.738 (5.06)	—	—	—
Industry Employment	—	—	—	—
Industry Employment (−1)	—	−0.301 (4.337)	—	−0.131 (1.03)
Industry Employment (−2)	—	−0314 (4.523)	−0.195 (2.381)	—
Industry Employment (−4)	−0.2999	— (4.183)	—	—
$\bar{R}^2$	0.192	0.255	0.172	0.099

Numbers in parentheses are t-statistics.

employment growth. Total employment is measured as the total number of hours worked in a month. Expected employment growth is estimated outside the event period using regressions of employment growth in the industry on aggregate employment growth and lagged employment growth in the industry. These models are reported in Table 15.5. The difference between expected and actual growth is the excess employment growth.

The effects of trade restrictions on employment are qualitatively similar to their effects on stock returns. The cumulative excess growth in employment is consistently negative across all three interval (Table 15.6). The point estimates suggest that, on average, the imposition of across-the-board trade restrictions is associated with a decline in employment of 0.08 percent per month. Although the results are not statistically significant, they nevertheless support the free trade advocates' contention that trade restrictions reduce the economy's efficiency and employment level.[10]

ALTERNATIVE WAYS OF CIRCUMVENTING TRADE RESTRICTION

If a trade restriction can be circumvented, it will not improve the industry's domestic profitability and employment outlook. In this section, we discuss how foreign producers apparently circumvented United States trade restrictions in the case of color TVs, footwear, autos, and steel.

Table 15.6 Effect of Micro Trade Policies on Employment Growth Cumulative Average Prediction Error (CAPE) Time Series Expectations Model

Cumulative period in the event interval	Industry Indices			
	Steel SIC331	Automobile SIC371	T.V. SIC365	Footwear SIC314
	CAPE	CAPE	CAPE	CAPE
EM-12 to EM0	−0.95	−18.62	−7.67	−7.80
	(−0.19)	(−0.57)	(−0.96)	(−0.14)
EM-12 to EM6	−5.35	−17.29	−1.00	−10.42
	(−0.91)	(−0.35)	(−0.10)	(−0.13)
EM-12 to EM-1	−1.74	−16.60	−3.51	−9.94
	(−0.37)	(−0.55)	(−0.46)	(−0.20)
Average error (APE)	−0.28	−0.91	−0.05	−0.54
Auto-correlation lag2	−0.08	−0.43	−0.12	0.24
	0.02	−0.04	−0.05	−0.12
Var (APE)	1.79	18.20	04.88	12.94

t-values are in parentheses—none Significant at a confidence level of 95.0%.

EM-12 = 12th month preceding the event month.
EM0 = the event month.
EM6 = 6th month following the event month.
EM-1 = 1st month preceding the event period.

Var(APE) = Variance of prediction errors in the event interval
Auto Corr = Auto-correlation of prediction errors (lag = 1 month)

The initial response to the imposition of the orderly marketing agreement for Japanese-produced color TVs was a sharp decline in colour TV imports from Japan but an increase in color TV imports from the rest of the world, particularly Taiwan and Korea. New orderly marketing agreements were negotiated with Taiwan and Korea in 1980, and the number of finished sets imported was substantially reduced. However, both United States and foreign-owned domestic producers began production of TVs in the United States, exported incomplete sets to use foreign-manufactured components, and then "reimported" the TVs for final assembly; reimported TVs were not covered by the trade restrictions, and only the foreign value-added is subject to a 5 percent tariff. In short, the color TV restriction was easily circumvented at a cost of a 5 percent tariff on foreign value added.[11]

In 1977 orderly marketing agreements were signed with Taiwan and Korea restricting the imports of nonleather footwear to their 1976 levels.[12] In 1981, United States trade negotiators were successful in securing a "voluntary export restraint" by the Japanese automobile manufacturers.[13] In neither case did the trade restrictions specify the quality of the units imported. The quantity restriction induces a substitution effect toward the higher-quality items, as shown by Falvey (1979) to result from Alchien and Allen's (1972) proposition that the imposition of quotas and/or transportaion costs increases the average quality of the imported product. The change in average quality may result in a significant erosion of the protection that may have been afforded by a restriction that maintained constant composition of the imports.

The effort required to prevent circumvention of trade restrictions is illustrated by the domestic steel industry, which prevailed upon the Johnson Administration to negotiate a 3-year voluntary restraint agreement with Japanese and European exporters, causing the Japanese and Europeans to alter the composition of their exports from lower-valued to higher-valued steel: the value of steel imports increased substantially (Canto, 1984). When the voluntary restraint agreement lapsed, and steel imports again began to increase, the industry asked for policies designed to protect it further againat foreign competition.

In 1978, the steel industry was provided with a new form of protection—trigger prices, a minimum price based on estimated Japanese cost of production at a standard volume, keeping European steel at a "fair" price, actually higher than their marginal costs. This may have helped United States producers, but it provided incentives to other foreign producers, such as Canada, Korea, and South Africa, to enter the market. The trigger price mechanism broke down after 3 years. The imposition of new import quotas in 1982 was the culmination of a legal process that began in January 1982 when United States steel companies filed unfair trade practice petitions. The plea for protection was prompted by compelling evidence that Europe and other governments were responding to the worldwide recession and overcapacity in steel by subsidizing producers in their own countries. At the same time, new steel-producing countries from the Third World, including Brazil and Rumania, began penetrating the United States market. In response to a combination of falling output and eroding market share, the steel industry sought protection under the Trade Act of 1979. On October 21, 1982, quota negotiations were finalized, limiting European steel imports to about 85 percent of 1981 levels.

Import restrictions, if effective, afford some protection to the protected industries. However, the restrictions also create benefits for those able to circumvent the restrictions. In some instances foreign producers take advantage of existing loopholes within the law, as was the case of the color TV industry. At other times the circumvention is not as simple and easy, but the quality of imports may change to mitigate the cost of restrictions, as with footwear and autos. The restriction in tonnage on imported steel was partially offset through a change in the composition of steel imported by the United States, where total tonnage declined, but the value of the tonnage increased by approximately 30 percent. In addition, countries not subject to the restraints were able to increase their exports to the United States market. In all cases, the value of trade restrictions to domestic producers was sharply curtailed. The evidence presented in previous sections suggested that complete circumvention was not prevented.

CONCLUSIONS

Specific industry trade policies are most significantly related to those interest groups directly affected by competition from abroad. A decline in employment and/or stock returns in an industry relative to the rest of the economy tends to increase the probability of a policy reducing international trade in that industry as orderly marketing agreements or quotas are imposed to protect domestic employment.

These results are consistent with the view that the activities of special-interest groups influence the shape of industry-specific trade legislation. Furthermore, to the extent that changes in domestic and/or international demand and supply conditions affect the income levels of the special-interest groups, the structure of protection will change in response to the different pressures. It is worthwhile to note that while capital and labor argue that imports are a cause of injury, no relationship is evident between the growth rate of imports relative to the growth of all United States imports and industry-specific trade restrictions.

Finally, the analysis of the impact of industry-specific trade restrictions suggests that the minimum requirement for an effective trade policy (i.e., one that improves the industry stock return and/or employment in trade-affected industries) was not evident. In addition, the negative and significant results are consistent with an ineffective policy where circumvention is largely effective but costly. A positive and significant result is consistent with a protectionist policy where circumvention is fairly costly. The least negative results occur in the steel industry, where different restrictions have been steadily blocking the flow of steel into the United States. The results suggest that the United States steel industry may be getting close to building a barrier that will prevent the inflow of steel. However, the cost of constructing the barrier may very well exceed the benefits achieved. To the extent that other domestic producers, such as the domestic auto makers, have to use the more expensive steel, their products will become less competitive. Our results suggest that protectionist policies have failed to protect capital and/or labor in the protected industries. The results are consistent with the arguments of free trade advocates who stress that trade restrictions impair the efficiency of the economy to the extent that restrictions are effective. Further, the benefits of the access to foreign goods and markets are lost to the protected economy. Production incentives shift away from those goods produced most efficiently domestically without producing significant benefits for interest groups hurt by foreign competition.

NOTES

1. For a discussion on the politics of special interest groups, see Brock and Magee (1978). The analysis of rent-seeking behavior can be traced to Krueger's (1974) seminal paper. Krueger's analysis has been further refined and generalized by Bhagwati and Srinivasan (1980).
2. The CRSP data file lists the SIC code for each of the stocks listed. Using the SIC classification, a value-weighted industry index of monthly returns was constructed.

3. Industries were excluded either because they were not listed in the CRSP data file (i.e., the meat industry) or because the restrictions were not precise enough to determine their effects (i.e., the interest equalization tax and the foreign direct investment programs designed to restrict United States financing of foreign direct investment by United States firms). Finally, in some cases where CRSP data were not available for the SIC three- and/or four-digit classification, we used a broader classification hoping to capture the effects of the trade restriction (i.e., agricultural products SIC 01 instead of a narrower classification).
4. The selection criteria for the firms included in the matched sample were data availability and the absence of trade restriction during the relevant time period.
5. Ray's analysis uses a large number of explanatory vaiables than ours (including capital intensity, concentration ratio, fraction of work force that is skilled), but in contrast to our analysis, he does not include a measure of total labor equipment and/or profitability like the stock return variables we employ.
6. The exception being the cases of perfectly inelastic industries where growth and profitability will not be closely related.
7. In a recent paper Canto et al. (1985b) present international evidence supporting these arguments.
8. Rafael Eldor (1984) demonstrates that higher beta firms enjoy higher effective protection from equal tariff treatment. However, we are attempting to explain the likelihood, not the level, of trade intervention.
9. To minimize the problem, one should ideally use maximum-likelihood techniques for each of the policies or events selected. One possible reason for a change in event period length is that speed of adaptation to events for an industry or a firm may be changing over time. The impact of a possible misspecification of the event period, if any, is being minimized by examining the effects of the event (trade restriction) over three different intervals in the event period.
10. Jenkins and Montmarquette (1979) estimate social and private costs of job displacement, which according to our results may result from barriers to trade. These costs are higher for older workers, which it would appear are more likely in mature industries such as those we analyze.
11. For a discussion of the color television industry case see Canto (1983).
12. For an analysis of the shoe restriction see Suh (1981).
13. For a detailed study of the automobile industry see Canto et al. (1985a).

REFERENCES

Beaver: "Econometric Properties of Alternative Security Return Models," *Journal of Accounting Research*, 19(1) (1981), pp. 163–183.

Bhagwati, J.N.; and Srinivasan, T.N.: "Revenue Seeking: A Generalization of the Theory of Tariffs," *Journal of Political Economy*, 88 (Dec. 1980), pp. 1069–1087.

Brock, W.A., and Magee, S.P.: "The Economics of Special Interest Politics: The Case of the Tariff," *American Economic Review Papers and Proceedings*, 68 (May 1978), pp. 246–250.

Brock, W.A.; Magee, S.P.; and Young, L.: "The Progressivity of Endogenous Tariff Policy in General Equilibrium," in V.A. Canto, and J.K. Dietrich, eds, *Industrial Policy and International Trade* (JAI Press, 1985).

Brown, K.; Lockwood, C.; and Summer, S.: "On Examinations of Event Dependency and Structural Change in Security Price Models," presented at the Western Finance Meetings (June 1983).

Brown, S.; and Warner, G.: "Using Daily Stock Returns: The Case of Event Studies," *Journal of Financial Economics* 14 (March 1985), pp. 3–31.

Canto, V.A.: "United States Trade Policy: History and Evidence," *Cato Journal*, 3(3) (1983), pp. 679–698.

Canto, V.A.: "The Effects of Voluntary Restraint Agreements: A Case Study of the Steel Industry," *Applied Economics*, 16(2) (April 1984), pp. 175–186.

Canto, V.A.; Eastin, R.V.; Laffer, A.B.; and Kadlec, C.W.: "A High Road for the United States Automobile Industry," *The World Economy* (1985a).

Canto, V.A.; Dietrich, J.K.; and Mudaliar, V.: "The Determinants of Trade Intervention in Industrial Goods: A Cross Country Comparison," working paper, University of Southern California (1985b).

Eldor, Rafael: "On the Risk-Adjusted Effective Protection Rate," *Review of Economies and Statistics*, LXVI (May 1984), pp. 235–241.

Fama, E., Fisher, M.; Jensen, M.; and Roll, R.: "The Adjustment of Stock Prices to New Information," *International Economic Review*, 10(19) (1969), pp. 1–21.

Jenkins, Glenn P.; and Montmarquette: "Estimating the Private and Social Opportunity Costs of Displaced Workers," *Review of Economics and Statistics*, LXI (Aug. 1979), pp. 342–353.

Krueger, A.O.: "The Political Economy of the Rent-Seeking Society," *American Economic Review*, 64 (June 1974), pp. 291–303.

Leroy, S.: "Expectations Models of Cost Prices: A Survey of Theory," *Journal of Finance*, 37 (March 1982).

Marvel, H.P.; and Ray, E.J.: "The Kennedy Round: Evidence on the Regulation of International Trade in the United States," *American Economic Review*, 73(1) (March 1983), pp. 190–197.

Peltzman, S.: "Toward a More General Theory of Regulation," *Journal of Law and Economics* 19 (Aug. 1976), pp. 211–240.

Ray, E.J.: "The Determinants of Tariffs and Non-Tariffs Trade Restrictions in the United States," *Journal of Political Economy*, 89 (Feb. 1981a), pp. 105–121.

——, "Tariff and Nontariff Barriers to Trade in the United States and Abroad," *Review of Economics and Statistics*, LXIII (May 1981b), pp. 161–168.

——; and Marvel, H.P.: "The Pattern of Protection in the Industrialized World," *Review of Economics and Statistics*, LXVI (Aug. 1984), pp. 452–458.

Ruback, R.: "The Effect of Discretionary Price Control Decisions on Equity Values," *Journal of Financial Economics* 10 (March 1982), pp. 83–105.

Stern, R.M.: "The United States Tariff and the Efficiency of the United States Economy," *American Economic Review Papers and Proceedings* 54 (May 1964), 459–470.

Suh, J.H.: "Voluntary Export Restraints and Their Effects on Exporters and Consumers: The Case of Footwear Quotas," Working Paper No. 71, Center for the Study of American Business, Washington University, St. Louis, Oct. 1981.

Index